W9-BMJ-512

(Continued)

Writing in the Real World

MAKING THE TRANSITION FROM SCHOOL TO WORK

Anne Beaufort

FOREWORD BY SHIRLEY BRICE HEATH

TEACHERS COLLEGE PRESS

Teachers College, Columbia University
New York and London

Published by Teachers College Press, 1234 Amsterdam Avenue, New York, NY 10027

Library of Congress Cataloging-in-Publication Data

Beaufort, Anne.
    Writing in the real world : making the transition from school to work / Anne
Beaufort ; foreword by Shirley Brice Heath.
      p.   cm. — (Language and literacy series)
    Includes bibliographical references and index.
    ISBN 0-8077-3900-6 (pbk. : alk. paper). — ISBN 0-8077-3901-4 (cloth : alk. paper)
    1. English language—Business English—Study and teaching. 2. Business writing
—Study and teaching. 3. Business writing Case studies. I. Title. II. Series:
Language and literacy series (New York, N.Y.)
PE1479.B87B42   1999
808'.066650'07—dc21   99-43189

ISBN 0-8077-3900-6 (paper)
ISBN 0-8077-3901-4 (cloth)

Printed on acid-free paper
Manufactured in the United States of America

07   06   05   04   03   02   01   00   8   7   6   5   4   3   2   1

Contents

Foreword

AMERICANS HAVE A SPECIAL PENCHANT for beginnings. They mark the "firsts" of nearly everything they do or have been, and they note milestones by calling particular attention to "new beginnings" along the way.

Researchers, especially those in education, favor not only starts of various sorts, but also early development. This book, remarkable in many ways, is perhaps most noteworthy for how it steps away from beginnings.

Beaufort, drawn to understand learning curves of high challenge, entered education research with a perspective unfamiliar to those accustomed to a "start at the beginning" approach. She selected as fieldsite an environment where demands for writing shifted by audience, function, and ideological climate, sometimes within a single week. Through observation, intensive follow-up interviews, and text analysis, she began to grasp the strategies high-level writers use to advance their skills and remain competent for the protean shapes of their jobs.

Several research methods Beaufort used to understand ongoing and high-challenge writing achievement merit particular note. Whereas most scholars give relatively little attention to either spatial or surrounding communication channels of a writer, Beaufort helps us grasp both space and access as dynamic and highly interactive. Close proximity and open physical space shared by workers characterize contemporary offices of movable partitions. From conceptual knowledge to organizational layout for grant applications, the writers Beaufort studied learned through their ready access to one another. In addition, the organization's writing amounted to collaborative achievement for all members sharing the goal of sustaining the nonprofit. Such joint project development is the norm in workplaces of the information-based postindustrial economy.

In addition to close observation of environmental factors not generally accounted for in studies of writing, Beaufort's iterative data analysis took her back for regular informational interviews with the writers. Beaufort stimulated their reflections through her own ever-tentative analysis of their data. In much ethnographic work, such feedback interviews rarely appear as *regular* steps within data collection. Beaufort's visual depictions of genres, constituencies, and knowledge domains derive from her *ongoing* input from the writers she studied.

It is one of the many ironies of research within the United States that little scholarly attention goes to *adult learning*. The phrase triggers thoughts of *illiteracy, adult basic education,* or *night school* and not the constant learning demands within today's workplaces. Technology has brought rapidly expanding access to information bases and a dizzying increase in speed expectations; learning curves grow steeper with the need to keep technology up to date in order to accomplish old and new tasks. Why is it that scholars who focus on learning have not jumped at the opportunity to study ongoing learning in response to rapid and high-challenge demands? The easy answer is that beginning learning presents fewer challenges; acquisition and onset of skills make themselves more accessible for measurement. Advancement of learning presents a host of other problems: absence of a uniform baseline of experience, strong probability of learning as internal strategy-building rather than observable skill development, and need for measurement of generative capacity for advancing knowledge. The latter two, in particular, sit at the heart of what some call lifelong learning.

WRITING IN THE REAL WORLD is an important contribution to *adult learning*—a much-needed field of study in the United States. A popular bumper sticker in the late 1990s asserts, "Technology drives the future: the question is—who steers?" Beaufort's work helps us think in smart new ways about advancing our steering expertise as well as writing our own tickets into the future.

Shirley Brice Heath
Stanford University

Acknowledgments

A BOOK CANNOT BE WRITTEN without the support of many.

First, I thank two teachers who captured my attention and taught me things that led eventually to my undertaking this enterprise. Miles Myers and Jim Gray showed me, in the Bay Area Writing Project Summer Program in 1976, that (1) I was a writer and (2) the teaching of writing was an infinitely interesting subject for investigation.

Second, I thank John Ackerman, Carol Berkenkotter, Patricia Bizzell, Michael Carter, Linda Flower, Tom Huckin, Jean Lave, Lucille McCarthy, Carolyn Miller, Barbara Rogoff, James Slevin, Peter Smagorinsky, Michael Smith, and John Swales for the articles they have published that led to the framing of the investigation I undertake here. I look forward to the day when I can thank each of them in person.

Mentors have been numerous. Steve Athanases, Arnetha Ball, and Shelby Wolf, who went through the Language, Literacy and Culture program at Stanford University a few years ahead of me, were immensely helpful, as were classmates Betsy Burris and Carrol Moran. Members of my dissertation committee—Melanie Sperling, Michael Tratner, Elizabeth Traugott, and Ramon Saldivar—paid great attention to little details as well as the hard questions a researcher must answer. And since my first attempts at describing an emerging research question on a February morning long ago, Shirley Heath, my mentor, has been the one who has kept me expanding the vision of the work and believing in it.

Then there are the people at the nonprofit agency I call the Job Resource Center (JRC), without whose assistance I would have no story to tell: Leong, who wisely pointed me in the direction of the four writers when I approached him with my research project; Mei, who replaced Leong and graciously allowed me to continue the project; and, most important, the four women who, for purposes of this text, call themselves Ursula, Pam, Selma, and Birgitte. They were the ones who squeezed me into already long and stressful days and willingly subjected themselves to my probing the nooks and crannies of their lives at work and their past lives as writers. I am deeply grateful for their patience, their willingness to be open, and, ultimately, for the friendship they gave me.

I am also very grateful to the funding agencies that provided research moneys to keep me and the project going: Stanford University's School of Education, the Research Foundation of the National Council of Teachers of English, the Spencer Foundation, and the College of Arts and Sciences Mellon Fund at American University. A number of individuals and organizations provided me quiet, rural environs for deepening the work as well: Nancy Wolf, Esther Wanning and Carol Press, Larry Lawlor, the Rising Phoenix Women's Retreat Center, Dayspring, and the Rolling Ridge Retreat Center.

My editors at Teachers College Press, Carol Chambers Collins and Cathy McClure, have been extremely helpful, as has the art director, Dave Strauss, and my graduate assistant, Lacey Wootton-Don, has been a first-rate editor and proofreader. Finally, my circle of friends, who know who they are, held me up through the work in countless ways. But no one deserves as much gratitude as my husband, Guy Wulfing, who met me when I was just 3 months into the Ph.D. work, who has had to go to a lot of movies alone, and who has yet to experience life with his partner under "normal" conditions. He is the one who gave technical, artistic, editorial, and moral support, sustaining me in every way a partner possibly could through the entire process.

Writing in the Real World

MAKING THE TRANSITION FROM SCHOOL TO WORK

CHAPTER 1

The Question of Expertise in Writing

I put so much into studying Shakespeare and memoriz-
ing passages from Shakespeare, and knowing that it
wasn't going to do me any good at any time. When I first
had those secretarial jobs, I would just laugh in my
head, well, at least I can quote Shakespeare. Here I am,
typing away. But, . . . what I studied . . . has nothing to
do . . . with anything I'm doing now.
                        —Ursula, Transcript of interview

AT JOB RESOURCE CENTER (JRC),[1] a small, nonprofit organization in the
heart of a major urban center in the United States, four women worked
the long hours common to the American workplace. Three of the women
managed employment training and literacy programs, and the fourth,
assistant to the executive director, managed all public relations communications and the director's correspondence. On any given day, a visitor was
likely to see each—Selma, Birgitte, Pam, and Ursula—at her computer for
as much as 4 to 6 hours, producing texts essential to the agency's functioning: reports to government and private agencies on funding received,
requests for new funding or donations to fund-raising events, inquiries
to public officials and business leaders about potential relationships, and
press reports on newsworthy events and accomplishments. Producing
texts so vital to the agency's business required advanced levels of writing skill.

Yet the writers produced such texts amidst obvious distractions:
ringing phones, interruptions from co-workers, and tight deadlines.
Other struggles that impeded writing tasks were less obvious: prior writing experiences limited to academic writing and unfamiliarity with such
genres as responses to requests for proposals (RFPs) or press releases.

Moreover, writers in workplaces that depend on the effects of the written word must understand complex webs of social relationships that undergird their texts and must juggle competing and often contradictory rhetorical purposes within a single text. For writing to be effective, composers have to learn to adapt, quickly and effectively, the style, length, and content of their texts, and they must do so in less than optimal working conditions.

All four writers in this study graduated from schools ranked in the top 10% of higher-education institutions in the United States. Two held a master's degree. Each of the four was recognized within JRC for her writing skills. Yet overt and covert indications of struggle surrounding writing tasks in such environments lead to the question of just how writers transform and advance literacy skills they learned in college to meet the demands of their current situations.

Two of the four writers followed in this study—Ursula and Pam— graduated from college within 2 years prior to the start of this study. Relatively new to workplace writing, academic writing still fresh in their memory, they faced new writing challenges on a daily, weekly, and monthly basis. The other two—Birgitte and Selma—further away from college graduation and longer in the job at JRC, were not newcomers to workplace writing, but JRC's needs and external pressures continually presented them with new writing demands.

Told here is the story, unfolding over more than a year, of four writers making transitions from academic to professional writing to meet the needs of their particular institutional context. Rather than a tale simply of workplace writing, this study follows in close detail a boundary crossing that all writers at advanced levels undertake, often several times during their careers. In its broadest sense, this is the tale of the dislocated writer: the poet, the essayist, the businesswoman who suddenly finds herself having to write a letter with legal import, or the researcher who needs grant-writing skills to secure funding for a new project. Just what does learning to write in new genres and new social situations entail? In particular, this study takes up three questions:

- What are the distinct and overlapping knowledge domains an expert writer draws upon in a given writing situation?
- How can transfer of learning be fostered to give writers flexibility and versatility in handling a variety of occasions for writing?
- Which individual traits and environmental conditions in informal and formal settings foster ongoing development of writing skills?

Answers here regarding the complex cognitive and social processes involved in ongoing development of writing skills enable new perspectives on writing curricula and pedagogy, not just for academics and workplace trainers, but also for individuals who want to improve their writing skills or are faced with unfamiliar writing tasks.

THE NEED FOR THIS STUDY

All of us, in academia and in business, have had to stretch and reach to keep our literacy skills current with the arrival of the Information Age. We must read and write the new forms of "text" spawned by new technologies (e-mail, interactive multimedia texts, on-line databases, virtual reality simulations, etc.). We also must decide how to manage the massive amounts of information we receive electronically each day—more than our grandparents received in a week or month. The technical complexities of many of these materials challenge the brightest and most educated (Bernhardt & Farmer, 1998).

Surveys of writers in work settings suggest writing as increasingly significant in the Information Age (Anderson, 1985; Ede & Lunsford, 1990; Faigley & Miller, 1982). Anderson's survey of surveys indicates that 38% of those surveyed spent, on average, more than 20% of their time on the job writing, and 42% said writing was of great importance. Ede and Lunsford's poll found workers saying they spent 44% of their time on writing activities, and 86% felt writing "very important to the job." Furthermore, the Secretary's Commission on Achieving Necessary Skills (SCANS) Report, produced by the U.S. Department of Labor (1992), suggests that in the Information Age, all workers need a wide range of writing and critical thinking skills, given three factors: (1) the technological complexities of most jobs, (2) the availability of such aids to communication as e-mail and word processing, and (3) the need for participatory management across all job levels rather than the traditional hierarchical structure in which workers merely followed orders from higher-ups. The demand on workers in all vocations to keep pace, to perform at higher and higher levels of literacy, continues.

Leaders in business and government complain that college graduates cannot handle important workplace writing tasks and therefore cost companies time and money. According to a representative sampling of 26,000 adults in 1992 by the U.S. Department of Education, testing them on three aspects of literacy—prose literacy, document literacy (i.e., reading graphs and charts), and quantitative literacy—only half of college graduates reached Levels 4 and 5 on measures of prose literacy and only 10% reached Level 5. (For an in-depth look at the results of the National Adult Literacy Survey of 1992, see Barton & La Pointe, 1995.) The test does not measure writing skill in any extensive way, but a look at the competencies established for Levels 3, 4, and 5 gives some cause for alarm. For example, Level 3 proficiency includes being able to write a brief letter explaining an error made on a credit card bill. One in three 4-year college graduates could do this task successfully. Level 4 of prose-literacy proficiency requires stating in writing an argument made in a lengthy newspaper article. Only two in five graduates of 4-year colleges could successfully complete this task. And national surveys of elementary and high school students' attitudes about writing and their views of themselves as writers repeatedly show an increasingly negative attitude about writing from grades 4 to 12 (Applebee, Langer, Mullis, Lathan, & Gentile, 1994).

Data from other sources corroborate this concern. For example, a growing concern that CPAs do not possess the written communication skills needed to serve the public led in 1994 to grading candidates' writing skills as part of the Uniform CPA Examination (May & Menelaides, 1993). Types of problems employers find in employees' writing and potentially harmful effects also surfaced in a study of 52 cases nationwide of company-produced documents that led to lawsuits. Seven key writing problems led to the lawsuits: (1) unclear purpose, (2) unfocused writing, (3) poor organization, (4) difficult language, (5) excess verbiage, (6) improper or ineffective choice of words, and (7) grammatical errors that misled readers (Shea, 1992).

Within academia, concern about the situated nature of writing has led some to question the validity of generic writing courses (Petraglia, 1995). Since writing outside academia must be context-specific, the argument is made that little transfers from the typical first-year college composition course. Perhaps writing instruction should always be located in context-specific disciplines and professional development programs. But there is even some doubt whether any professional writing courses taught in formal educational settings can accurately simulate workplace writing situations (Freedman, Adam, & Smart, 1994; Knoblauch, 1989).

There has been a burgeoning of studies of workplace writing since the mid-1980s, both for purposes of professional training and for purposes of making comparisons between academic and workplace writing. These studies begin to give us a sense of how writing may differ in different social contexts or discourse communities. To briefly summarize, in the workplace the purpose for writing is to take action rather than to leisurely reflect on thought processes or on artistic expression (the latter are qualities usually valued by English teachers), and this difference is reflected in the content, form, and tone of much business communication (Broadhead & Freed, 1986; Johns, 1989; Woolever, 1989). Although texts may be written by an individual, frequently they are a collaboration of a group of employees, and almost always the text of a business communication reflects the point of view of the institution rather than of the individual, leading to a very different sense of authorship in the workplace than in academia (Ede & Lunsford, 1990). And there is greater complexity associated with issues of audience and purpose in workplace writing than in the writing for most undergraduate classes, where writing tasks are directed to a single audience, the teacher, and written for a single purpose, displaying knowledge (Beach & Anson, 1988; Faigley & Miller, 1982). Also, as Flower (1989) points out, "In school writing the social, rhetorical context is often buried and the student is used to dealing with assignments, not problems" (p. 20). Each of these studies offers a valuable, yet incomplete, picture of what is involved in workplace settings for writing.

DEFINING EXPERTISE

This study examines advanced levels of writing literacy in one professional setting. The data can be compared with other research on expert performance and we can begin to theorize what expert writing performances entail. As Robert Gundlach (1998) points out, there is no master narrative about learning to write, but we can advance the story another chapter with each report of research.

Current debates in cognitive science about the general characteristics of expert knowledge usually are cast in terms of a continuum of skills—general versus context-specific skills or declarative (content) versus procedural knowledge. The general skills model of expertise (Newell & Simon, 1972) proposes the expert as someone with problem-solving skills (e.g., setting goals, developing strategies, and monitoring progress) that cut across disciplines or contexts. Experts see abstract principles and procedures that can be applied in a given situation. In contrast, the context-specific model of expertise proposes no universals, only very specific forms of knowledge that apply in specific, or "local," situations.

Recent research suggests a view of expertise combining general and local knowledge. As Perkins and Salomon (1989a) explain, general skills in a given area of expertise work as a "mental gripper" by which both novices and experts get a handle on new problems or learning situations. Then as specific knowledge within a domain or with a particular type of task grows, the expert uses more and more local knowledge and skills. For example, novices learning to drive a car apply the general rule that one should shift gears at a given speed, whereas expert drivers make seemingly intuitive, more context-specific decisions about shifting gears based on road conditions, the sound of the engine, and so on (Dreyfus &

Dreyfus, 1986). (See Sternberg & Forsythe, 1994, for a discussion of different views of expertise still under debate in cognitive psychology.)

Expertise in Writing

To return to college graduates experiencing difficulty writing in advanced academic programs or in a new workplace culture, we can assume that they know something about writing. The question is, does the knowledge used to write academic papers and pass essay exams at the undergraduate level also provide expertise for professional writing situations? Do different writing situations and genres require different types of writing knowledge and skill?

Theorists since antiquity have taken a generalist view of writing expertise. Drawing from Aristotelian rhetoric and the nineteenth-century work of rhetorician Alexander Bain (1886), current traditionalist teachers emphasize general rules of grammar, spelling, and punctuation, and teach essay forms such as Bain's modes of discourse (description, exposition, argument). In the early 1980s, influenced by cognitive psychologists' work on the ways in which the brain processes information, Flower and Hayes (1981) proposed teaching, in addition to correct forms, a general model of the composing process (i.e., procedural knowledge) that takes into account long- and short-term memory issues in order to diagnose and overcome common problems of writer's block or lack of fluency in composing. Others in composition (Elbow, 1981; Murray, 1980) popularized a simpler procedural model for teaching the writing process—prewriting, drafting, revising—that soon became a standard addition to writing curricula. But general kinds of writing knowledge do not explain all that expert writers do, whether they write in professorial garrets or executive suites.

A context-specific view of writing expertise arose in the early 1980s, concurrent with changing views in linguistics, philosophy, literary theory, and science about the nature of truth and the nature of spoken and written language. To explain writing expertise more fully, social constructionists (Bizzell, 1982; Heath, 1982) look to the ways writers and writing are informed or constrained by cultural institutions.

But exactly what constitutes local, or contextual, writing knowledge is problematic. Some theorists (Flower, 1989; Miller, 1984) focus on rhetorical problem solving (e.g., how to address a specific audience or what types of persuasive argument can best be used for a particular purpose). Others (Bizzell, 1982; Rafoth, 1988) raise the issue of how cultural and social norms influence acts of writing, and invoke the notion of discourse community as an all-encompassing term for the latter.

The term *discourse community* came into use in composition studies in the early 1980s, borrowing from Hymes's (1974) notion of speech communities and from Fish's (1980) notion of interpretive communities. The term generally has come to refer to a group of people who follow a set of common practices for communicating through written text. And while there is no universally agreed-upon or precise definition of the term, composition theorists who appropriate the term (Bartholomae, 1985; Bizzell, 1992; Brodkey, 1987; Cooper, 1989; Faigley & Hansen, 1985; Porter, 1992) generally use it to extend traditional rhetorical concepts of audience and purpose to include a sociological or cultural perspective. Swales (1990) gives the example of a discourse community of stamp collectors organized to obtain rare stamps who communicate with each other across national boundaries via a newsletter with its own in-house jargon and discourse forms.

To add another layer of complication in discussions of a writer's contextual knowledge, theorists working from a postmodern perspective have created new understandings of genre that encompass traditional notions (matters of form and other textual features) as well as notions of social and cultural practices in which genres are embedded (in other words, discourse community issues) (Bakhtin, 1986; Devitt, 1993; Schryer, 1993). Berkenkotter and Huckin (1995) point out this all-encompassing view of genres: "Genres are the intellectual scaffolds on which community-based knowledge is constructed" (p. 24). This work has been useful in terms of reconceiving genres, not as fixed forms constant across time and cultural contexts, but rather as shapes and patterns of texts almost as fluid as holograms, changing across both time and contexts. This more fluid, contextually based notion of genre also will be an important consideration in the study that follows. However, extending the notion of genre so broadly as to include social context or the discourse communities in which genres are situated collapses in effect two very broad concepts into one even broader concept that becomes unwieldy to operationalize. So in this discussion, in order to parse as clearly as possible what writing expertise entails, the notions of genre and discourse community, although closely linked, will be viewed as separate but intertwined concepts.

Just as a synthesis of the general versus local knowledge view of expertise has been attempted in the cognitive sciences, likewise in composition studies several arguments have been made for a view of expert writers' knowledge combining general knowledge and local knowledge. Carter (1990) was the first to suggest viewing composition theory in light of the general versus context-specific debates in cognitive psychology on the nature of expert knowledge. He makes the case that the whole matter of general knowledge (i.e., cognitive and traditional approaches to teaching writing) versus local knowledge (i.e., social constructionist approaches to teaching writing) should be considered not as an either–or debate, but as a continuum "that grows increasingly contextual with greater [writing] experience" (p. 280).

Smagorinsky and Smith (1992) divide Carter's continuum from general to context-specific writing skills and knowledge into three parts: (1) general knowledge (e.g., knowledge of the basic expository structure of the five-paragraph essay and of the prewriting, drafting, and editing stages of the writing process); (2) task knowledge (e.g., ability to distinguish modes of expository discourse and appropriate rhetorical strategies of analysis, observation, etc., for a given writing task); and (3) community-specific knowledge (e.g., knowledge of how an argument is made within a specific field such as law or film criticism). This study will refine further their continuum from general to specific writing knowledge.

Smagorinsky and Smith (1992) also point out areas of dispute among composition scholars about just what expert writing knowledge really consists of. Grammar, mechanics, and vocabulary certainly constitute basic declarative knowledge every writer needs and can transfer across all contexts (Teich, 1987). But beyond this point, no clear agreement exists as to whether writers use general writing process strategies or more task-specific writing processes. (For contrasting views, see Flower & Hayes, 1981; Applebee, 1986; and Broadhead & Freed, 1986.) Furthermore, although composition textbooks continue to propose modes of discourse as generic textual forms for students to emulate, theorists have for some time debunked the use of the formulaic discourse modes as models for writing. But composition teachers do not agree on forms of writing to teach or whether in fact the forms can be taught explicitly.[2]

No doubt the murkiness in our understanding of what constitutes expert writing performance exists in part because writing is a very complex task calling upon a number of different cognitive processes and domains of knowledge, all of which are closely interwoven. It is also a task that is very hard to study because of the elusive nature of both the cognitive and cultural components. For example, how does one determine the boundaries of a discourse community: Is it as broad as a particular culture? Or narrowed to one institutional site of composing (the design department of a particular town's branch of the Ford Motor Company, for example)? Or is it some intertextual space between two U.S. corporations with at least 2,000 employees, say, or all automotive companies? In other words, what is the appropriate contextual space to consider in determining social influences on writing activities, and what are the criteria for determining those boundaries? As Harris (1989) says, given the fact that "the borders of most discourses are hazily marked and often traveled . . .

the communities they define are thus often indistinct and overlapping" (p. 17). The complexities of these theoretical problems replicate themselves in the difficulties with empirical research on writing behaviors. Often the time and complexity involved in looking across all domains of knowledge that the writer must use prohibit a comprehensive look at the factors involved in writing production at one site of composing.[3]

In sum, what constitutes writing expertise has not been sufficiently illuminated by current theories and models of writing practice. Generalized views of writing capture only part of the picture of what is going on, and in fact there is little basis for labeling someone "an expert writer." Rather, what can be described are expert writing performances in a given set of localized conditions (Bazerman, 1994). Far more emphasis in composition pedagogy has been placed on generalized rules and forms for writing than on the specifics of contextualized writing knowledge. There is a need to operationalize situation-specific types of writing knowledge (e.g., discourse community knowledge) and to understand the linkages between general and specific knowledge required for successful accomplishment of writing tasks—whether in school or professional settings.[4]

THE RESEARCH STUDY

To return to the problem of our four writers and the advanced level of writing skill they must develop to succeed at JRC, it is necessary to delineate the overlapping yet distinct knowledge domains they must become competent in and to understand how they do or don't succeed in gaining that knowledge. By analyzing this group of writers in a particular institutional context for an extended period of time, collecting data from a variety of sources, I was able to document aspects of writing expertise and the processes employed for gaining that expertise. Although a report from one field site is hardly evidence to be universalized, this study adds to existing knowledge of what is involved in expert writing performances and suggests implications for educators and managers who work with writers new to particular writing situations.

Ethnography was the research methodology of choice to provide the broadest possible view of what was going on at the research site. Studies of writing that have employed ethnographic techniques have been done in settings as diverse as a school on an island off the coast of Maine (Lofty, 1992) or within an Amish community (Fishman, 1990). Others who do intensive work within organizations and societies—journalists, teachers, social workers, therapists—will recognize many of the characteristics of research methods that lead to ethnography: (1) intense immersion in a particular situation under consideration, (2) merging of outsider–insider roles by the observer, and (3) casting of wide nets in terms of considering what might be useful data (Geertz, 1973). Scientific rigor applies throughout: testing hypotheses, triangulating data in order to corroborate patterns that emerge, and making overt the relations between researcher and subjects and the ways in which the researcher herself is the instrument of research. While not attempting any universal or necessarily quantifiable results, ethnography particularizes abstract concepts at a moment and place in time.

I will leave the details of the evolution of this particular ethnography for Chapter 8. Methods used at this cultural site, the Job Resource Center, consisted of, on average, one day a week of observation and interviewing for a 12-month period and attendance at special events such as the annual fund-raising dinner. As much as her work demands would allow, each of the four writers met with me almost weekly—sometimes for a quick 20-minute interview, other times for as long as 2 hours. Interviews consisted of a combination of open-ended questioning, stimulated recall of what was going on in the writing of texts they had given me, and on one occasion a sorting task to determine how each writer categorized texts. The data gathering resulted in 49.5 hours of taped conversations with Selma, Birgitte, Pam, and Ursula and another 16 hours of taped interviews with others with whom I could triangulate my data—co-workers, bosses, people outside JRC who received the agency's writing in one form or another, and professional writers considered to be experts in discourse communities similar to or interfacing with JRC. Field notes and approximately 3,710 pages of text produced by the four writers mostly between July 1992 and August 1993 completed the data.

No doubt, when I approached each of the writers, her conception of what "participation" would entail was entirely different from what evolved over the course of the year. But by virtue of perseverance and an empathy for day-to-day pressures born of my own work experiences, I was able to gain entrance to the organization. Within a few months, after showing up every Tuesday, I became so familiar around the office that most of the staff of JRC would greet me in the hallways or chat with me at the copy machine or microwave. I was also blessed with good fortune. It is often difficult to conduct extensive research in a workplace setting, given the press of day-to-day concerns and myriad demands on employees' time, but my four informants and JRC's executive director believed in the value of the research and were also sufficiently curious about outcomes to cooperate with my efforts.

A brief autobiographical note to explain personal experiences that led to this study also may interest the reader. After a shift from teaching junior high English to teaching college composition as a part-timer, in the summer of 1976 I participated in the Bay Area Writing Project. Jim Gray's fundamental belief was that one had to write to be a good teacher of writing. For 6 weeks, we wrote and wrote, and we shared our writing publicly. From my beginnings publishing work written that summer, I gradually built a writing portfolio and transitioned for economic reasons into a staff writer/editor job for a large public utility company.

In my 9 years as writer and editor at that company, my writing skills were constantly stretched and challenged. I had to run the gauntlet of lawyers and technical experts who could find potentially damaging innuendoes in a simple expository sentence. I had to master the news story, the feature story, the 5-second sound bite, and the press release. The latter—a seemingly simple genre—caused endless grief. No matter how hard I tried to come up with the perfect lead, my boss—a seasoned PR man of 30 years—could always write it better.

The year before I began doctoral studies, I worked at a small, high tech company as a trainer and writing consultant to engineers, account executives, and marketing managers. Occasionally I would ask if they remembered college teachers talking about a "thesis statement" and if they saw any similarity between a "thesis" and "the point" of a memo or report. They stared at me blankly. Although I didn't know it at the time, a research question was starting to emerge.

What follows then is an ethnography of workplace writing in the 1990s that examines the issue of learning to write in new genres and in new social contexts, and the issue of that difficult boundary crossing from writing in school to writing in business situations. At issue are both writing literacy at advanced levels and learning processes associated with gaining advanced levels of writing skill in informal instructional settings. When we understand the socialization processes for learning to write at professional levels and the nature of context-specific writing tasks, we can shape curricula and foster mentoring relationships to promote more effective writing in the twenty-first century.

Also at issue is a theoretical debate in anthropology and cultural studies on the nature of truth. In light of postmodern theory, can we approximate the truth of "the other"—in this case, the four writers at JRC? Can I, as ethnographer, as participant-observer, find ways to understand others' experiences with writing, and in the telling accurately reflect that lived-through experience? And is ethnography a viable genre for the study of text production? Debates rage in composition research among cognitivists, social constructionists, and critical theorists on the appropriateness of widely varying methodologies for understanding the composing processes of writers and the meanings of the written texts produced. What does a full-scale ethnography of writing contribute to these debates?

Chapter 2 contextualizes the particular site of composing in this study, while Chapter 3 examines the ways that several discourse communities of writers and readers define their writing practices and genres of communication. Chapters 4 and 5 tell how these four women acquired advanced writing skills. Chapter 4 gives a broad overview of different roles apprentice writers assumed and stages of their socialization process into new discourse communities. Chapter 5 looks more closely at the processes three of the writers went through in learning to write in new genres over the period of a year.

Chapter 6 alters the time frame of the study. Retrospective accounts of the informants about their earliest and most memorable experiences with writing, both inside and outside school settings, and writing samples from those years enable us both to glimpse the developmental process entailed in coming into a set of writing skills and to contextualize local conditions for writing that occur in American high schools and colleges. Contrasts in the ways that writing works in school and on the job, as evidenced from the accounts recorded in Chapter 6, receive attention in Chapter 7. Also explored in Chapter 7 are matters related to the transfer of writing skills from one social context to another and the implications of this ethnography for curriculum development and instructional design for university writing program administrators and business communications consultants. Chapter 8 offers a self-reflexive analysis of the process of researching and writing this ethnography.

This ethnography is a testament to using multiple lenses for understanding acts of writing. The contributions of literary and rhetorical theory to understanding meaning making in relation to texts is one such lens, along with the perspective from cultural anthropology on what constitutes a "culture" and the contribution of ethnographies of communication on specific relations between culture and communication processes. The contributions of cognitive science to our understanding of both how learning takes place and what "knowing" really means are also helpful. All these lenses undergird this attempt to understand the complicated interactions of text, context, and learner at advanced levels of writing literacy.

CHAPTER 2

Setting the Stage: The Cultural, Social, and Physical Terrain of Job Resource Center

... believing, with Max Weber, that man is an animal suspended in webs of significance he himself has spun, I take culture to be those webs, and the analysis of it to be therefore not an experimental science in search of law but an interpretive one in search of meaning.
— Clifford Geertz, *The Interpretation of Cultures*

THE LIGHT-RAIL TRAIN dumped its load of passengers underneath the city. Moving up the escalator stairs, passing through the gate, I was greeted by the sounds of Mozart—a pleasant surprise at 8 a.m. The music was being played by a slender, disheveled violinist poised at the entryway, open violin case at his feet. Stepping into the open air of the plaza, I scurried past sleeping human hulks huddled under thin blankets or worn-out sleeping bags on the half-circle of benches around the perimeter of the plaza, drawing my own coat a little tighter around my body as an involuntary shiver passed from head to toe.

I walked the eight long blocks to the nonprofit agency I will call the Job Resource Center (JRC), passing a McDonald's; a bank; three high-rise tourist hotels; souvenir shops; an Irish pub; two Vietnamese, three Chinese, and one Thai restaurant; a church well known for its community activism and eclectic ministry; two theaters; several sidewalk shoeshine stalls; an antiques store; a hair salon; a few more homeless people sleeping in doorways; several upscale restaurants serving pastries and espresso to their morning customers; four corner liquor stores; two food markets

13

displaying huge baskets of Chinese eggplants, squash, and oranges on sidewalk tables, their signs in Chinese characters; and numerous residence hotels or apartment buildings, their entryways gated and sometimes filled with debris the wind and passersby had deposited.

I walked at a brisk pace. Occasionally a panhandler or drunk attempted to step in my path and solicit a donation. Mostly, though, the passersby were tourists, maps and cameras in hand, businesspeople with briefcases and satchels at their sides, children with backpacks on their backs headed for school, grandparents or mothers with a young child on either arm along with white plastic bags laden with purchases from the nearby market, or street people searching the trash containers for recyclable cans. By early afternoon, when I took a break from collecting data and walked to the Vietnamese restaurant for a $3 plate of rice and broccoli beef or to a cafe for a sandwich, several women were pacing back and forth at adjacent street corners, their body-hugging garments a giveaway to their occupation.

JRC, a nonprofit with approximately 50 employees, looked like just another small office crowded in between other buildings. But unlike neighboring businesses, JRC's outreach was both to the immediate neighborhood and to the entire immigrant and unemployed population of the city. Its simple glass front and the straightforward lettering of the sign, "Job Resource Center," painted on the glass belied the layers of organizational complexity both internal and external to the agency. Like the surrounding environs, JRC had a whole lot more going on than an initial impression might reveal.

Inside JRC, a row of chairs lined the wall opposite the receptionists' desks in the front area. Sometimes, there was a welcome calm. Most days, at any given time, there would be a handful of individuals seated there, clipboards and intake forms in hand, expressions of intense concentration or concern on their faces. For most of them, being able to take an employment training course at JRC would mean an opportunity to get off public assistance or stop a drain on the meager resources of a newly immigrated family. But four out of every five who applied would be turned away—sometimes because their English was too low even for the beginner classes, but most often because there just weren't enough enrollment slots for everyone.

Sometimes they sat in pairs, one person interpreting the English on the form to the other in a native language—Mandarin, Vietnamese, Russian, Spanish. Or the two receptionists, Flo and Phara—both graduates of JRC—interpreted the procedures to applicants who spoke Cantonese. Chinese and Vietnamese immigrants filled about 43% of JRC's classes, but an increasing number of Eastern European and Central American immigrants filled the classes as well.

Phones rang incessantly. The same greeting was given over and over, rapid-fire, the pitch of the receptionist's voice rising as "JRC" rolled off her tongue a hundred times a day in the midst of stuffing invitations to the upcoming fund-raising dinner, dubbing 100 tapes for a new training program for nonnative speakers on use of the telephone, or answering visitors' questions.

On the wall above the row of chairs in the reception area were honorary plaques and certificates indicating the 25-plus years of service JRC had given the community and the acknowledgments received from city, state, and national leaders in job training and development. There was a photo of the Secretary of Labor, at JRC on a visit several years earlier, flanked by JRC's executive director and board president. At the end of the row of memorabilia on the wall was the white board where staff signed in and out as they came and went during the day from meetings with city council members, labor leaders, potential funders, and local business partners—activities that all supported the writing and fund-raising activities of the organization.

Beyond the receptionists' desks were the staff mailboxes and a copy machine at the beginning of a long hallway leading to more staff offices; a small room with the heavy-duty copy machine and a microwave and small refrigerator for staff use; and a large open area ringed with long tables and chairs that was used for staff meetings, an occasional potluck, the monthly celebration of staff birthdays, or a press conference. Furnishings were not plush. Desks and chairs usually didn't match, and except for an occasional poster or bulletin board, the off-white walls were bare. But there was an IBM computer on every manager's desk (the result of a large grant from IBM several years earlier) and there was a laser printer for every two or three computers, signs of the organization's reliance on production of texts that would lead to the funds to pay the building overhead and employees' salaries.

INFORMANTS IN THE STUDY

Selma, one of the four informants in the study, had an office in the back area of the first floor. She had once shared a large office space with two English as a Second Language (ESL) teachers and two job developers, but now that she was managing additional staff from another program, she'd moved to a private office more centrally located between offices of both programs.

She was usually in her office by 8:30, having dropped her 2½-year-old daughter at a day care center at 7 a.m. and ridden the light rail from the suburbs into the city. On the train, she scanned the daily paper—

especially the local news and business section—looking for trends in employment, the economy, or government policy that could affect the programs she managed or provide statistics for the needs section of the grant proposal she had to write in a few weeks. Or she would indulge in a few more pages of the lawyer thriller she currently was reading.

Selma was considered an old-timer by most of the staff. She'd been at the agency 5 years and had risen from a position as administrative assistant for the executive director to program manager for several training programs for immigrants. She was the agency's institutional memory, unofficial historian, and all-around generalist. She could assist the executive director in budget analysis for an upcoming board report, cajole with perfect calmness two very agitated ESL teachers having a disagreement over use of classroom space, listen sympathetically to a new employee's job stress, represent JRC at meetings with city agencies that distributed state and federal funds to nonprofits like JRC, explain the upcoming training class to a potential client, fill in as secretary at a board meeting if the administrative assistant was out sick, or call local leaders to solicit letters of support for an upcoming grant proposal. She also was called on frequently to edit others' writing, as she had a reputation for being good with grammar. She was calm, rock-solid in the midst of the pressures of the job.

In the last year Selma had had to take over management of the programs of another manager who left the agency and was not replaced. She accepted the increased responsibilities without a salary increase, knowing the agency needed to trim costs wherever possible at that time. Although overall JRC had a very good track record for operating in the black, this had not been a particularly good year in the fund-raising arena or in the economy in general. Over the course of a year, Selma would write five major grant proposals—two fairly routine annual requests to a local government funding agency, and three to state and federal agencies for programs that would break new ground for JRC. Writing these grant proposals was her most critical job responsibility. Grants from various government and private agencies were the lifeblood of the agency, which provided its services at no charge to clients. We will see that even though she was an old-timer in the organization, Selma continually had to take on new writing responsibilities.

Birgitte, another program manager and informant in the study, also had a private office—a little cubbyhole off the hallway on the way to Selma's office. Birgitte usually arrived at work a little later—around 9 a.m.—preferring to drive to the office from her apartment on the western side of the city rather than take city buses. She stayed later in the evening. She also worked a 4-day week in order to spend Fridays on her personal writing projects at home—the freelance articles for community newspapers and short stories she wrote "for fun."

Birgitte also fit the old-timer category by JRC's standards—she'd been there 4 years. Unlike Selma, who rose through the ranks, Birgitte was brought on board when a small grant of seed money allowed the agency to start a new program—a program to help African Americans in a housing project start their own small businesses. Birgitte's job was to get the program off the ground—with assistance from a community organizer working part-time at JRC—and simultaneously to start developing a broader funding base to keep the program on its feet and growing. Within 6 months of starting that program, she and the executive director were actively seeking funding for another new program, one that would take advantage of the fact that the computer classrooms were idle in the afternoons while adult students were out in their internships at various work sites in the community. Children's Computer Networks (CCN), as the program was dubbed, would allow students in grades 3 to 5 to come to JRC's classrooms after school to learn computer skills, science, and writing skills.

CCN took off with a bang, and soon Birgitte was managing a myriad of tasks: recruiting and training teachers, building curricula, lobbying with other community organizations (schools and youth agencies) to join JRC as partners in the program, and churning out two or sometimes three grant proposals a month to private and corporate foundations for additional funding so that CCN could keep a financial base and grow.

In the midst of a huge stack of papers on her desk, a current writing project waiting to be finished on the computer screen behind her desk, the ringing of phones, a half-eaten lunch, and constant deadlines, Birgitte managed to describe a funny incident that happened recently, crack a joke, or otherwise entertain and assist other employees who dropped by her office. Typical of the kind of collaborative effort on writing projects at JRC was another staff member's visit to Birgitte on this particular afternoon to brainstorm on a new program idea. One of the bright-eyed young students in CCN popped his head in to say "hi" on his way to class. And her colleague and community worker, Betty, came in to discuss a problem in the field. Birgitte had a reputation among the staff as having the most creative flair in her writing as well as good technical skill with language, in spite of the fact that English was not her native tongue but rather was one of four languages she was fluent in.

The other two writers who are the subject of this study—Pam and Ursula—started working at JRC about the same time, just a few months before I began collecting data at the agency. They were considered newcomers, and their offices were upstairs, on the second floor, next to five classrooms that usually were occupied with some 200 adult students in any given week.

Pam was usually in her office early—by 8 a.m.—unless she had a breakfast meeting with a business partner at one of the downtown hotels. Her commute was easy. She lived in an apartment just around the corner from JRC, tolerating the unpleasant aspects of an inner-city environment because of her commitment to community activism and her involvement in a nearby church whose other members, like Pam, believed in living among those they sought to help. Frequently she and I started my weekly visits at JRC at a favorite cafe a few blocks from the agency. Amidst other regulars, I attempted to balance tape recorder, notebook, and writing samples Pam had given me with our muffins and coffees on a tiny round table in the corner—the only table near an electrical outlet where I could plug in my recorder.

Pam began at JRC as a job developer, one of six or seven staff members whose task was placing graduates of JRC's 12- or 18-week training programs in paid jobs. After working 3 months on the first floor in the job developers' offices and just a few weeks prior to our first meeting, Pam moved upstairs to join the staff of Project Advance as program assistant. The program director was in the midst of working on a huge federal grant proposal with an outside grant writer and brought Pam in as part of the writing team—the beginning of a long apprenticeship for Pam in grant writing. Project Advance was just completing its first 3 years of federal funding to work with local businesses and labor unions in a partnership program to increase literacy skills of entry-level employees in the workplace so that they could perform better on the job and eventually qualify for promotion to higher-level jobs. Initially, the program served small businesses: baking companies, local clothing manufacturers, and restaurants. With the second round of funding, JRC started similar workplace literacy programs for housekeeping and food service personnel in five downtown hotels.

In addition to getting her first exposure to grant writing, Pam had to learn all the facets of Project Advance, manage the four ESL teachers who conducted on-site language classes for the city's businesses, build contacts with both the work-site managers and labor leaders, and oversee curriculum development and testing and evaluation procedures. She was a quick learner and strong writer, though, and within 2 months in the new position, as a result of her boss's promotion to become the new executive director of the agency, she would take over as program manager.

Pam was Chinese-American, as were a number of the staff at JRC, including the executive director and two-thirds of the board. JRC began in the mid-1960s as a community agency geared solely to addressing the language-training needs of a wave of Chinese immigrants, some 19,000 strong, in the early 1960s. Initially the agency offered its services out of a church in the city's Chinese district. Within the past few years there'd been an attempt to shift and broaden the mission and client base of the agency—symbolized by a new name, which, unlike its original name, was devoid of reference to the Chinese community, and also symbolized by the new location in an area that represented a cross-section of the city's ethnic groups. But a recommendation by a Caucasian board member to move the annual fund-raising dinner out of the city's Chinese district eventually was vetoed for fear of losing the strong base of support in the Chinese community: Some leaders in the Chinese community would not attend the dinner if it were held outside the Chinese district. Internally at JRC the Chinese influence was still present as well. Chinese-speaking staff members often addressed each other in Cantonese as they chatted in the hallways or across desks, and the smells of soy or bean sauce and ginger wafted from the microwave at lunch time.

Perhaps the person most acutely aware of the Asian influence on values and operations at JRC was Ursula, the fourth writer in this study and also a newcomer to the agency. In her position as administrative assistant to the executive director, Mei, and as secretary to the board, Ursula was expected to be able to think as her boss would think and speak and write in accordance with Chinese cultural values in a myriad of interfaces with JRC's external audiences—politicians, business and community leaders, suppliers, and the Chinese and mainstream press. And yet the Chinese way of thinking was new to her and at times left her baffled by her boss's expectations. She explained to me some months after she'd been in the job what she gradually had learned:

> I guess the values of JRC, what I feel are the values, is that there's a real commitment to providing something to the community.... *It's a cultural thing with the Chinese that you give back to the community and you support your own, and you help your own people become more self-sufficient.* (Ursula, 1/12/93, p. 3, emphasis added)

As with any cultural value, though, there were subtleties involved. Ursula told me of an idea put forward in a recent board meeting that the agency expand its services to include counseling, an idea that quickly was rejected. All the Chinese members on the board said, "We're not social service. We're job training." And the executive director added, "Asian people don't like to talk about their personal problems.... We don't do that" (Ursula, 1/12/93, p. 3). And yet, clients' needs were to be taken into account in all their dimensions in the day-to-day life of the organization, even to the point that Mei asked Ursula to intercede with an insurance company that was hassling one of JRC's clients.

There is a fine line, though, between help that leads to independence and help that insults self-pride, and this fine line kept the agency on its toes as ongoing changes in the environment pushed it to continually re-think its mission. Re-revising the agency's mission statement was another of Ursula's tasks. At a managers' meeting with Mei, there was a half-hour discussion among the managers about wording. The current mission statement read:

> JRC helps economically and/or educationally disadvantaged indi-
> viduals improve their potential through language instruction, job
> training and other activities so that they may enhance their value as
> productive members of society.

The proposed revision was as follows:

> JRC seeks to empower the community by providing education and
> job opportunities to those who need it. Our goal is to provide eco-
> nomically and/or educationally disadvantaged individuals with
> language instruction, job training and other support services so
> that they may become self-sufficient.

Did JRC "empower" people or did they "provide job training and educa-tion"? Another manager had a problem with the word *disadvantaged*. As Selma reported to me, "She thought that was us imposing a term that, that implies some kind of inferior status, and she thought that was a negative" (Selma, 4/20/93, p. 6).

The staff never resolved all the issues about wording of the mission statement in that meeting. When Ursula began working on a new bro-chure for the agency 2 months later, with the back-and-forth debates about the organization's self-image very much in her mind, she changed the mission statement so it read:

> JRC provides job training to empower the community. Our goal is
> to implement innovative programs that equip the work force with
> skills to succeed in a competitive job market.

She wasn't fully satisfied with the statement and would wait for further inspiration to find better words. The mission statement was only two sen-tences long, but it had a powerful focusing effect within the organization:

More time was devoted to those few words than to any other text of comparable length during the year of my observation.

Ursula's office was next door to Mei's office and was shared with the two bookkeepers for the agency. She was a focal point for a lot of the activity within JRC. She got the requests from other staff for assistance on the Macintosh computer (others at JRC worked on PCs); requests for help with office tasks from the receptionists, whom she supervised; and a steady stream of requests from Mei, from board members, and the general public. If the receptionists didn't know whom to refer a caller to, Ursula got the call. She also dealt with building maintenance (problems like a leaky roof or getting the building to meet city codes), all correspondence on behalf of the executive director, all public relations materials and activities, and coordination of special events such as the annual fundraising dinner, a job fair for high school students, and graduation ceremonies for JRC students. Because writing was central to her job—taking as much as 50–70% of her time—she had been hired specifically because of her BA in English and her desire to use her writing skills in her work.

When we met for the first time, she had been on the job 3 months and was on a steep learning curve. She usually did three things at once, talked fast, and laughed a lot. If anyone could see the humor in a situation, it was Ursula. Our initial interviews took place for 15 or 20 minutes at her desk—preferably when Mei was out of the office and not likely to come in with an immediate need—but still there were many interruptions. The pressure of the job was great, but she was excited to be working in an agency she respected and to be treated as a professional. When things got too crazy, she'd join a fellow smoker for a cigarette break downstairs, outside the building.

THE PHYSICAL CONDITIONS FOR WRITING
AT JOB RESOURCE CENTER

It's frustrating, I work, *I write under conditions that I'm not used to which is that I have tons of interruptions and I have a million things on my mind.* When I was in school I had a habit of just sitting in a cafe in the corner for hours to do my writing. . . . In this room, there's always people coming and going, the phone rings all the time. (Ursula, 7/14/92, p. 1, emphasis added)

The physical layout and the resources for writing at JRC affected the writing practices there probably as much as the organization's goals and values. So I turn now to a description of those material conditions for writing as the four informants perceived them.

Each manager had her own computer workstation, and Selma and Birgitte had private offices, but all four writers groaned when I asked about writing conditions at JRC. Even a private office did not guarantee a lack of interruptions—either the phone ringing or a co-worker wanting to talk about something. It was part of the culture at JRC to be responsive, accessible, helpful. As Pam explained:

> It's one of these atmospheres where things come up and everyone wants to deal with it and talk about it or whatever, then people just can interrupt you in the middle of anything and say, "Oh, can I interrupt? I have to. . . . " You know . . . they want to talk about it right there, right then. . . . *It's just constant interruptions around here.* (3/16/93, pp. 2–3, emphasis added)

Ursula described a similar scenario:

> I was just trying to write a simple letter . . . and I could not think of how to say, write that letter, shoot . . . *and I had like this major block and then just when I would think of something the phone would ring or somebody would ask me a question,* somebody comes to the Macintosh and they don't know how to use the Macintosh and it just, my blood pressure was coming out of my head, 'cause I can't, I can't concentrate. (1/12/93, p. 8, emphasis added)

Birgitte said,

> I can only write if I know that I won't be disturbed for a certain amount of time. . . . I can crank out a letter. But if it's something that—that's longer and involves structuring and organization, then I really need quiet and . . . *just to know that I might be interrupted is enough to throw me.* (4/20/93, p. 8, emphasis added)

And for Selma it was also a problem—not only the interruptions, but also the pressure of knowing that a lot was riding on the writing:

> *For me it takes a great deal of discipline to sit down and write and tune everything out* and . . . try to concentrate on only what I'm doing when there's a lot of other things going on that I know need to be taken care of. We have some program problems. . . . *It's hard to block those things out and just think about what you're writing.* I mean it happens

when you're in school too. It definitely happened to me in school
too, but when it's work and there's money tied up to it and a deadline and all that stuff, somehow to me there's more pressure. (11/
24/92, pp. 11 12, emphasis added)

Each of the writers developed her own ways of handling this obstacle
to writing. Pam went to a nearby restaurant to get her thoughts organized. Birgitte and Selma stayed at home some days to write. Ursula
stayed after hours to work when the phones had quit ringing or came in
on a Saturday morning. But writing had to be accomplished at the office
during business hours, too, so they all needed to learn the mental discipline of keeping their train of thought in the midst of interruptions. Pam
noticed this skill in her boss and other project directors: "When stuff like
that comes up, they just stop whatever they're doing, deal with the issue,
and then try to go back and focus" (3/16/93, p. 3).

This is a skill Ursula had been trying especially hard to develop since
coming to JRC, and she told me one day in March about an incident that
showed her progress:

I wanted you to be there to watch me 'cause you would've
laughed, 'cause I was going to the Macintosh and looking in there
at a letter, then I was looking in the file, then I typed a sentence
and then, oh, then I'd call somebody and ask them a question, like
no wonder it takes me so long to write, I'm all over the place. Then
I had this brilliant idea . . . then I thought I should do this and
call this person, *I was all over the place. And then writing in between.*
(3/16/93, p. 9, emphasis added)

A set of circumstances that 2 months earlier made her blood pressure
come "out of [her] head" she could now handle comfortably, and with
amusement. She had grown much more accustomed to a frenetic environment in which writing was a task done intermittently, squeezed between
other tasks, and under great pressure.

Another aspect of the physical environment supported writing,
though. The same people who interrupted and caused one to lose a sentence forming in the mind could serve as sounding boards to bounce
ideas off in the brainstorming stages of a writing project, or would read
a piece of writing in draft stage and offer editing suggestions. Someone
was always around to read a piece, and all four writers relied on others
to catch typographical errors, awkward phrasing, or grammatical errors.
Referring to a letter she wrote to President-Elect Clinton, Ursula said of
her co-worker Jan, "Thank God she caught 'United Stated.'" All four writ-

ers quickly learned what the strengths of different staff members were: So-and-so was good at grammar, and Oliver was Mr. Suave when it came to saying something nicely, and Jan was a pro at proofreading, and another manager had a great ability to envision how a plan might work. The four writers also relied on each other: Pam was good at structuring points in a logical sequence; Ursula would eliminate any unnecessary words and make sure the precise word was used to convey the *intended* meaning; Birgitte knew how to make something sound exciting; and Selma was expert on grammar and on thinking through the practical issues associated with a proposal.

There was also the added boon of the files, both paper and computer. Expediency and efficiency drove most processes in the office, so "plagiarizing" was the norm. With the aid of the cut-and-paste function of word-processing programs, sections of text were transported readily from one document to another, to be used over and over. There were also the file drawers where copies of all important documents were kept—an excellent source of information on a new genre or a way of handling a particular rhetorical situation. Whenever Ursula had to write something new, if her boss didn't dictate a few key phrases or the gist of the content, she went to the files. For example, this is how she figured out how to write her first press release: "There were already some on the Macintosh from the woman who had the job before me, so the format I got from her" (8/5/93, p. 4). Ursula also referred in one of our conversations to her "snagged programs file"—a file of brochures, program flyers, and annual reports she'd started collecting from other nonprofits, all to serve her when she got the time to revise JRC's existing information packet. Models usually were readily available for most types of writing at JRC.

The use of text over and over—or borrowing heavily from models— was due partly to the fact that certain situations arose repeatedly—hence Ursula's computer subdirectory of different types of letters, including the Ima Donor letter and the We Care, Inc., letter. Having standard texts and standard verbiage, or as Pam called it, "a well-oiled language machine" that spewed out the routine documents, also helped writers at JRC to have more time for new thinking and originality when necessary.

There was also the issue of making use of available technology to create texts. A computer technician was on staff to deal with hardware problems, but software had to be learned without any assistance. All four writers came to JRC familiar with a word-processing program, but each learned other software programs to create the various types of text needed at JRC. Selma learned Harvard Graphics so she could produce charts on JRC's finances. The three writers who produced proposals used Lotus 1–2–3 spreadsheets to produce budgets and charts depicting class schedules, curriculum modules, and client demographics. Ursula had to master a graphics program to aid her in producing the quarterly newsletter. The task of learning the program wasn't easy and typified the trial-and-error method the writers resorted to for teaching themselves these technological skills:

> The first newsletter I learned Pagemaker while I did it. . . . It was hard. But *I got a book and I just screamed and cried a lot and figured it out.* (10/20/92, p. 11) *I was here every Saturday and Sunday for a month, trying to figure it out.* (11/3/92, p. 1, emphasis added)

Pam, who liked to play with computer graphics in her spare time as "therapy" and who liked to think visually, was perhaps the master at computer graphics, but even she got frustrated at times. One day, explaining the format of a flyer to me, she said:

> I was tired of trying to do columns 'cause we were trying to do a folding brochure and the [computer] program was making me crazy 'cause it was taking too long, so I said, *"Forget it. I'm just going to do it . . . on just a straight page,"* 'cause I had to get it out really fast. (10/27/92, p. 4, emphasis added)

Computer tools were a "mixed blessing" to writers at JRC. Learning to use them could be painful. But once learned, they saved time and increased options for formatting text and were an integral factor in the material conditions for writing at JRC.

In fact, the two critical aspects of the physical environment at JRC that bore on writing activities were time and space issues. Time was always short. There was more work than hours in the day. So any tool that was a time-saver—formulaic texts like Ursula's "Ima Donor" letter, or computer programs—was a boon. Time also was gained by distributing different tasks associated with a writing project among several people, each with different areas of expertise. The space factor was a mixed blessing: On the one hand, close proximity allowed for efficient division of labor and collaboration; on the other hand, the open offices and easy access to colleagues brought constant interruption to a task that often required single-minded absorption. Material conditions also affected substantive issues such as choice of communications channels and socialization processes, as we will see in Chapters 3 and 4.

A DAY AT JOB RESOURCE CENTER

People could wear many hats at JRC. A staff of about 50 provided services to approximately 1,000 adults and 400 children in the course of a year, through a dozen different programs—all organized, however, around the central mission of the agency: job training and employment assistance to help people become self-sufficient. It was one of the oldest nonprofits of its kind in the city. Its track record—measured by funding levels (approximately $3 million in grant money or donations annually) and by success in placing graduates in paid jobs (about 90% success rate)—had earned it a solid reputation not only in the Chinese community, but among local and national funding agencies.

The second floor of JRC was the floor with all the classrooms, the true heart of activity. In the morning, adult students worked on language skills, computer skills, and general office skills. At noon, 15 of the staff gathered in another of the classrooms for the monthly staff meeting. Each staff member took a turn at running a staff meeting. That included preparing and distributing an agenda, presiding at the meeting, and writing up minutes for distribution afterwards. Today it was Donna's turn to preside. She sat at the head table, along with Mei, and others sat at tables arranged in a U around the perimeter of the classroom.

The meeting began with Mei giving kudos to Ursula and the others who had helped make the Job Fair on Saturday a success. There was a round of applause, and Ursula blushed. A visitor from a national political advocacy organization for Asians was then introduced, and she explained that grant money was available to educate Asian immigrants about their employee rights. Donna suggested that this information be incorporated into JRC's classes. After the visitor left, Mei also excused herself, and the meeting continued through two more agenda items—ideas for creating fee-for-service programs and reports from program managers on goals for the upcoming quarter. The fee-for-service idea generated lively discussion for about 20 minutes, and an ad hoc committee of teachers, job developers, and other staff agreed to continue the planning the next week. An intern from the local college was introduced, and Chris announced that the YMCA needed volunteers for a preliteracy program. The meeting adjourned promptly at 1 o'clock.

The staff meetings were a good window into the way JRC functioned as an organization. There were three levels of management: the executive director, the program managers, and everyone else. Mei held managers' meetings monthly to deal with difficult policy, program, or budgetary issues. (Ursula called them "Amazon meetings" because at the time it was an all-female staff at the manager level, and she said, "The discussions are incredible.") On the critical issues that could make or break JRC, Mei held a tight rein. On other issues, she strove to allow staff freedom and growth opportunities. For example, the rotating leadership of the staff meetings and the openness of the agenda were attempts at staff development and at allowing new ideas to be developed. Several staff told me there was room to try new things here or to try one's hand at something new. Want to learn to write grant proposals? Join the committee that's researching new funding sources in the *Federal Register* once a week. Want to write? Submit an article for the newsletter. Want to get involved in the community outside JRC? The mayor's task force on homeless people needs volunteers.

As staff members left the meeting, afternoon classes got under way. Adult students were out at job sites for their internships. CCN students came bursting through the doors at 3 o'clock—third and fourth graders from the East Indies, Mexico, Cambodia, Vietnam. They had book bags on their backs, hands filled with snacks. They bounded up the stairs to their second-floor classroom for a science lesson on mold. Their teacher, Juan, had assembled several lemons with mold growing on them, a bag full of mushrooms, and small hand-held microscopes. After dropping their book bags and coats at the computer workstations around the room, they assembled around the front table to see what Juan had in store.

> JUAN: Is mold a plant or animal?
> BOY: Plant.
> JUAN: How many types of mold are on this lemon?
> GIRL: Three?
> JUAN: That's a good guess. But actually, the three different colors
> you see are really young mold and old mold.
> GIRL: [Touching mold on lemon] Oooh, it's mushy.
> BOY: It stinks.
> GIRL: [Looking at mold through microscope] It looks like gold.
> (6/12/94 field notes)

After students had a chance to examine the mold growing on the lemon, Juan brought out a handful of mushrooms for them to examine and led them in a discussion of this type of mold. Students were inquisitive: "Why are mushrooms so expensive in the store?" Juan explained that it's hard to grow them. This prompted another question: "If they're so hard to grow, how come mushrooms are growing in my backyard?"

After a lively exchange between teacher and students, the students were directed to take a piece of paper and draw the mushroom, labeling the parts they'd named. Then they went to the computers to compose reports about the lesson. One student wrote:

> Today I learned that mushroom takes a long time to grow. And they grow in the night not like ordinary plants that's why they have green and the mushroom is white. I also learned that some mushrooms are even poisonis.

While Juan helped students with their reports, Joel, another JRC staff member, had walked to one of the hotels five blocks away and was conducting a Project Advance class with Spanish-speaking employees who worked in the steward's department. He had prepared a worksheet listing the different types of tableware they had to be able to identify in order to set tables for banquets correctly.

JOEL: What is number 5, Jose?
JOSE: Wine basket.
JOEL: Alonzo, what is number 2?
ALONZO: Ladle.
JOEL: Everyone say "ladle." (2/3/93 field notes)

After they'd worked through the vocabulary on the sheet, Joel held up various serving dishes he had on a table at the side of the room—another vocabulary-building exercise—and then gave them a grammar lesson on the uses of the articles *a* and *an*. He reviewed the rules and then said, "Would you say *a* dinner plate or *an* dinner plate? *A* oyster fork or *an* oyster fork?"

The manager for the work team participated along with his staff. Ages, it appeared, ranged from early 20s to 50s. When Joel passed out another worksheet that tested their ability to use *a* and *an*, the manager muttered, "If we flunk this, do we stay after school?" Laughter accompanied the joke. It appeared there was an easy rapport between teacher and students, between manager and employees.

Back at JRC, the day was winding to a close. Most everyone worked hard. In the opinion of people I talked to, there were few slackers. Each employee's motivation was slightly different. Among the four writers I followed over a 12-month period, I saw individual motivations and career goals emerge in our conversations. But what they said was true of the staff of JRC as a whole, and what I saw in them as well was a core belief in the value of helping other people. Yes, it was a job to pay the bills, but all seemed to have chosen this nonprofit, JRC, because they took satisfaction in its mission. As Selma put it in her succinct way, "I think that most people are here because they feel a sense of helping people who need help, especially newcomers" (2/16/93, p. 7).

As the lights were turned off when the last employee left for the day and the building alarm was set, at least one individual in another part of the city also was getting ready to go home from work because of the training she had gotten at JRC. Mary Xu, 23, had immigrated to the United States with her family 2 years earlier. Soon after her family's arrival, her father became ill and was diagnosed with terminal cancer. Mary suddenly became the person who needed to support the family, but her English skills were limited, and she had no local work experience. She was torn between the need to care for her dying father and the need to make progress in acquiring language and job skills. Finally she decided to enroll in the full-time, 18-week program at JRC.

Two years had passed since then. In a few weeks, Mary would be honored in a celebration with the governor at the state capitol for receiving the city's Private Industry Council award for "Alumna of the Year," an award given to an exemplary graduate of an employment training program. Her father passed away when she was midway through the program at JRC. But she persevered, graduated with her class, and found a job as an administrative assistant at the Neighborhood Self-Help Center. At the JRC banquet a few months later, she would receive the JRC Alumna of the Year Award. Handing her the commemorative plaque, Mei would tell the 500 people in attendance, "Mary has overcome tremendous obstacles and has been able to thrive in this society. We at JRC are proud to have been able to make some difference in her life" (9/23/92, field notes).

Like any institution and any group of individuals, JRC was not without its tensions and its internal struggles over its identity, personnel issues, and allocations of resources. The mission of the organization was carried forward amid personality conflicts, successes and failures, and learning by trial and error. As I became more insider than outsider to the organization over the course of the year, the public image I have depicted here became layered in my understanding with its private side, through asides about internal politics and organizational crises the four writers would share in the midst of our conversations about their writing. It was the public image of JRC, however, which by and large shaped the writing tasks of the four women I followed. Always the standard upheld in any written document, that image was in fact a large part of the reality of the organization, and it was against this image that writing tasks proceeded. Hence, without further discussion of the institution's more private side, which would serve no constructive purpose in this study, I proceed.

CHAPTER 3

The Institutional Site of Composing: Converging and Overlapping Discourse Communities

> When writing is studied as a reflection and manifestation of culture, researchers emphasize discovering what writing means to participants and what patterns of literacy behavior participants display in making sense of their world.
>
> —Carolyn L. Piazza, "Identifying Context Variables in Research on Writing"

A HUGE BANQUET ROOM on the third floor of a restaurant in the heart of the city's Chinese community bustled with activity at 6:30 on a Tuesday evening in September. Thirty-five round tables, each seating 15, were almost full, and a number of guests were still coming off the elevator to stop at the greeters' table. Above the hum of voices, a drum beat to the winding gyrations of a Chinese dragon on the stage, and waiters brought steaming bowls of wonton soup to the tables.

Ursula spoke with Mei, the executive director; then with the board president; with the master of ceremonies (a local TV news reporter); with Selma, who was handling the raffle; and with the banquet manager from the restaurant—all within a space of 5 minutes. She was too nervous to sit down at one of the tables. She had had the job of coordinating this annual event, the twenty-sixth anniversary fund-raising dinner—but her first, since she'd been at Job Resource Center (JRC) only 4 months. At stake was JRC's reputation in the community and about $50,000 in contributions toward JRC's annual budget. Represented in the audience were all of JRC's key supporters: elected officials, labor leaders, business partners, community organizers, government bureaucrats, heads of philanthropic organizations, leaders from school-based vocational training programs, the news media, and, of course, JRC employees.

By 7 o'clock, the first course finished, the entertainers yielded the stage to the president of the board and then Mei, who took the microphone and welcomed guests in Cantonese, then in English. The board president spoke of weak economic conditions, rising unemployment, and government budget cuts that created even greater challenges than those encountered in the past 26 years. Mei spoke of strengthening partnerships with business and other nonprofits.

Following a round of polite applause, they left the stage, and waiters circulated throughout the room, placing dishes of fish, chicken, duck, vegetables, and rice on the lazy susans on the tables. Quickly, conversations resumed and even the ethnographer stopped note taking for some dinner and a chat with the president of one of the Chinese family associations.

After 30 minutes, the master of ceremonies took his place at the podium on the stage to begin the evening's program: a keynote speech by a political candidate and the presentation of awards to the president of a local foundation, the chancellor of a local community college, a fire commissioner, the CEO of the Private Industry Council in one of the cities JRC served, a local businessman, and, finally, Mary Xu, alumna of the year. Mei and the president of the board, standing on the platform with the emcee, supplied the award plaques and handshakes. The councilman spoke of "keeping the American dream alive for new arrivals to our community." The foundation president said, "No organization we've supported has been more successful than JRC." The CEO said she was impressed with JRC's "attention to people most at risk of failing in the community." The chancellor of the local college spoke of his immigrant grandparents' sacrifices for their children. Several of the speakers referred to the recent riots in connection with the Rodney King beating trial and reiterated the theme for the dinner—"Diversity Now."

At 8:30 the entertainment resumed, and Ursula sat down, finally, at a table with fellow employees. By 9:30, the entertainment and raffles over, only a few guests and employees of JRC remained as waiters cleared the banquet tables.

THE WEB OF DISCOURSE COMMUNITY INTERACTIONS

An anthropologist viewing this event might examine its ritualistic nature. An accountant might consider the balance sheet on the morning after. A politician might count potential constituencies reached. A journalist might note whether any political contender made a significant claim in a speech. And an ethnographer of communications will consider the event in terms of the ongoing web of communication between one institutional site of composing, JRC, and four other institutional entities represented at the event, each with its own distinct web of communications practices.

This event was the result of a massive communications effort. Ursula had created over 500 pieces of correspondence (some accomplished through mail-merge computer software, some carefully crafted as one-of-a-kind text) and put together three publicity pieces: a press release, the invitation, and the evening's program brochure. She also had collaborated on the speeches for the president of the board and Mei. Although not involved in the creation of texts directly related to the dinner, each of the other three writers, Selma, Birgitte, and Pam, was involved with those who attended the event on an ongoing basis through written communiqués. For them, the evening offered a chance to add a face-to-face conversation to the numerous communications in writing.

In fact, if we wish to understand the institutional site of composing at JRC, we must look also at four major overlapping sites of composing—or discourse communities—that were represented at the fundraiser and in large measure shaped JRC's external written communications: (1) the federal and state agencies that dispersed vocational training funds to JRC, (2) the city government in JRC's locale that dispersed local and federal money to agencies such as JRC, (3) philanthropic groups that also funded JRC programs, and (4) the business community, an aggregate discourse community made up of unique smaller discourse communities that shared some communicative goals and activities in common with the larger entity. These discourse communities are shown in Figure 3.1.

While these four discourse communities may at first glance appear too amorphous to aid analysis of writing practices, the data will reveal that their communicative practices around written texts differed enough to warrant viewing each as both overlapping with the others and as a unique discourse community in itself. Harris (1989) argues that the boundaries of a discourse community should be drawn around a specific group of individuals (such as one corporate division—public relations, or marketing, for example) so as not to become so all-encompassing as to become meaningless. However, I use the term here to describe groups

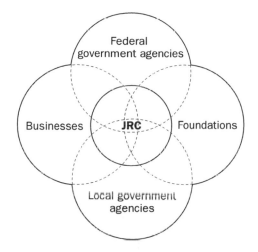

Figure 3.1. Overlapping discourse communities. JRC, the nonprofit agency studied here, had both unique characteristics and characteristics that overlapped with those of the discourse communities with which it interfaced.

whose boundaries are expansive and permeable but nonetheless recognizable by virtue of differing writing practices.

Nonetheless, it is no easy task to develop a working definition of discourse community, that is, to isolate those particular aspects of a social group that bear upon writing. A synthesis from the work of anthropologists (Basso, 1974; Chin, 1991; Heath, 1981), rhetoricians (Bazerman, 1988; Rafoth, 1990), and sociolinguists (Gunnarsson, 1997; Swales, 1990) who have focused on writing in relation to social contexts leads me to suggest three features critical to any discourse community:

1. *communications channels*—oral and written—whose interplay affects the purposes and meanings of written texts (Basso, 1974; Heath, 1983)
2. *norms for genres* that may be unique to a community or shared with overlapping communities (Swales, 1990)
3. *writers' roles* (including how these roles are distributed) *and tasks* as defined by the communicative situation (Basso, 1974; Heath, 1983; Swales, 1990)

The distinguishing features of discourse communities can be recognized and understood only with an understanding of critical factors influencing

Influencing factors

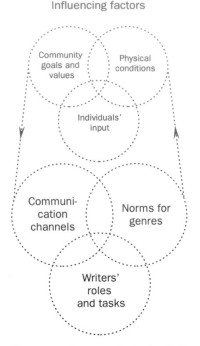

Elements of communicative activity

Figure 3.2. The dynamic elements of discourse communities. Influencing factors give rise to the three elements of communicative activity.

discourse communities. In the data and literature, I've identified three such factors that seem to be most salient.

1. a set of underlying *goals and values* for the community that influence all aspects of text production (Rafoth, 1988; Swales, 1992)
2. *physical conditions,* such as spatial arrangements for working and tools for communication (computers, faxes, etc.), that influence writing activities (Chin, 1991; Gunnarsson, 1997)
3. *individuals' input*—previous experiences, personal goals, and skills as brought to bear on community writing practices (Bazerman, 1988)

I will develop and explain these features and factors throughout the rest of this chapter. Figure 3.2 depicts these six elements in dynamic relation to one another and will serve as the lens through which the writing activities in the study are analyzed in this chapter.

JRC's mission as a community-based, nonprofit provider of job training and job-related literacy training required the organization to accomplish three overarching goals: (1) to conceptualize and implement solid training and placement programs that gave JRC a niche among a number of competent, competitive vocational and language-training service providers, (2) to raise over $3 million annually to fund the programs, and (3) to create visibility and goodwill among its constituencies and thus a climate of political/social support. From these three goals, all communication—oral and written—stemmed.

Written text at JRC had high stakes: people's jobs at JRC and a segment of society dependent on the agency's services. Responsibility for a particular program meant responsibility for all writing to support the program—business correspondence, grant proposals, and mandatory reports to funding agencies. Each of the four writers had to interact with at least two of the discourse communities that overlapped with JRC, as well as understand the ways in which the agency's own ethos, mission, and history were played out in the creation and use of texts. By looking at JRC both as a discourse community itself and as sharing writing practices with several other discourse communities, we will gain a broader understanding of this particular writing site. I turn first to a description of those discourse communities external to JRC with which it had significant interactions and then, within this broader context, to an examination of JRC as a discourse community in its own right.

The Discourse Community of a Federal Agency

Leong, the former executive director of JRC, and Donald, a college professor and professional grant writer, both held Ph.D.s, had responsible managerial positions at their respective jobs, and had written numerous successful grant proposals to federal agencies. But both also indicated that learning to respond to a federal government request for proposal (RFP), the genre that would secure entrance into the discourse community of a federal agency, was not easy.

> [Federal] proposal writing is unlike anything that any of us have been trained in. . . . I remember writing my first proposal, I just couldn't understand how anyone would want something that illogical presented to them. (Leong, 9/15/92, p. 7)

The federal ones, they're absolutely the worst. They look like they're designed to scare people off. (Donald, 2/25/93, p. 10)

The specific discourse community investigated here is the U.S. Department of Education's workplace literacy program. The data are not intended to be a generalized characterization of communications in all federal agencies. However, those I interviewed both within JRC and outside the organization who had applied for grants from a number of federal agencies tended to speak of those instances of writing under the single label "the federal grant proposal." So in referring to the genre and the social entity, I will use the terminology and distinctions my informants did.

Before the proposal actually was written, a number of research steps were required, including researching sources of funding. This research required a combination of document literacy and technical literacy: Sources such as the *Federal Register,* the *Catalog of Federal Domestic Assistance*, and the computer-based information program, *Federal Assistance Program Retrieval System*, were not user friendly. Texts were laden with technical jargon. Another experienced government grant writer, Anna, explained the challenge the writer faced in this way:

The thing to realize when you're writing a government proposal is that governments speak in code. In order to be understood by everybody, they're understood by practically nobody. . . . I remember spending hours looking at their definitions of what's the difference between a goal and objective and a mission. (1/19/93, p. 1)

Research also entailed becoming knowledgeable about both theoretical bases for program activities and current practices in vocational and literacy training. The U.S. Department of Education expected that programs proposed would be innovative, so research was a critical task in the process of writing a successful federal grant proposal.

Another form of research—networking—was also essential for writing a successful grant proposal because the RFP didn't contain all the information grant writers needed about the standards of evaluation. This fact was learned only as one became an insider to the discourse community.

In their preliminary attempts to respond to federal RFPs, Birgitte, Selma, and Pam wrote solely from the information in the RFP, and the grants were turned down. In fact, if we compare Selma's first proposal to fund a family literacy program for preschoolers and their parents, which was *not* successful, with the proposal she subsequently wrote for a different type of family literacy program, which *did* get funded, we will see the difference both library research and networking made. To put together the preschool family literacy proposal, she spent a few days in the library looking up material about existing programs and then called some of them. She also had one meeting with the state consultant to show him an executive summary—but that meeting was on Friday, and the proposal was due Monday. She had begun to take some of the steps toward writing a successful proposal but had not allowed herself enough time or gone far enough in researching this particular discourse community.

Birgitte went through a similar process the first time she applied for a federal grant. She attempted to respond in a 3-week period to an RFP for preventing high school students from dropping out of school. Here is her account of the process of putting the proposal together:

> Leong put it on my desk. And then I guess about 3 weeks before it was due, we got around to talking about it. And we realized that we needed partners. . . . So we called somebody there, and we got some meetings together and talked about how it should be structured . . . then I wrote a couple of pages of a draft, outlining the partnership and then we met again, and I think I just wrote it based on the second meeting, and I spent a week writing it and getting the data. (8/4/92, pp. 7–8)

In September, word came that the proposal was turned down. I discussed the readers' comments—two sets of comments from two different readers—with Birgitte. They pointed to what they saw as flaws in the program design and mandated requirements in the RFP that hadn't been addressed. Reflecting to me on what she saw, she said:

> We just sent it into like a black tunnel. I think ideally, next time around, we would contact somebody who has been a grader before or who knows what the commission is really looking for, because we really had no idea. And also somebody who can lobby some for us. (9/29/92, p. 3)

Although Birgitte had been very successful in writing grant proposals to private philanthropic organizations, that knowledge did not serve her well enough to be successful in writing to a distinctly different discourse community. Both Birgitte and Selma did too little research—in particular, not enough field research—to write successful federal proposals the first time they made the attempt.

Another issue is the structure of the federal grant proposal. At a glance, a number of subsections of the federal RFP that must be addressed one by one in the grant proposal appear redundant. And the sections do not necessarily build on each other in logical sequence, yet the writer must attempt to create a coherent text. These factors require that the writer not only decipher the meaning of the surface language of the RFP but also understand what Donald referred to as the "deep structure" of the proposal's sections. He said:

> I've had to really analyze and think about it, and it seems to me that in every grant that I've ever seen or ever written . . . it can be boiled down to maybe a half a dozen critical functions that need to be accomplished. . . . It's the underlying structure . . . in an RFP . . . if you filter through a little bit of the surface jargon. (2/25/93, p. 6)

But that knowledge of how the genre works does not come readily. He confessed:

> Probably not till about 3 or 4 years that I felt like I really knew what I was doing, other than just kind of thrashing about and writing stuff that sounded impressive. . . . It's easier to take on the flavor of the lingo than to really hook into what's going on at the level of discourse function. (2/25/93, p. 9)

The process by which the proposals were read and scored also influenced the norms for the genre of the federal grant proposal. Tom, who had been an evaluator for grant proposals in the U.S. Department of Education, described to me a long process that started even before the week spent in Washington, with a 43-page, self-study workbook sent in advance to train readers in their job duties. On the first day in Washington, they were given another training session, including coaching on what to look for in this specific set of proposals and a practice proposal to evaluate. The next day, evaluation began in earnest. He said, "We are given review criteria and forms that have explicit language that we should use against which to judge the proposals" (3/11/93, p. 3).

In teams of three, the readers were given a stack of seven to nine proposals to take back to their hotel rooms and evaluate by Friday. Each member of the team would read each proposal and rate it independently. Then the three evaluators would meet to decide on a consensus score. Tom said, "Then you get into a discussion about . . . what makes one proposal better than another" (3/11/93, p. 6). These discussions were made difficult by the fact that the readers came from different backgrounds. Generally, he said, federal agencies tried to get experts in the appropriate field of endeavor to read the proposals: academicians, program administrators, technical assistance people like himself. But each reader, he said, had a different internal standard about what made a good program, that is, different background knowledge and experience, making coming to a consensus difficult.

Donald, who also had been a reader for Department of Education grant proposals, offered a description similar to Tom's of the evaluation process for grant proposals and the effect it had on the proposal writer who was aware of that process.

> You can pretty much envision . . . who the reader's going to be and what context they're going to be reading this thing in. They're going to be sitting in a conference room somewhere or a hotel room for 3 days with a stack of about 20 of these, *reading through them with a rating sheet, trying desperately to figure out what the hell this thing is about, and then what's this next one about.* (2/25/93, pp. 9–11, emphasis added)

Also important to an understanding of the norms for the federal grant proposal is seeing the relationship between oral and written channels of communication. In JRC's experience with the Department of Education, oral communication between grant requester and grant maker normally was limited to answering technical questions. Usually, texts from JRC to the Department of Education were the sole form of communication between the two entities. The grant proposal was a document of extreme importance: It served to "level the playing field" of institutions across the country vying for federal funds.

From "decoding" the language of the RFP, to researching the unwritten expectations of the evaluators, to figuring out the complexities of a program plan that involved hundreds of people over as much as a 3-year time span, to gaining a national perspective on the social issue at hand and then writing a document that could be 100 pages long (for the federal grant Donald was working on, he would end up with a 60-page narrative, supplemented by another 60 pages of charts and supporting documents)—grant writing was a communication process that entailed multiple layers of complexity and placed a number of literacy demands on the writer. Gaining a broader view than just the peculiarities of the RFP— including an understanding of underlying values and goals that drove the discourse community—was ultimately what was required to become a successful participant in the community. Neither the RFP that initiated this labor-intensive process nor the 3- or 4-inch-thick proposal that eventually was mailed to Washington could be viewed in itself. Each had to be understood in relation to the web of discourse community practices in which the genre was embedded, some of which have been described here. The proposal was a yardstick by which all parties staked their claims—the grant seeker, in terms of promises to deliver a set of goods; and the grant maker, in terms of looking for the best idea among hundreds to spend taxpayer dollars on and keep a nation on its feet. To make matters more complex, federal agencies were not always uniform in their defining characteristics as discourse communities. The grant writer had to be able to discern where those differences lay.

The Discourse Community of City Government

It would be easy to imagine that city government would follow discourse practices similar to the federal government. However, as a writer at JRC would find out over time, there was a different set of communicative practices associated with written text in the discourse community of city government in JRC's locale. Two key factors provided explanations for the differences between the grant-making practices within the Department of Education and within JRC's city government. First, being two city blocks from one's audience rather than a few thousand miles, one did business differently—even when it came to the written word. Second, the values and goals of the city and federal discourse communities differed.

Within 2 weeks of the deadline for the federal workplace literacy proposal that Pam assisted Donald and Mei with, another proposal was due—for the same program at JRC, but to a different funding source: the city's Community Development Block Grant (CDBG). The money came from a branch of the federal government, but cities handled the allocation of the funds. Mei had made Pam responsible for all but the budget on this proposal to the city, which was basically an update of the previous year's proposal. Pam had 4 days in which to meet the deadline. Here's her description of the process of putting together the first draft:

> A lot of it was from other proposals. Some of it was from the CDBG proposal that Mei had written last year. And then some of it was from the latest proposal that we had just written, the federal one. And then some of it was just the same lingo. . . . You know, the big phrases and catch words that we throw around in the office. (7/20/92, pp. 1–2)

The city proposal did not require an original or new program idea. And the "genre" of city grant proposal, in contrast to the federal proposal, had a looser set of norms. In fact, the city's RFP was much less specific than the Department of Education's, with its seven sections and 39 subsections. Nor were the city proposals evaluated on a point system, which also allowed for a more flexible genre.

But like the federal RFP, the city RFP used confusing jargon and called for apparent repetitions in different sections of the proposal. Pam had attended the bidders' conference the mayor's office held a few weeks earlier, but she was still not altogether sure what the various sections of the RFP called for. Following the meeting with Mei, Pam would produce three more drafts. Whole chunks of text were moved from one section to another—the overlaps among the eight categories left a lot of room to maneuver. Mei edited some of the wording to take out some colloquial expressions Pam had used and to incorporate appropriate phraseology. Pam spent a half day filling out charts and forms. Finally, the deadline came, and there was no more time to perfect the text. Three copies were made and hand-delivered to the appropriate agency.

But the grant-seeking process did not end there. After the staff of the mayor's Office of Community Development reviewed the proposal and wrote a one-page recommendation regarding funding, the proposal was forwarded to the Citizens Committee, a 20-member panel of private citizens appointed by the mayor. They read the proposals, negotiated any changes they felt should be made in the staff recommendations, and prepared a public document summarizing their recommendations. JRC's proposal was recommended for funding, but at $67,000 instead of the $113,000 requested.

At this point, the process moved into the political arena. Mei called the head of the mayor's Office of Community Development, explaining the need for the full amount of funding requested. She had Pam prepare a letter to a member of the city council with whom Mei had close connections. A few weeks later, the mayor and the Citizens Committee held a public hearing for organizations that wished to appeal the funding decisions. Some 100 nonprofit groups sent representatives to the hearing. Pam was in the city council chambers at City Hall at 5 p.m. to get in line for her allotted 3 minutes before the Committee. When that attempt was unsuccessful, Mei tried once again, through telephone conversations with key city supervisors, to get the funding amount increased. Ultimately, the proposal was funded only at the $67,000 level.

When Pam repeated the process of applying for the same CDBG funds for Project Advance the following year, she assigned a staff member under her to go through last year's proposal and note changes that needed to be made in light of the current RFP. Pam input those changes, made a few other additions, and finished the proposal in an 8-hour day, 4 days less than it took her the year before with the same proposal. She reflected on the difference from the process a year earlier:

> Last year I was really excited because I was really idealistic, and I wanted to show that we had this good model and that it really was meeting people's needs—and this year . . . it's gonna have more to

do with Mei's political clout in getting the funding than it is in our writing it. (7/20/93, pp. 2–3)

The change is indicative of Pam's growing awareness of the dynamics of the discourse community of her local city government and how text functions within that community. The funding usually remained stable from year to year on these local government grants—as long as the agency delivered what it had promised the year before. And text was only a starting place in the whole process. After the initial review of the text by local bureaucrats, text became one element in a complicated political bargaining process, facilitating the face-to-face and telephone conversations in which the hard bargaining took place. The ultimate decision makers for city grants were elected officials, and a decision might have determined their re-election. Birgitte summed up this aspect of grant writing to city agencies:

> If you look at a city council member, they all look at JRC, and they'll say, "They've had 10,000 students. They represent a lot of potential voters. I want them to like me, so I'm going to vote for their proposal." (9/29/92, p. 4)

Charles, who was second in command at the mayor's Office of Community Development, confirmed these perspectives of writers at JRC:

> Some folks come with perceptions that if they lobby hard politically, it doesn't really matter what they put down on paper. . . . We have a number of situations where existing agencies do not write the best proposals, but by the weight of their services that they've provided we will give a little bit more . . . consideration to them. (6/9/93, pp. 4–5)

Even apart from the political maneuvering associated with a city grant proposal, it also took on different textual features from those of the federal proposal. The two main reasons for the differences in genre features and roles of the grant proposal in these two discourse communities had to do with community goals and values and differences in physical proximity, which in turn affected the interplay of oral and written communication. The implicit value demonstrated in the grant-making process at the Department of Education was one of "leveling the playing field" among all grant seekers; hence the elaborate structure of the RFP and the point system for scoring the proposals. The federal grant request also had to carry its weight much more by virtue of the written text because of the lack of physical proximity and lack of personal connection between grantor and grantee. However, as Birgitte indicated, at the local level the dual purposes of the grant-making body—to disperse funds and to seek election votes to stay in office—produced a different set of communicative practices. Phone and face-to-face communications played a crucial role in the political process associated with the city's grant-making process. The purpose of the city grant proposal was to instigate a political process, so its formal features were much looser than those of a federal grant proposal.

The underlying goals of this city discourse community changed the writer's role and the norms for the text considerably, too, with fewer incentives for creativity and lower writing standards. However, although the genre constraints for a city proposal in JRC's locale were less daunting than those for a proposal to the U.S. Department of Education, the novice writer at JRC had to learn a number of intricacies of discourse community practice at the local government level, including

- determining how to fit an agency's program goals within the values and goals that drive the city government
- understanding the interrelationship of written text and oral communication within the discourse community
- writing to audiences that varied widely in their background knowledge on the community issue being addressed and their knowledge of JRC (Citizens Committee versus elected officials)
- understanding a genre that was a complicated mixture of both flexible and standardized features

The Discourse Community of Philanthropic Foundations

JRC was new to the foundation world, having relied on government funding for most of its 26-year history. But in the year or two preceding this study, Leong and Birgitte had been successful in attracting several grants from local foundations. Exactly how to enter the relationship with foundations, including the appropriate discourse, was something they were still in the process of learning as I began collecting data, and they had a number of unsuccessful proposals to foundations. However, as I looked at the successful responses and talked to experts in the world of foundation giving, a profile began to emerge of a discourse community that differed from government agencies. What follows is a generalized account, illustrated with the particular case of JRC's relationship with one foundation.

If the grant proposal itself was of primary importance for federal grant decisions, and oral negotiations were a big factor in allocation of city funds, the personal relationship counted most in foundation giving. Text was a facilitator of that relationship but was not the ultimate deciding factor as to whether a nonprofit like JRC would receive a grant. Whether the foundation was a charitable trust established by one individual or a consortium of trusts organized into a community-based foundation such as the Metropolitan Foundation, the program officers or grant administrators at the foundation usually wanted some personal contact with the people and program they were considering funding. They sought assurance of the credibility of the request and that the foundation's philanthropic interests were being served, using written and oral channels of communication.

> Because our nonprofit community is diverse in size, cultural identity, and fundraising experience, the Foundation makes every attempt to understand the fundamental merits of each applicant and concept rather than relying exclusively upon written proposal materials. (*How We Can Serve You*, Metropolitan Foundation, p. 3)

The establishment of that personal relationship no doubt varied in each case.

JRC's first communication with Metropolitan, the letter of intent, was written without any extensive groundwork, either through research of the Foundation's printed materials or phone contact. Some foundations did not want personal contact initially, so JRC was not off base in using a letter of intent as its first step in the communication process. But as soon as the rejection letter came, the board president arranged a meeting with Shawna, the grants officer at the Foundation, who explained the two reasons the letter of intent had not been received favorably: first, JRC had not demonstrated an adequate financial base for its program, and second, she had a personal bias against an aspect of the program design. She suggested steps JRC could take to remedy both problems.

In an interview with me over a year later, after the grant had been awarded, Shawna explained her perspective on the process:

> *We were in a period of courtship for a number of months before they came back to me with a proposal that I felt that I could argue for competently.* And that's not unusual either—for a period, an interactive period of working with one another, with them getting to know me more, with me getting to know them more and what they're trying to do. (3/2/93, p. 13, emphasis added)

In fact, Shawna saw her role as someone looking for "a germ of an idea," something unique or "cutting edge" that fit within the broad mission of the Foundation. In a letter of intent, she was interested in the idea rather than the quality of the writing. She said:

> We get very sophisticated grants written by professors at [the university] to more bureaucratic grants written by the school district, to very cutting-edge grants written by nonprofits, to grants written on the back side of a note pad from grassroots organizations. *And we look very seriously at all of them.* (3/2/93, pp. 1–2, emphasis added)

Shawna had a Ph.D. in education with an emphasis in program evaluation and had worked in the nonprofit sector prior to joining Metropolitan. It was her role to evaluate the idea, see if it had a workable kernel, and bring her expertise in program design, management of nonprofits, and financial planning to bear on the initial request. She wrote down her questions after reading the letter of intent, called the organization, and sometimes arranged a meeting; she also talked to possible clients, board members, competitors, and other community leaders to get a sense of the organization and the need they were proposing to address. In some cases she would help the organization rethink its need and produce a new request.

As the relationship developed and the idea took shape, written documentation became important, and a formal proposal was requested. But in marked contrast to the numerous sections and subsections to be addressed in a response to a federal government RFP, Metropolitan's booklet *How We Can Serve You* gave several suggested formats for a proposal to the foundation under the subheading "How Your Story May Be Told." Here is one sample format—the most extensive of the four samples:

- statement of purpose
- organizational background
- project objectives
- methods
- personnel
- evaluation
- future funding

Shawna stressed that the proposal should be free of jargon—also a marked contrast to proposals written for federal grant-making agencies. Length usually ranged from five to 15 pages. The grant proposal was a flexible form with few rigid features. From Birgitte's perspective, grant proposals to foundations also left much more room for what she called "imaginative" writing: She could use anecdotes of program successes for persuasive appeal.

Once Shawna received the proposal, she wrote a one- to three-page evaluation of its strengths and weaknesses; the proposal then would be reviewed either by her peers for requests under $25,000 or by the Foundation board of directors for larger requests.

If the proposal was funded, the paper trail continued—part of an unspoken, unwritten "rule" of appropriate etiquette in the ongoing relationship between grantor and grantee. JRC sent Shawna a letter any time the program reached a milestone—if another funder came on board, for example, or a new phase of the program began. Birgitte explained what she tried to accomplish in those reports:

> *You should . . . make them feel that their contribution was key.* And you also want to tell them that you're headed in a good direction. And you want to tell them about other funding opportunities that might be emerging. *So they feel that you're . . . not just using them,* and you're also out there trying to get more. (11/17/92, p. 1, emphasis added)

Once a relationship was firmly established with a foundation, it was maintained through both oral and written communication. As Anna, the grant writer, points out:

> The goal of this phone call business is that you want the foundation to tell you what they want you to write in the proposal. You want them to write your proposal for you. So you start off by asking them questions, but pretty soon they're asking you questions, and they're telling you what you need to do instead, and they're guiding you and directing you the whole way through. That's called a relationship with a foundation. (11/15/92, p. 13)

While soliciting funds from foundations involved less bureaucracy, the communication process nonetheless required an understanding of the unique characteristics of philanthropic organizations as discourse communities and a number of strategic moves on the writer's part. As Maggie, a grant writer for another agency similar to JRC, explained:

> I recently got a $25,000 grant from a corporation on the basis of basically a two-page letter of intent that took like an hour to write. I got a $2,000 grant from a foundation after a 15-page detailed narra-

tive proposal that took me 4 days to write. . . . *It's so much a matter of getting to know which foundation is funding your area, what their procedures are, whether they approve or disapprove of you lobbying their boards, you know every single one is different.* (11/10/92, pp. 3–4, emphasis added)

The challenges for the writer entering the discourse community of private foundations require "wearing a different hat," as Maggie put it. At the very least, the writer who wants entrance to philanthropic discourse communities must

- research the idiosyncrasies of the foundation through print documents and networking
- develop a positive working relationship with foundation personnel through face-to-face or phone communication
- write flexibly, meeting the specific formal requirements of a given foundation and conveying both good business acumen and passion for a good cause through a combination of rhetorical strategies

As Anna said:

The relationship that you're building is a long-term relationship. They may say no to you the first year. They may say no to you the second year. They may say no to you the third year. *But your real goal is not to get funding that first year. Your real goal is to become friends with that foundation, to have them respect you, to approach them, to be a peer with them, to become their colleague.* (11/6/92, p. 16, emphasis added)

The Discourse Community of Business Partners

Ursula handled most of the external correspondence, often ghostwriting for Mei. Mei would call on her car telephone and say, "Would you write a letter to so-and-so and cover these three points," and Ursula would jot down the three points on the back of an envelope and prepare a draft that would be edited and refined through several more exchanges.

As Ursula built up a computer file of business letters, she created subdirectories for different categories of routine business letters: thank-you letters, requests for information, donor letters, rejection letters. Whenever possible, she used the same basic text as a starting point, modifying it slightly to fit the particular situation.

But some rhetorical situations would never be routine and required an in-depth understanding of the social context for the communication. For example, a simple letter was often only the tip of the iceberg: Much more was communicated by what was not said or by the very fact that a letter was sent. For example, Ursula told me one day:

> I'm working on a corporate letter for this fund-raising dinner. . . . I have no idea how to write this kind of letter. So I went into the file and looked at what they did last year, and sort of plagiarized from that, and then I got a lot of input from other people. . . . It has to be a sell letter about JRC but it has to have what they get from giving us money. And the problem has been that I really don't know the format. (7/21/92 p. 1)

Another day Ursula showed me a letter written to a tenant who had broken a lease. She talked about the "psychology" behind the letter—Ursula's term for the relationship she was watching her boss orchestrate via the letter.

> Dear [Client]:
>
> Congratulations on your move to a new, expanded facility. All of us at JRC are proud of you and your success.
>
> In our September meeting between you, Peter, Selma and my-self, we discussed the fact that JRC may not be able to rent the base-ment immediately since JRC was operating under the assumption that a new tenant would not be necessary until the fulfillment of your lease (April 1, 1993). Subsequently, Peter and I had a conversa-tion and we arrived at a mutual agreement that you will cover the rent through November 30, 1992 if we are unable to locate a new tenant.
>
> It has been a pleasure working with you over the years and we wish you continued prosperity.
>
> Sincerely,

In essence, Mei was being tough with the tenant about a contractual agreement; she convinced the tenant in a phone conversation to make a large donation to the annual fund-raising dinner in order to compensate for JRC's lost income, in addition to covering rent through November. The letter confirmed the oral agreement and therefore would serve as protection if any legal dispute arose. But Mei also wanted the letter to further the relationship, so to Ursula's draft, Mei added, "We will miss you, so visit us when you're in the neighborhood"—a sentence loaded with implied meaning that would be considered inappropriate to state directly in this discourse community. Mei also instructed Ursula to send flowers to the former tenant's new office location.

In January, close to the Chinese New Year, Ursula received numerous letters from Chinese family associations asking JRC to contribute "letters of proclamation" for the souvenir programs of their banquets. Initially Ursula had no idea how to write these letters or what they should say, so she called a Chinese board member who was familiar with one particular association to ask what they had done. She said:

> He kept saying that they, well they bought this building. I was try-
> ing to figure out what he meant by the fact that they bought this
> building, and then *I realized that, culturally, that's really important,*
> self-sufficient, 'cause they have a building. . . . *There was a click when*
> *I got it, I got what point of view.* (1/26/93, pp. 1–2, emphasis added)

New rhetorical situations like this one arise frequently in business correspondence. Each requires knowledge of the specific context of the communication: the history of the relationship, the areas of mutual and individual concern, and the art of polite negotiation, or, as Ursula put it, "how to keep people's interest and flatter and remind of past obligations and the whole you owe me one I owe you one kind of thing" (7/20/93, p. 11).

In fact, at first glance, "American business" may appear to be too large and amorphous to be considered a discourse community. Certainly individual business entities—both for profit and not for profit—have goals unique and values. JRC, as we will see, functioned much differently in some of its written communication practices from, say, IBM or Procter & Gamble. But some principles for external communication at JRC did *not* vary with rhetorical context and formed a set of practices commonly referred to as business communications. Whether the term applies solely to discourse practices of American businesses as compared, for example, with Japanese businesses is beyond the scope of this study. Nonetheless, for purposes here, the features of those external communications that JRC had with other business entities seemed to form an aggregate of written discourse practices, which I will enumerate briefly.

Ursula had to learn such business community norms as matters of politeness or correct etiquette and the rhetorical negotiation of conflicting interests. What may have seemed on the surface like a matter of phrasing or style was in fact an issue tied to overall norms for the business letter genre. Leong explained:

> Writing business letters . . . what . . . level of friendliness you display and the kind of courtesy that you have to accord business colleagues . . . all those are acquired skills on the job. . . . How do you write someone to tell them we thank you for applying for a certain vacant position, but we really do not find them suitable. . . . I think those are a little bit more challenging 'cause then it's not just reviewing the facts. . . . You have to state the fact, yet you have to say it in such a way that it doesn't hurt people. And of course, legally you don't leave yourself vulnerable to any kind of a possible lawsuit. (9/15/92, pp. 21–22)

A business letter Ursula drafted for her boss provides another example of a seemingly small matter of word choice that in reality tied directly to the discourse community goals of polite, face-saving communication. In a letter to the local congresswoman, who had just been reelected for another term, Ursula had written:

> On behalf of JRC, I wish to extend our congratulations to you for retaining your seat in the House of Representatives. We look forward to two more years of your representation in Congress.

Mei crossed out "retaining your seat" and wrote in "a splendid victory." Ursula was able to laugh about that:

> Yeah, that sounds like she just made it [laughs]. Lucky you, didn't get kicked out of office. *See, I have that almost kind of dry way of writing sometimes, and I'm just the facts ma'am, and she's good with . . . saying things a little bit more flowery in a way that's more acceptable.* (1/12/93, p. 1, emphasis added)

Mei also crossed out the second sentence and substituted, "Your leadership in advocating for excellence in workplace education and job training programs will be especially important in the upcoming years." The purpose of the letter was twofold: to continue a mutually beneficial relationship and to keep JRC's objectives visible. The second objective, which Mei's added sentence addressed, Ursula had missed, forgetting, as she told me one time, "the big picture." Reflecting on Mei's edits to her earlier letters, Ursula said:

I'm shortsighted, but she's got the big picture going and she's making all these big connections. . . . She thinks that way. Everything's
give-and-take and everything has a repercussion, and everything
you do now is gonna affect you later. . . . So, leave doors open in letters and think of ways, bring in ideas that are of relevance to them
and us. (8/5/93, pp. 12–13)

Ursula had to learn another type of business writing in order to fulfill
her duties at JRC, a type of writing largely for symbolic purposes, which
Leong explained this way:

You know, like PR material type of things, *where the form itself is
more important than the contents of the writing*. . . . *You're legitimate*, you
have something printed. You know, stationery and stuff like that.
(9/15/92, p. 3, emphasis added)

What Leong was referring to included minutes of board meetings, press
releases, brochures, and a quarterly newsletter called "New Beginnings."
This category of business writing entailed distinct genres, along with a
set of linguistic features and rhetorical aims as complex as those of the
business letter.

The board minutes were a case in point. The straightforward purpose
was to record the business discussed and decisions made as a tool for
internal efficiency and accountability. But the minutes also served as a
public record of JRC's activities—a conflicting purpose. They were sent
to auditors and to funding agencies, and, given this external audience,
they were edited to present an image of JRC in keeping with its public
face. Organizational difficulties and internal politics were left out of the
public record.

Normally Ursula drafted the minutes, which Mei carefully edited
before they were sent out. Ursula quickly developed a sense that the less
said, the better. When a co-worker sat in for Ursula at a board meeting
and wrote up the minutes, Mei was alarmed: "Too much detail," she said
to Ursula. The symbolic function of the minutes—to present a positive
public image—had to predominate over the secondary purpose of documenting the meeting proceedings—another example of dual and conflicting rhetorical purposes the writer must negotiate so that the text ful-
fills the community's needs.

In sum, business as a discourse community has a number of sub-
groups, all of which have idiosyncratic written communication practices.
However, some norms appear to apply to all business communications:

- politeness
- deference to persons of higher rank
- flattery of the audience and appeals to self-interest
- negotiating conflicting purposes of sender and receiver

THE INTERNAL DISCOURSE COMMUNITY
AT JOB RESOURCE CENTER

Not long after arriving at JRC, Pam received a forceful introduction to its norms and standards for internal communication:

> Memos. People hate them. "Aw, another memo!" I've heard all these comments, although when I first came here, I just figured that everyone just writes memos because they have to have a paper trail. I mean I . . . figured since we have all these . . . federal contracts you're supposed to account for everything, right? So I just naturally assumed that everything had to go in writing. So I was generating all this paperwork, and . . . finally one of the [job] counselors took me aside and just said, "I don't want to ever see another damned memo on my desk. You have something to say, you come and talk to me about it." I was just like going, "Oh, hmm, *I sure didn't divine the culture of this organization very well.*" (Pam, 8/11/92, p. 4, emphasis added)

Material conditions (number of employees, physical layout, etc.) and underlying discourse community values unique to JRC dictated the norms of the discourse community within the institution.

JRC was an organization of approximately 50 full- and part-time employees, and most of the organization's activities and staff were centered in its 2,000-square-foot headquarters building in the heart of an urban area, with a satellite office with a staff of 10 in a nearby city. At the main office, physical proximity and the small staff allowed much business to be conducted face to face. Colleagues met by chance in the hallway, or someone could be sought out easily in an office or the computer room. Smokers taking a break exchanged information in front of the building, and others met across the street at the cafe, over coffee or lunch. Pam said, "Hanging out. Passing each other in the halls. That's how information gets transmitted" (8/11/92, p. 4). Managers held regular staff meetings as well—sometimes weekly, sometimes every other week.

Leong, who directed JRC until 2 months after I arrived, explained his own preference for face-to-face communication:

I don't write memos to people when I tell them to do something. I'd rather sit down and talk to them about it, and if [we] need to, then we'll write something down. That way *it becomes an interactive type of a session instead of I'm telling someone to do something. . . . In the whole process of talking, you get more things clarified.* (9/15/92, p. 1, emphasis added)

Although Mei, his successor, put more things in writing, oral communication still predominated for relaying information internally. Oral communication had more immediacy, but the preference for face-to-face talk was also indicative of the organization's cultural values.

In March, Pam told me of a discussion during an all-day staff retreat about the agency's self-image:

There was a big debate over what metaphor we should use to see ourselves. Are we a family, or are we a company? I think there's still some tension about that because we all want to be very compassionate and liberal and like a family and take care of each other. But at the same time everybody really wants us to be more like a corporation and be professional and formalize and have systems and goals. (3/2/94, p. 4, emphasis added)

The pull between the intimacy of a family and the more professional image of a corporation was at the heart of the conflict over whether to communicate internally in writing or orally. Pam explained:

Since we're so small and we're like a family, people sort of view writing in two ways. One is they feel threatened because something's down on paper, like when it's codified, it's somehow a threat. Or, that it's a way of being efficient. If we were a corporation people would have no problem with a memo or a notes. But here there's . . . this attitude towards memos, like, "Why? Why did you have to write this and you couldn't tell me?" *'Cause if you're a family you just see each other around the house and just mention things. But if you're more of a corporation, there has to be some kind of formalized system.* (3/16/93, pp. 1–2, emphasis added)

Pam liked the idea of JRC as a family, but she preferred to put things in writing because it was more efficient. She managed a staff of six instructors who were often out at the workplace sites where they conducted classes, so catching people could be difficult. In a 3-month period, August through October, Pam wrote seven internal memos.

These memos had various purposes. In the sales pitch, she carefully spelled out the reasonableness of the request. The memos to another manager contained important information that needed prompt action. Two memos were gentle reprimands and reminders to staff of matters already mentioned orally. The request to the bookkeeper was one of the few standardized internal communication procedures: Financial transactions were always in writing. And Pam's upcoming absence from the office prompted a memo. Pam felt each issue warranted written instead of oral communication.

However, she continued to get flack from her staff for her memos. One of the instructors asked Pam to handle more things orally; as a teacher, she felt she had too many papers to keep track of. Pam related the conversation with the instructor:

> You know, it takes me 10 times as long to do it verbally and catch everyone and have to listen to everything that they have to say. *She says, "I know it's less efficient, but it's a better way to get us to do things."* *And so I have to change my style.* (3/2/93, pp. 11–12, emphasis added)

Over the course of the year, Pam experimented with different solutions to the negative attitudes in the office about memos. She tried different formats for memos, using informal, script-like fonts, icons, or other bold graphics to make the communication seem less "threatening." She used humor: "Which one of you has time to do this? Don't say 'Pam!'" (8/11/92 memo). When making a request, she was conciliatory: "Let me know how else I can help coordinate this process and make life easier for you" (7/30/92 memo). If she was addressing just one person, she tried to adapt to the particular individual's communication style. Another strategy was to save up the items she needed to communicate, writing one longer memo rather than a series of short ones—"so that people don't have tons of paper flying across their desks"(4/20/93, p. 6). She also was learning how to position her messages in memos differently:

> . . . *now the kind of memos I write it's like, "Well, this is to inform you of something, and we'll talk about it later."* You know, whereas before it was like, "This is what I need. Give it to me." [laughs] (4/20/93, p. 6, emphasis added)

In reality, though, no matter what efforts were made to write a friendly, nonthreatening memo, at JRC the very act of putting something in writing conveyed the importance of the matter. Ursula was on very good terms with Birgitte and talked to her all the time. But when she had to deal for the third time with a member of Birgitte's staff failing to set the building alarm after a weekend class, she wrote Birgitte "a nasty memo." When Selma had to handle a personnel dispute with two of her instructors, she put in writing the agreements made in the previous day's meeting for written documentation in case any personnel action had to be taken.

In addition to memos regarding day-to-day business, managers at JRC also had to write procedural documents (Ursula wrote the employee handbook and personnel procedures), monthly reports to Mei (who in turn wrote the director's report to the board), and minutes of the staff meeting (this duty rotated among the staff).

Even within an organization as small as JRC, some internal events required the formality of written communication. Putting requests or actions in writing was a tool for holding people accountable. (See Yates, 1989, for documentation of the rise of this practice of internal written communication as a part of the "systematic management" philosophy that began to appear in the 1880s in American business.) It was also a means of being fair. Pam said:

> It's . . . to ensure that everyone gets the same information. . . . I mean I find out that when I tell people things, that's fine, but then some people ask me more probing questions and then they get a different story, and then they talk to each other. It's like, "Well, hey, I didn't know that. And what about this?" And you know, so at least *at the bare minimum I want a fair distribution of information.* (3/16/93, pp. 10–11, emphasis added)

But probably the most important feature of the internal discourse community at JRC was the sometimes prolonged face-to-face interaction accompanying all internal texts. For example, in producing a two-page memo confirming the pay rate for and procedures for hiring workplace literacy instructors, Pam had to go through extensive negotiations with the bookkeeper, Mei, Ursula, and the other program managers. She said:

> It was like all this talk, talk, talk, talk . . . just to produce this one little memo saying, "This is what the person's status is. Please pay them." *I had to spend 2 months negotiating all these different things with all these different people* . . . and then I thought, this is really how it is in business, you know? . . . *I could write the most clear memo, but if somebody doesn't agree with it or they find one little flaw, then I'm going to have to change it all over again.* [laughs] (8/5/93, pp. 15–17, emphasis added)

While written communication was secondary to oral communication and while the format of most internal texts was loose (writing in bullet form and in incomplete sentences was perfectly acceptable), the social relations at JRC associated with those texts (down, up, and across ranks) could be as complex as those associated with the documents for external audiences. A complex set of institutional purposes had to be accomplished: accountability, record keeping, fairness, legal protection, efficiency, analysis. At the same time, the "human factor" had to be taken into account—that is, people's individual needs and communication styles. The writer needed to develop a sense not only of what internal matters to put in writing, but of how to handle multiple and sometimes conflicting discourse community norms, even in a small organization that considered itself "family." JRC's internal discourse community was the most intimate and idiosyncratic of the five discourse communities the four writers had to understand.

DISCOURSE COMMUNITY RECONSIDERED

The usefulness of discourse community as a conceptual lens for understanding writers and writing has been debated considerably in composition studies. In addition to the problem of too few studies attempting to operationalize the concept, some in the field have argued on philosophical and political grounds against the notion. Claims as to the consequences of discourse communities fall to either side of an ideological fence. One side views attempts at defining discourse communities as recognition of clearly identifiable systems of rules, therefore engendering a rigid and untenable formalist position (Nystrand, Greene, & Weimelt, 1993). Others (Kent, 1991) have argued that discourse communities' dynamic, changing nature leads to the problem of relativism. The biggest debate, though, centers on what constitutes a discourse community. Or, to return to the central question of this chapter, how can we identify those borders at which textual practices change?

From a purely methodological standpoint, discourse community is a conceptual frame that is hard to "see." Like culture, a discourse community can be examined partially through its artifacts—written texts—but as this study demonstrates, the artifacts are only the tip of the iceberg. Short time frames or too structured a research methodology will prevent an understanding of the full range of factors shaping the communicative behaviors of members of a given discourse community. Like anthropologists who must "go native" in order to fully understand the people they are studying, the writing researcher must be willing to sit for a long time in one spot, with antennae extending wide, in order to pick up knowledge that is largely tacit to the participants in the community and rarely talked about in any systematic way.

Only JRC's practices as a discourse community could be examined in detail in this study; other discourse communities revealed themselves only as their practices overlapped with JRC's. But the particulars of each community's practices are of secondary interest here: the primary question is whether a conception of discourse community, if stabilized, can provide a useful heuristic for writers and teachers of writing in aiding those border crossings from one set of writing practices to another, crossings such as the four writers at JRC encountered. As Rafoth (1998) points out:

> The conceptual metaphor of audience inevitably orients our thinking toward readers and questions about their possible response to texts, stereotypes about their likely attitudes and beliefs, and musings about whether they really exist at all—*all important questions, but only features of some larger picture which concepts of audience never quite seem to capture.* (p. 142, emphasis added)

Cognitive psychologists talk about the notion of high-road transfer—the ability of an "expert" to recognize similarities in different situations because knowledge in long-term memory is organized into useful categories of "abstract structural attributes" (Perkins & Salomon, 1989b; Salomon & Globerson, 1987). Does the notion of discourse community qualify as such an organizing schema for writers to use in making sense of local conditions for writing that are new and unfamiliar? Or, to put it another way, what does discourse community knowledge add to the picture of what expert writing performance looks like?

Loosely, I have taken a discourse community to represent that social entity within which a set of distinctive writing practices occur and beyond whose borders different writing practices occur. But a summary of the data in relation to the six elements that guided my analysis of community practices will illustrate more precisely the meaning of the term as I'm using it here.

Communicative Practices

Here I summarize the key aspects of discourse community observed at this research site, which can be parsed for a full understanding of how such a community is functioning.

Communication Channels. What to put in writing and when in a chain of events to commit something to writing were practices associated with writing which the savvy writer could maneuver. A back-and-forth between oral and written communication occurred in most of the occasions for writing observed at JRC. Texts either supplemented oral communication or paved the way for face-to-face or phone communication. As a result of the intertwining of oral and written communication at JRC, no text could be viewed apart from the web of oral interactions of the community.

Norms for Genres. While underlying rhetorical purposes for the genre of the grant proposal were the same (to persuade the granting institution of the credibility and worthiness of the request for funds) and the types of information included in the proposals were similar (goals, program elements, outcome measures, etc.), the surface features of the grant proposals varied widely among federal, city, and foundation proposals. Differences in the genre's features were a manifestation of differing needs and purposes of the respective discourse communities that "owned" the genres.

Writers' Roles and Tasks. Overall positioning of writers within the discourse community in relation to social hierarchies affected the types of writing tasks. For example, at the banking institution where Ursula had worked prior to JRC, writers' roles conformed to a rigid social hierarchy. Because of her low-level status in the bank, Ursula was not allowed to write except on rare occasions, and her editing suggestions routinely were rejected, again due to her social position within the organization. But at JRC, even employees whose jobs required little writing were given opportunities to write for the newsletter or to a client, and they were valued as editors of others' writing. In line with the community's values, writing at JRC was a shared community responsibility, with some members taking leadership roles as writers and others taking lesser writing roles.

Factors Influencing Discourse Communities

Understanding the dimensions and meaning of the discourse community's practices around production of text came about in the context of looking at several critical undergirding factors.

Community Goals and Values. Grant-writing and grant-making activities varied widely among the three types of organizations: federal agencies, local government, and private foundations. Federal bureaucrats had the responsibility to execute congressional laws fairly and impartially, city officials had the dual demands of keeping their elected positions and executing their duties in accordance with their constituents' wishes, and private foundations carried out the missions of key philanthropists. These differing goals led to different writing activities and to different norms for a common genre, the grant proposal.

Physical Conditions. Physical proximity also played a role in the activities centered around grant making. Close proximity between JRC and both city and private grant makers enabled intense negotiations. Physical proximity of employees at JRC also influenced the interplay of oral and written channels of communication within the organization, and enabled collaborative writing practices. On the other hand, physical proximity also meant constant interruptions during periods of writing.

Individuals' Input. In an organization the size of JRC, one writer's skills or one manager's communicative style could make a difference. Leong and Mei both were disposed to face-to-face communications. Ursula, the English major, would not allow any of JRC's public documents out the door without careful editing. Birgitte's creative vein lent a boost to foundation grant writing; others tried to mimic her grant proposals. Whether the contributions of these individuals to discourse community norms would outlast their individual stays at JRC is beyond the scope of this study. But individuals' influence on the community practices must be considered in order to see the dynamic nature of those practices.

In sum, the data here suggest the following working definition of discourse community:

> *A discourse community is a social entity distinguished by a set of writing practices that result from the community's shared values and goals, the physical conditions for getting writing done, and individual writers' influence on the community.*

In addition to these defining features of discourse community observed in the data, several overarching themes emerged with regard to the nature and functioning of discourse communities:

- *Discourse communities at the site of this study could not be viewed in isolation but had to be considered in a broader cultural context of overlapping discourse communities and the conditions influencing each.* Rather than a circle complete unto itself, a discourse community must be viewed more as a

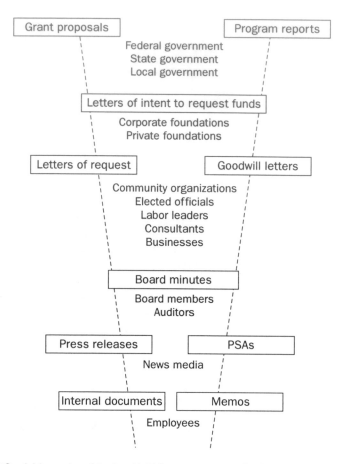

Figure 3.3. A hierarchy of texts. At JRC, resources and writers' roles are assigned on the basis of the importance of the constituency and the text to the discourse community's achieving its goals.

Venn diagram (refer back to Figure 3.1), placed within overlapping discourse communities that are influenced by one another. Even the internal communications of an organization are influenced in part by practices of external discourse communities—for example, the use of "standard" formats on some internal memos, a carryover for Ursula and Pam from practices they'd observed at other organizations, and the "standard" practice of meeting minutes, typical of American business. The external communication practices at JRC resulted almost entirely from standards of discourse communities external to JRC.

- *Within the discourse community at JRC, texts were given relative impor-*

tance according to the importance of their functions in relation to the community's values and goals. At JRC, at least 10 genres were used (memo, letter, meeting minutes, speech, press release, public service announcement, brochure, proposal, report, procedure manual), along with numerous subgenres of those genres. The relative importance attached to those texts, and hence the amount of time dedicated to them and the degree of perfection expected, were in direct proportion to how crucial the text was to the organization's survival. Texts associated with bringing in financial support (grant proposals, letters of intent, reports) had the highest priority, and texts for the purposes of goodwill or image (press releases, newsletters, brochures) had lower priority. Figure 3.3 depicts the particular hierarchy of texts at JRC. In addition, standards for content, formatting, and correctness varied according to the relative importance of the text. Despite an overall desire for all written communication to appear "professional," the meaning of "professional" was both ill defined and context-specific. A letter to President-Elect Clinton was carefully edited and proofread, whereas a letter to a job applicant might be dashed off.

   • *Viewing rhetorical context and discourse community issues as separate but related concepts enabled a fuller interpretation of writing events.* For example, the specific relationship between JRC's executive director and a particular city council member determined the tone of a letter of request to that council member. Matters of how formal or informal the language or formatting of a text was, how direct or indirect a request was, or how explicitly the truth was stated also were determined by the immediate rhetorical context for communication—the writer's purpose and the writer's relationship to the specific audience for the text. However, another level of decision making was involved in the creation of texts. At the discourse community level, issues of overall community goals, values, and norms for texts were placed against specific rhetorical issues. For example, the letter Ursula wrote to the Ning Yung Association required not just figuring out the immediate reason for the letter, an annual ritual, but also realizing that this writing event was part of a whole web of communications—oral and written—between JRC and other community organizations. Rhetorical situations exist in the immediate occasion for writing; discourse community practices have an extended history beyond the single communicative act.

   I turn now to a consideration of how the writer new to this particular site of composing, JRC, grew in understanding and mastery of the knowledge and skills necessary to succeed as a productive participant in the discourse community.

CHAPTER 4

Creating a Fit: Socializing Writers into the Community

This is to verify that Jenny Jones served as Development Director at Job Resource Center (JRC) from February 18, 1992 to July 31, 1992.... Unfortunately, funding for the Development Director position was not extended and we have not filled the position since.

THIS IS THE BEGINNING of a letter that conveys more by what is *not* said than by what is said. Jenny Jones was terminated from JRC after 4 months on the job for failure to fulfill the duties of her position successfully. Although neither Jenny nor those who supervised and worked with her would be likely to think of the problem in terms of the process of socialization into a discourse community, I argue that Jenny's situation was a case of her failure to learn the social dynamics shaping the discourse community at JRC. What emerges from the comments of community insiders who worked with Jenny is a picture of someone who chose to remain at arm's length from the discourse community. This distance—and the associated behaviors—inevitably led to her termination. Here is what her co-workers and bosses said:

> That was one of the complaints about her interpersonal skills . . .
> she didn't talk face-to-face with people. She did a lot of memo writing. (Ursula, 8/11/92, p. 3)

> She did not learn from people. (Leong, 9/15/92, p. 19)

I think the weakness in her writing is she couldn't learn. She's not willing to ask, and she's not willing to be told. . . . *She really didn't allow herself to socialize to learn. I think that was the problem.* I didn't think it was her grammar or anything like that. (Mei, 10/20/92, p. 31, emphasis added)

We don't know the reasons for Jenny's distance from her colleagues, for her working in isolation. But we can see the effects: She did not learn JRC's programs well enough to write about them accurately and authoritatively; she did not learn about the needs of JRC's partners—the overlapping discourse communities of private and corporate foundations she was asked to communicate with; she did not study and master the genres used in JRC's discourse community (letters of intent, proposals, PR materials); she did not pick up on the preferred method of communication within JRC: face-to-face conversation. By not adapting to several discourse communities, Jenny failed as a writer and as development director at JRC.

We have seen the complex array of expectations and norms of overlapping discourse communities affecting the writers at JRC. Assuming a willingness to learn, how do individual writers master the knowledge and skills specific to any or all of the discourse communities they must participate in? What hinders or helps the process of socialization into new discourse communities? These are the questions that guide the discussion of the data in this chapter. But first, the distinct categories of knowledge that were necessary for expert writing performance at JRC, in addition to discourse community knowledge, must be delineated.

KNOWLEDGE DOMAINS FROM WHICH EXPERT WRITERS DRAW

In Chapter 1, I pointed out the usual categories of knowledge that psychologists assign when studying learning—declarative versus procedural knowledge, or general versus local knowledge—as well as debates in composition studies concerning the knowledge and skills associated with expert writing performance. In studying the writers at JRC, who included newcomer and old-timer, novice and expert, I observed five domains of context-specific knowledge critical to full participation in the community: discourse community knowledge, subject matter knowledge, genre knowledge, rhetorical knowledge, and process knowledge. The domains, both overlapping and distinct, existed in a kind of symbiotic relation to

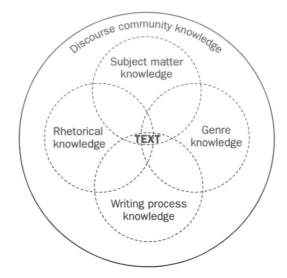

Figure 4.1. Five context-specific knowledge domains for writing expertise.

each other, as depicted in Figure 4.1. Each of these knowledge domains also represented a continuum from general knowledge to more context-specific knowledge. Becoming expert within the community, handling the most difficult and important writing tasks, involved a movement from more general knowledge brought from other contexts to increasingly context-specific knowledge and expertise unique to JRC. But first, I will describe the five domains of knowledge the writers in this study drew on.

Discourse Community Knowledge

As we saw in Chapter 3, JRC as a discourse community shared some writing practices in common with overlapping communities—federal and city funding agencies, philanthropic foundations, and businesses. To be successful, the writer had to grasp the complexity and variety of each discourse community she needed to interact with.

For example, we have seen Selma and Pam learning that norms for a grant proposal to a federal agency differ from those for a grant proposal to a local government agency because of differing goals and processes for communications. Birgitte, over time, refined her methods for approaching foundations and communicating with them orally and in writing; Ursula gained a great deal of knowledge about matters of decorum and social rank that infused writing practices in the business community; and Pam wrestled with norms for communicating internally at JRC.

Subject Matter Knowledge

When Pam came to JRC, she had no experience in vocational training, adult literacy training, or grantsmanship; her academic background was in linguistics and anthropology. Within 4 months at JRC, she found herself in charge of the workplace literacy program.

> ANNE: How much did you know about workplace literacy before?
> PAM: Zero. [chuckles]
> ANNE: So what have been the sources for you to learn about all this stuff?
> PAM: Reading proposals, so I know what we specifically are about, and then all the literature that comes out from the National Workplace Literacy program. Things about what other programs do.
> ANNE: Do they publish regularly?
> PAM: Well, there's like two books I'm referring to. When I say all the literature [laughs] it's like nothing. Nothing! [laughs] And they're little pamphlets. It's just, "This is what they're doing in Arkansas. This is what they're doing in Wisconsin." . . . *Most of it's from talking to people.* (9/22/92, pp. 2–3, emphasis added)

So Pam was faced with two challenges: Not only did she need to learn about a subject area new to her, but the information was largely in oral form or diffused nationwide. She focused on learning the basics of the day-to-day operations of a workplace literacy program. The instructors who delivered the program, who were trained in ESL, had greater depth of knowledge, and Pam drew on their expertise for a deeper level of understanding to analyze training results or write a proposal for a new training program.

Pam also had to learn financial concepts such as "indirect costs" and "leveraging" funds. In October, she attended a workshop on proposal writing, which began to fill in some gaps in her knowledge. After that workshop and a year of working with Mei on budgets, Pam had sufficient background knowledge to put together a program budget on her own.

Selma faced a situation similar to Pam's when she came to JRC. She had an academic background in Near Eastern studies and had worked for an Israeli travel agency prior to JRC; she also had to learn about ESL and vocational training. After several years as an administrative assistant at JRC, during which she absorbed a lot of information about JRC'S programs, she became program director for the clerical and medical-assistant training programs and learned the intricacies of government training programs funded through the Private Industry Council and the U.S. Department of Labor.

Pam and Selma also talked about the depth of subject matter knowledge required to actually put one's own ideas in a proposal rather than recycle old ideas. Only after 2 years of writing proposals for various training programs and another 3 years before that being on the periphery of the proposal-writing process was Selma willing to put her own ideas into a proposal. After a year of working with workplace literacy programs, Pam said, "Maybe someday I'd like to get to that stage, you know, when I'm not just taking other people's ideas" (8/5/93, p. 5).

Because she wrote publicity for all the programs, Ursula needed to know something about each of the five programs JRC ran. She explained the importance of that knowledge in commenting about a fact sheet she edited when new on the job:

> I really didn't know much about the organization. . . . I just used a lot of their language that I hate now—it was all over the place. But I didn't want to go too far out of the bounds, 'cause I didn't know anything yet. *Now that I know more about all these programs I've written many things about [them] and I used a whole different way of describing them 'cause I understand them.* (8/5/93, pp. 6–7, emphasis added)

Ursula was a stickler for conciseness and precision in word choice. But until she understood the subject matter and the lingo, she was unable to utilize fully her skills as a writer and editor. With specific knowledge of JRC's vocational and literacy training programs, she could use jargon skillfully and also choose when *not* to use jargon.

Birgitte ran two programs at JRC: one to build kids' computer and literacy skills, and the other to help unemployed adults start their own small businesses. Her academic training and work experience prior to JRC were in political science and public policy. As she and Leong were starting to talk to foundations about their idea for the kids' program, she went to a Foxfire training program to gain background in ways of tapping kids' home and community knowledge to build literacy. She also started talking to principals and teachers at elementary schools in the city about after-school programs, slowly building her knowledge base about literacy and after-school programs. At the same time, she recruited Gilda, who was already working on self-employment training for low-income individuals. By working with Gilda, Birgitte developed her own knowledge of small business programs.

For all four writers at JRC, subject matter knowledge was a necessity for handling writing tasks successfully. Means for acquiring that knowl edge in a workplace setting included library research, talking with subject matter experts, reading, and observing.

Genre Knowledge

The genres on which most of JRC's business depended were the grant proposal, the business letter, and the report. No writer had to master every genre, but each writer had to master several in order to function effectively. Furthermore, genre knowledge and discourse community knowledge were integrally linked; for example, as Chapter 3 illustrated, the grant proposal took different forms and varied in length and purpose depending on the discourse community addressed. Reports and business letters also varied depending on the context of the communication. And each of these genres spawned subgenres with more specific characteristics than the main genre.

Pam's introduction to the federal grant proposal—within a few months of her starting to work at JRC—is a good example of what can be a long road to genre mastery. Her first assignment was to draft several sections of a proposal that would end up totaling over 100 pages. The professional grant writer, Donald, wrote most of the text and edited Pam's portion. Here is *her* report of the writing process:

> I wrote one section of the proposal, and it was . . . really hard because it was such a deadline and such pressure to it. It was the first time I'd ever done it, *so I just wrote everything out there, and I just said,* "Well, you guys fix it." So they did, and they cut and redid it. (Pam, 7/14/92, p. 2, emphasis added)

According to Donald:

> She took on doing some of the pieces of the plan of operation. . . . She wrote well, but she tended to write quite—let's see. It was real wordy. It was real voluminous. It wasn't . . . tight enough. . . . I'm sure she was looking at the lingo in these things and then sort of trying to emulate it, which is, I think, based on my own experience in learning how to write these things, that's . . . what I did too . . . *sort of trying to imitate another grant, and not really quite understanding that there is a kind of a deeper level that's going on there. . . . She was . . .*

> *sort of throwing everything in—the kitchen sink,* and . . . not being able
> to filter out. . . . "Maybe I'll just mystify them and bury them in an
> avalanche of data and planning-sounding language, then they'll
> just give us the money." (Donald, 2/25/93, pp. 3–4, emphasis
> added)

On the heels of contributing to this federal proposal, Pam assumed most
of the responsibility for a smaller but very similar grant proposal to the
city, which was touched on in Chapter 3. Here's her description of trying
to accomplish that writing task:

> I think the hard thing for me is that some of the things that I would
> say in one section I would also say in another section, so I tried to
> figure out, . . . should I really bang them over the head with this
> need in this section, or do it in another section. And then what I
> usually end up doing is writing everything on everything, and then
> later I go back and compare it with the RFP and see if it really goes
> there or if I should just ax it. (Pam, 7/14/92, p. 5)

Her understanding of the genre of the grant proposal at this point can be
characterized as surface knowledge.

Four months later, in November, she had an opportunity to attend a
3-day workshop on grant writing for nonprofit organizations. On the one
hand, she realized that she'd already assimilated a lot of information on
the genre of the grant proposal as she'd worked with Mei. On the other
hand, the information at the workshop took her to a deeper level of understanding, not just of financial terms, but of the genre itself: "It was
like [the instructor] was naming all the things that I had observed Donald
and Mei doing, so . . . *she sorta demystified what it was that we had been doing
already*" (11/10/92, pp. 1–6, emphasis added). Pam commented several
months after attending that workshop:

> I'm one of these people who needs to see the overview, so that I
> can understand what I'm doing at each part. . . . *I didn't know what I
> was doing when I was writing those first [proposals]. . . . After that class
> I had a sense of, "Oh, I'm writing this [section] 'cause it's going to lead to
> this."* (2/3/93, p. 1, emphasis added)

Her understanding of the genre had deepened.

A year after she was introduced to the genre, Pam had a chance to
write another grant proposal—this one a modification of the one done
the year before. Rereading what she'd written a year earlier, she said, "I

went through and I thought . . ., 'Aaah—I wrote this? This is really lame!' . . . There was just a lot of really bad—like it didn't really answer the question very well" (7/20/93, p. 1). As she faced this proposal-writing task, she was well on the road to understanding a difficult genre; simultaneously, she was teaching a member of her staff the genre, parceling out parts of the writing task just as Mei and Donald had parceled out parts of the writing task to her a year earlier.

Birgitte's experience learning the genre of the grant proposal began in a job previous to JRC. Reflecting on that time period several years earlier, she said:

> I don't think I really thought about [grant writing] as being dramatically different from anything else I'd written. We did a lot of practical-type writing in graduate school. It's . . . like anything else. You think through the project. Which is the best way of presenting, describing the project to somebody who doesn't know anything about it? And then you make an outline, and then you write it. You get an idea of how long it should be. I spent some time in the Foundation Library . . . but not so much to write a proposal. More to figure out who was likely to give me money. (11/24/92, pp. 2–3)

Several months later we had this conversation:

> ANNE: This was the very first proposal you wrote [at JRC]. I'd love for you to scan it and tell me do you see things in there that you do differently now?
>
> BIRGITTE: *It's boring. It's really boring. And I'm not saying I couldn't write anything that's boring at this point, but it doesn't engage you. It doesn't sound like a distinctive, innovative program. . . . There's a lot of information, but if I were a program officer and I read it, this wouldn't move me in any way. . . .* Overall it's reasonably well written, but it just has no lingering effect. . . . *I think I'm more aware of—like you want to write something that makes the audience remember your project.*
>
> ANNE: Where did you get that awareness from?
>
> BIRGITTE: *Maybe from writing fiction. And from writing other types of writing. And from reading other people's proposals. . . . I'm using more stories in my proposal* . . . because I think it's all people will remember when they're done reading is the case story, or some little anecdote. People don't remember numbers. (1/19/93, pp. 2–3, emphasis added)

In the last few years Birgitte had taken fiction-writing classes and had started writing short stories in her free time. This genre enabled her to see how narrative could be embedded in the expository prose of the grant proposal.

We also have seen Ursula's struggles with the fine points of the business letter in all its permutations. When I was asking her about her understanding of the notion of genre, she said:

> It's funny. . . . I said sort of kiddingly, "[Genre] seems like too good a word for [business writing]." This business category I wouldn't even include if I didn't have this job. . . . I would never think of that as a style of writing but now I know that it is. (12/8/92, p. 1)

What Ursula thought of as "styles of writing" were in fact genres. Genres may be shared by several discourse communities, so that a writer may come to a new discourse community already equipped with some relevant genre knowledge. But the writer must be sensitive to the ways genres are tailored to a specific community of writers and readers, as in the case of the federal grant proposal and the city grant proposal. As local knowledge grows (i.e., knowledge of a genre's use and particular norms within a given discourse community), communication becomes more effective.

Rhetorical Knowledge

In addition to a writer's need for subject matter knowledge and genre knowledge, each instance of writing requires attention to rhetorical challenges: how to juggle between the writer's purpose and the audience's need. After creating the program for the annual dinner, Ursula realized that she had been approaching the project from the perspective of a "consumer," as if she were attending the dinner; she didn't think about including a message from the director or a list acknowledging sponsors.

> But that stuff's gotta be there. . . . Stuff about JRC. . . . I'm really finally starting to learn what I need to, thinking from the right perspective. . . . I have always been thinking about just . . . what's practical for the people who are gonna be here, not making everything into a big JRC PR thing, which is my job. (6/9/93, pp. 4–5)

Ursula's first program brochure was for the annual fund-raising dinner in the fall. The program brochure she was referring to above, for a public event in the spring, she approached very differently. What changed was her understanding of the genre's rhetorical requirements: to guide some-one through the events, but also to educate the public about JRC's mission and goals. By her second year at JRC, she in fact was keeping the institution's point of view in mind, so that each instance of written communication was used strategically or rhetorically.

Rhetorical knowledge also includes a keen sense of the audience's needs. All of the writers commented that Mei "knows everybody"; this knowledge enabled her to tailor letters to the individuals being addressed. For example, Pam wrote a draft of a letter to send to people who had endorsed JRC's application for a grant. Then, as she explained:

> Mei would say, "Oh, . . . you should include labor in Nan's letter because that's something that's important to her," so Mei kinda just puts little points on each letter, like labor, you know, Asian, Hispanic. (9/22/92, p. 4)

Or, if the letter was very important and Mei did not know the individual personally, as in the case of the letter to the Secretary of Labor, she found someone who knew him to critique a draft and give specific feedback on how best to request him to speak at the annual fund-raising dinner.

Over time, the four writers developed personal relationships with many of the individuals they corresponded with, just as Mei had. Even if the writer did not personally know the specific individual(s) being addressed, as she became more familiar with JRC's relationships with other discourse communities, tailoring the written communication to that particular situation became easier. Mei commented at the end of the research project about Ursula's growing expertise in this area:

> MEI: What she's really learning is . . . I think generally, even though she doesn't know the person or the organization, . . . she's gotten a good sense of . . . how we would want to approach, let's say, a foundation, a business, a person. *If you compare her writing for the last anniversary and this year's anniversary, you could see automatically she approached it very differently.*
>
> ANNE: How would you describe the difference?
>
> MEI: *I think she has a very good sense of who she's writing to,* like she drafted a letter for me inviting people to be on [the] honorary committee and automatically she knew these are people we work with, at least they know something about us. So we don't have to say so much about JRC's work, maybe a global statement, but it's very warm, very genuine, and very upbeat, ver-

sus a more formal, cold, but technically correct letter. (9/24/93, pp. 6–7, emphasis added)

These writers learned, over time, how each specific writing situation could be used strategically to interpret and further JRC's aims—whether in a routine thank-you letter, program brochure, or letter of request.

Seeing the rhetorical moment from the discourse community's point of view also entailed letting go of one's own sense of self as the author of the text. When Ursula started her job, she was excited by the opportunity to use her writing skills: If a fact sheet could be improved, she would edit it. Here's what she told me about a letter she was working on with a board member:

I finally got it together. Between my ideas and his ideas. See, part of—what he gave me was, it was done last year. And I wanted to change that a little bit. Just because I wanted to have my mark on it, I guess. (7/28/92, p. 11)

Contrast that statement with this one, some 6 months later:

Even though I've always wanted a job where I could write . . . now that I have one . . . I'm just trying to get everything out. [laughs] I'm not trying to write great letters or to do anything really great anymore, only once in a while. (1/12/93, pp. 8–9)

Her sense of purpose shifted—both in terms of her own job duties and in terms of the purposes that texts served within the overall scope of the organization's activities. Writing had become a means to an end beyond the writer's own goals rather than a means of self-expression. And written text had importance within a much larger arena of social action.

Selma also described a similar shift in her attitude toward writing grant proposals:

It's hard not to look at it personally when you don't get [the grant]. But you know, with each rejection they get a little easier and you know, the more funded things I get a chance to read, the more I think, mine wasn't that bad. It just wasn't what they were looking for. (5/4/93, p. 5, emphasis added)

Maggie, who wrote for a nonprofit similar to JRC, told me that over time her writing for the organization became "more of a task and less of a mission," which, she felt, was how it should have been all along. The

shift that all these writers experienced may have been due in part to a
loss of idealism about the writing tasks—but also to a growing realization
of the function of text within the organization's overall scope of activity.
A writer thus may need to redefine standards for writing, with less pride
of authorship and more of a sense of moving through one of many tasks
to achieve the end goal. This shift to the institutional point of view also
enables writers to gain the appropriate rhetorical stance in their texts.

Writing Process Knowledge

We have already seen the working conditions impeding concentration
and efficiency that each writer had to learn to cope with. But each writer
also could describe ways in which her writing process evolved at JRC in
order to meet productivity standards and to deal with the types of writ
ing the job required.

In addition to learning to compose at the computer and to hold a
thought when interrupted in the middle of writing, Ursula learned a
number of other important procedural strategies:

- She lowered her standards for originality and style so that she
  could stay on top of a steady stream of writing tasks.
- She learned to give her boss just a skeleton draft when requested
  to write something. From the skeleton she got feedback on what
  her boss was looking for in the document, thus accomplishing the
  task with fewer drafts.
- She determined a weekly cycle for writing that fit the ebb and
  flow of her tasks. Monday she handled "little stuff," and Tuesday
  through Thursday she tried to address writing projects. Fridays,
  fatigue set in and she wasn't as efficient, so she dealt with the
  "little stuff" on Fridays as well.

For Birgitte, who had to write as many as two or three proposals a
month to keep her programs funded, efficiency evolved through breaking
apart the stages of writing a proposal or report and knowing her own
rhythm of productivity. She started by making notes—her initial thoughts
about key points and structure—on a yellow pad. After writing her key
points as an outline on the computer, she would start to compose, a section at a time, gradually erasing her outline. She also knew that she had
a warm-up period followed by a period of "maximum efficiency":

The way it normally goes is that I'll have this sort of initial period
where I'm not producing at the maximum level of efficiency, and I

know that, and I can sense it. And then it's almost like something clicks inside when I know that if I don't start writing now, I won't get done, and at that point . . . I'll just write and write and write. . . . Normally I write from 8 to 10 and maybe 12 hours a day. (7/22/92, p. 1)

In college, Pam outlined her papers in detail to organize her thoughts before writing. At JRC, she either did a very rough outline or plunged in, writing as fast as she could type and not worrying about sequencing, knowing that the cut-and-paste functions on her word-processing program allowed flexibility for rearranging and editing. She also learned not to write in linear fashion. When faced with a daunting report for the federal government, rather than figure out the key points before she started writing, she began with the simplest parts of the document: assembling data for the charts. Once that information was assembled, she could begin to write her way through the analysis.

Selma also adopted a writing style that kept her on target for deadlines. She waited "for the right moment"—but with a firm sense of how long she would need to accomplish the task—and at a certain point started the task even if inspiration had not hit. She also gauged how much time to spend on any one section of a proposal based on the number of points it could receive in the evaluation process:

"Evidence of existing or future labor demand," that could take a lot of research, and it could take a lot of writing, but it's only five points, so . . . you'll do the best you can and you'll go and dig up some statistics. But I wouldn't spend a week thinking about it. (8/4/92, p. 4)

Doing a good job, but doing so efficiently, was part of being a successful writer in this setting. Efficiency was a matter of learning the task's requirements but also learning how to handle the process of composing for a given task.

In sum, these five domains of knowledge—discourse community knowledge, subject matter knowledge, genre knowledge, rhetorical knowledge, and writing process knowledge—were necessary for the writers I studied to acquire within the local context for writing. While each knowledge domain contributes to and helps create the others, looking at each separately begins to give a picture of "writing expertise" in all of its complexity. Also, as I listened to the four writers react to texts they had written at JRC in the "early days" of their employment, they—

Table 4.1. Comparison of Novice and Expert Writing Knowledge

Knowledge Domain	Novice	Expert
Discourse community knowledge	• Little awareness of discourse communities	• Tacit knowledge of discourse community norms informs writing
Subject matter knowledge	• Borrows content from existing documents • Uses everyday vocabulary or uses specialized vocabulary awkwardly	• Creates new content based on insider knowledge • Uses specialized vocabulary appropriately
Genre knowledge	• Each text is a first • Focuses on surface features of genre • Bridging from more familiar genres	• Text is recycled if genre is familiar • Focuses on deep structure and purpose of genre • Versatile in many genres and subgenres
Rhetorical knowledge	• Writes from personal point of view • Focuses on generic audience and matters of correctness • Takes pride in authorship	• Writes from institutional point of view • Focuses on specific audience needs and social context • Writing is toward institutional goals
Writing process knowledge	• Uses similar process for all writing tasks • Writing task is labor intensive; hard to get started, easily sidetracked	• Streamlined writing process, adapted to specific tasks • Works well under pressure

and I—were able to see the ways in which their knowledge and skills had grown in connection with the writing tasks at JRC. None of the writers arrived at JRC a blank slate; each had had 4 or 6 years of training in academic writing at the postsecondary level and some exposure to writing in work contexts other than JRC. But each also could recount specific knowledge she had gained for accomplishing the writing tasks at JRC; this specific knowledge, from a cognitive perspective, would be considered "local knowledge." In fact, each probably started with some generalized knowledge in each domain that became increasingly localized knowledge through a process similar to the progression Dreyfus and Dreyfus (1986) have observed in studies of gaining expertise in other realms.

Table 4.1 gives an approximation of what the differences might look like, from novice to expert or general to local knowledge, based on comments of the four informants about their writing at JRC in the early stages and their representations, in retrospective accounts, of writing knowledge gained elsewhere. In each of the knowledge domains, a writer who is gaining expertise goes from surface-level to more in-depth knowledge; or, to switch metaphors, a writer "borrows" from knowledge acquired in another writing situation to get started in a new situation until he or she gains the local knowledge.

WRITING ROLES WITHIN THE ORGANIZATION

In order to build a conception of expert writing performance, it is necessary to think two-dimensionally: One dimension represents knowledge domains, and the second dimension represents the tasks or roles the writers take on that make the learning process possible. Writing involves dynamic mental and social processes; likewise, learning to write happens in the process of writing. Hence the importance of looking at functional roles associated with mastering the knowledge and skills evidenced in the work of the writers at JRC. Like the intersection of two lines on the x and y axes on a graph, roles and knowledge become conjoined at the point of action, so I turn now to an examination of specific activities undertaken at JRC in association with writing tasks. Also, like knowledge, writing tasks range from the simpler to the more complex. By distinguishing among different tasks according to their complexity, we can begin to understand the learning process that occurs when writers make those border crossings from one discourse community to another.

Many differing roles associated with writing tasks were evidenced in the data. I will explain each.

The first two roles, *observer* and *reader/researcher*, might be considered prewriting roles. Each of the four writers was constantly reading texts others in the organization wrote, reading general and trade publications, and gathering information through external contacts. Ursula's "snagging" of PR materials from other nonprofits, Mei's countless meetings and lunches in the community, and Selma's skimming of the newspaper's business section were all part of their ongoing, automatic scanning of the environment for information useful for writing tasks. And a more focused, project-specific type of reading activity also occurred, as we have seen in Selma's methodical survey of the literature on family literacy programs.

Mei explained the importance of the reader/researcher role at JRC:

I think JRC's strength is our ability to constantly learn the evolution of job training. And then as we update our knowledge . . . we have to be able

... to store all the information in a bank, and then we have to be able to sort and then pull out our own knowledge in a way that addresses the ... employment needs. (10/20/92, p. 7, emphasis added)

Observer of writing in progress was also an ongoing role for the four writers—partly through naturally occurring situations, partly as a result of Mei's drawing staff members together in meetings to discuss major projects. Both the physical layout of the offices and computing facilities—mostly in large, open rooms without partitions between desks—and the familial approach to the organization fostered writers' seeing each other's work on a regular basis. Texts in progress were routinely circulated among co-workers for feedback. As Pam commented, "Here writing is such a collaborative process anyway 'cause everybody in the office reads everybody's things, and comments on it and hacks and slashes" (7/14/92, p. 7). And more deliberate opportunities were created for newcomers to observe old-timers planning more complex, high-status writing projects; for example, both Ursula and Pam sat in on planning sessions for grant proposals within their first few weeks on the job.

Assisting with texts that others created also introduced novices to the organization's writing activities. For example, the *clerical assistant* role, the only one assigned solely to newcomers, provided Pam an excellent opportunity to see several facets of the process for writing a federal grant proposal:

So then my job was a lot of the follow-up work—faxing them letters to sign and doing revisions on letters. . . . I would follow up on . . . a letter from the mayor or from a senator and an assemblyman . . . and I would go around and pick up those letters. (7/14/92, p. 1)

Although these tasks involved minimal, if any, writing, right away Pam took on a supporting role that allowed her to see a number of steps and components in a grant-writing project. Pam also could have assumed one of three other closely related roles while revising the letter soliciting support for the grant proposal: *proofreader, grammarian,* or *editor.* An author at JRC did not necessarily have to be an expert in grammar or style; individuals among the staff had expertise in each of these skills, and that expertise was regularly drawn on. For example, regarding a proposal to the city government that she co-authored with Mei right after the federal proposal, Pam commented:

Mei was the only person who got involved in the editing. Drake, another instructor, proofread it. But that was when it was at its final

stage, and he just did grammar check and spelling check, and minor changes like that. (7/20/92, p. 5)

Three of the writers, Ursula, Selma and Pam, assumed one other
specialized role, *document designer,* which was linked to actual writing
tasks. All three learned computer programs for specialized visual dis-
plays of text: Ursula learned Pagemaker to do the layout of JRC's newsletter, Selma learned Harvard Graphics to make graphs representing JRC's
demographics, and Pam became an expert at Excel for reporting data in
chart form.

Next in terms of increasing complexity came several entry-level
writing roles for newcomers to JRC's discourse community, each entailing
a gradual increase in the amount of context-specific knowledge. Pam
described the *ghostwriter* role she played early in her work with Project Advance, when Mei needed some letters sent to participants in the
project:

> The content of those I get from Mei, . . . she just says, "Oh, this is
> the gist of what I want you to say," and "This is the tone." . . . She
> called me from Hawaii in like my first week here and she said,
> "Oh, why don't you write this memo to this guy, and let me tell you
> the story on this guy. He's a lawyer, and he went to this school, and
> he did this, and he's on this committee . . . so do you get it?" and I
> said, "Okay, I get it." (7/14/92, p. 9)

Here, we see Pam serving essentially as scribe—taking down Mei's
thoughts and turning them into useful prose. The *ghostwriter* role called
for genre knowledge and basic writing fluency (knowledge of syntax,
style, vocabulary, etc.) but did *not* require subject matter knowledge or
rhetorical knowledge.

The next three roles, also commonly assigned to newcomers to JRC,
entailed creation of content as well as genre and rhetorical knowledge,
but the texts themselves were what I call "low-status" texts, meaning
they were routine or were likely to have low impact on the organization's
functioning and success. Although very close to the ghostwriter role, the
role of *co-author/low-status texts* required the writer to have some input on
the content of the document. Early on, Ursula became co-author of a low-
status text, Leong's announcement of his accepting a new job. She described the writing task this way:

> I was given the instructions to draft it, and I did a very simple
> thing and I wanted his feedback before I got serious, this is more of

a reminder to him to tell me what you want. My instructions were, "Draft a letter that I'm leaving and the new executive director . . . " and that was it. (7/28/92, pp. 1–2)

The farewell letter involved more initiative on her part to come up with the content than ghostwriting situations in which she would be given directions to write a letter covering certain points.

The first step toward solo writing was handling routine correspondence and form letters, a role I label *author/low-status text*. For example, Ursula and Pam authored thank-you letters to participants in the federal grant proposal process; Mei would make only minor changes in wording or add a personal, handwritten postscript to these letters. Some press releases were also low-status texts: They were written about "minor" events, with little likelihood of the daily paper picking them up.

The *co-author/high-status text* role could occur when a newcomer was still getting acclimated to the organization, as evidenced in Pam's contribution to the writing of the federal grant proposal just a few months into her job at JRC. Of that project, Pam said:

I spent most of my time just sitting in on meetings that he would have with me . . . , and they would be discussing the aspects of the proposal, and I would give whatever input I had, *and I wrote one section of the proposal.* (7/14/92, pp. 1–2, emphasis added)

The next step up in responsibility, to *author/high-status text*, did not occur for either Ursula or Pam until a point that I demarcate as the "old newcomer" stage of development—approximately 12 months into their assignments at JRC. High-status texts were those most critical to JRC's survival, usually involving solicitation of funding for its programs. For Ursula, this milestone came when she assumed responsibility for the correspondence and publicity for her second annual fund-raising dinner.

For Pam the increased writing responsibility began a year after she'd taken on responsibility for Project Advance, when she started initiating the contacts and building support with labor and business leaders for the next workplace literacy proposal to the U.S. Department of Education. Not only did she assume the author/high-status text role, but she also moved in the direction of Mei's role as *negotiator*, which entailed getting the necessary external support to ensure a positive reception for the text. At the same time, she began to assume the role of *coach* to a staff member to whom she assigned the task of co-authoring portions of a low-status city grant proposal. She was transitioning between old newcomer and new old-timer as she assumed more responsible writing roles.

The *negotiator* role involved a combination not only of knowing how to speak the audience's language and appeal to their self-interest, but also of building positive personal relationships with the intended audience and trading, in Ursula's words, I-owe-you-you-owe-me political favors. All four writers pointed to Mei as an expert negotiator, and although they had only limited opportunities to observe her directly in this role, they saw the effects of her actions in her instructions to create texts resulting from her negotiations. For example, Birgitte said:

> I'm right now writing these letters to all these politician[s] who Mei knows. . . . I did a draft and then Mei added a bunch of stuff and took a bunch of stuff out. . . . She's a lot more tuned in to how you address politicians than I am. And she also knows some of these people personally. (9/15/92, pp. 8–9)

Anna, the professional proposal writer, talked at length about the negotiator role. Here are some excerpts of a scenario she gave me; although imaginary, it is true to her experience of writing proposals to foundations:

> You have your budget and you have your questions. And you call up Flo again and you go, "Flo, this is Anne Beaufort from da da da." And she goes, "Oh hi."
> "Thank you so much for sending me the information. I really appreciate it and I've been reading through it. I wonder if you could help me." Try not to ever ask anybody to do something they can't do for you. . . .
> Now, Flo says, "You know what? I think it would be a really good idea if you wrote that and addressed it directly to Mr. So and So."
> *Without even telling you they're helping you, they're starting to help you.* . . . The next time you call, you get to the person himself or herself. . . . It . . . puts you on the level of peer. *So you're two people who are now problem solving.* (11/6/92, pp. 13–14, emphasis added)

In this example, the negotiator serves as liaison from one discourse community to another. It is a role that occurs throughout the writing process and calls for problem solving, interpersonal skills, and good oral communication skills.

The final role, that of *inventor*, is one that old-timers assume, including, during the year of my observations, Birgitte, Selma, and Mei. Unique to the inventor role was the ability to conceptualize a new course of action, whether it be creating publicity or creating a program to match the agency's mission and funders' needs. Within the agency, Mei was the most expert in this role. Here's Pam perception of Mei's expertise as inventor:

> It's really, really hard to come up with a good proposal. Of course, if you don't have a good idea in the first place, it's . . . hard, but we're . . . lucky that *Mei's ideas are so tight, and she has worked them all out really well in advance,* so that when you go to write it, it's very obvious, you know. There's not a lot of explaining that you have to do to try to make it fit the request for proposal. (7/14/92, p. 2, emphasis added)

When I talked to Mei, she explained her thinking process in conceptualizing a program:

> The very basic is you have to really understand the purpose of our work . . . and second is with that understanding you have to be able to justify why we need this kind of work in . . . society. . . . That's more philosophical. . . . *I'm constantly looking at addressing more issues, but . . . I would only be willing to take on one issue at a time. . . . My background is genetics. And you never test two unknowns.* (10/20/92, pp. 14–15, 18, emphasis added)

The *inventor* builds on a strong experiential knowledge base as well as the ability to conceptualize and convey a vision of a new program, or convey a new idea in writing.

Having viewed both the types of knowledge gained on the job at JRC and the writerly roles assumed in various projects, we begin to see how everyday contexts for learning to write exhibit different characteristics from school contexts for learning writing skills. The knowledge gained was very concrete and situation-specific, rather than abstract in nature, and was for the sake of taking action to further the organization's goals through written texts, rather than gaining "knowledge for knowledge's sake." And as will become clearer in the next section, both the status of the learner and the process for learning also sharply contrasted with school writing experiences.

THE ROAD TO EXPERTISE

A parallel existed between the complexity of the writing role and the degree of context-specific knowledge required to execute that role. As reader, observer, document designer, proofreader, grammarian, or ghost-writer, any of the writers at JRC could draw on general knowledge of writing fundamentals acquired in school or other jobs: knowledge of grammar, syntax, basic vocabulary, computer knowledge, and generic writing process knowledge. For example, Ursula began revising the fact sheet on the agency, first working on spelling, grammar, and style, and then taking a closer look at ways to improve the content as she understood the agency better. The remaining roles all require some degree of context-specific knowledge, and we can begin to see the relationship between context-specific knowledge and writing role. As soon as they had some knowledge of JRC's programs and mission, Ursula and Pam moved into the roles of editor and co-author/low-status texts; assuming the more expert writer roles and those associated with high-status texts required increasing mastery of context-specific knowledge. Furthermore, the more context-specific knowledge gained, the greater the number of writing roles a writer could take on.

The data suggest, then, that expert writing performances at JRC required a combination of general and context-specific knowledge, but with heavy emphasis on the latter when writers assumed full authorship responsibilities.

With an understanding of the domains of knowledge and writing roles associated with expert writing performance at JRC, we can now turn to the question of how newcomers to this discourse community moved from limited to full participation, or from newcomer to old-timer status.

Already, the reader probably has sensed a dynamic process in which newcomers assume multiple roles from the start, sometimes even within a single writing project. In the types of apprenticeship situations Lave and Wenger (1991) offer as examples of situated learning or legitimate peripheral participation, "[a]n apprentice assumes several roles simultaneously: status subordinate, learning practitioner, sole responsible agent in minor parts and aspiring expert" (p. 23). The writing roles assumed by Ursula and Pam, the two newcomers to JRC, during the first 3 months of the research study (months 4–6 of their employment at JRC), in fact portray the situation Lave and Wenger theorize from their observation of other kinds of cognitive apprenticeships.

Ursula's Start at JRC

Ursula came to JRC with some business writing experience. After graduating from the state university with a B.A. in English, she had worked in two businesses as a secretary. Here's her description of what she learned from those first two jobs:

The first job that I had out of college was not a good example because people I was working for, English was their second language, it was a construction company, and they didn't care a lot [how things were written]. But the second job was this real cushy investment banker job and they were super anal about everything, so I learned a lot, just the style. . . . "Respectfully yours," there were different gradations of that, of how to end a letter, each one, depending on who they were writing to, how they did it. . . . The language was sort of almost legal . . . , "Per your request of October blah blah blah, our phone conversation on this," that kind of detail. (10/6/92, pp. 7–8)

At JRC Ursula was responsible from the start not just for typing others' letters but for creating letters, too. The social structure of the two organizations she'd worked for previously—one very hierarchical and the other much less so—led to very different apprenticeship experiences. She explained the situation at the investment bank:

A few times when I tried to make a suggestion, even if their writing wasn't good, they didn't want to know. Maybe they were using the wrong word, or maybe this could better be expressed this way, or this sentence is too long, or too many commas. If I took a comma out, they'd tell me to put it back in. (10/6/92, p. 9)

On her first day at JRC, Ursula's boss asked her to ghostwrite a letter for him, and his response was dramatically different from that at the investment bank:

He'd say, "Oh, that's great," and he'd sign it and that was that. [Not] "Could you put a comma here and bold this," it was just, "That's a good letter, this is functional and it'll get done." It was such a change. . . . *Within weeks of being here I was given more and more to do, and more trust,* and the whole thing, that I have a brain and that I'm trustworthy came in right away and I was so grateful. (10/6/92, pp. 8–10, emphasis added)

Ursula came to JRC strong in the basics of standard written English and with some familiarity with common business letter jargon and formats, and JRC immediately offered her a chance to learn more. Here is a log of some of the writing tasks Ursula participated in before she'd been in the job 6 months:

Text	Ursula's Role
July	
letter to Secretary of Labor	editor
newsletter articles	editor
graduation press release	author/low-status text
lead article for newsletter	author/low-status text
letter to labor union leader	co-author/high-status text
corporate donor letter	co-author/high-status text
August	
press release on new director	clerical assistant
press release on graduate	editor
letter for raffle prizes	co-author/low-status text
report to board of directors	author/low-status text
public service announcement	author/low-status text
letter to councilman	co-author/high-status text
board meeting minutes	co-author/high-status text
September	
annual dinner brochure	editor
press release on key speaker	co-author/high-status text
letter to honorees	co-author/high-status text

We see here five different roles, varying in levels of responsibility, that Ursula took on in connection with writing projects over this 3-month period: clerical assistant, editor, co-author/low-status text, author/low-status text, co-author/high-status text. In each role she was engaged in a legitimate activity of the organization, which, as Lave and Wenger (1991) describe it, is an authentic task, albeit smaller and easier than the old-timers' tasks. A few examples will illustrate the apprenticeship aspect of the learning.

The corporate donor letter for the annual fund-raising dinner was written cooperatively by Ursula and several of JRC's board members. The purpose of the letter was to persuade corporations to buy a table ($1,500 for 10 seats). Ursula didn't know how to write this kind of business letter, but she had two sources for ideas: last year's letter and verbal and written input from board members. In fact, one board member took last year's letter and drafted another version himself. Her concluding remark about the task was, "*I finally got it together. Between my ideas and his ideas*" (7/28/92, p. 11, emphasis added). In fact, the letter was a composite of the introduction from last year's letter (with sentence structure tightened up by Ursula); a second paragraph based on the board member's draft, but said in half as many words by Ursula, who also included her newly revised one-sentence statement from the fact sheet about what JRC does; and a final paragraph very similar to the one in the previous year's letter.

Ursula started the task by "plagiarizing" from the files to write a first draft. She then took the direction offered in response to her initial draft— input on content appropriate to the letter's audience and consistent with JRC's purposes—to draft a revision. She took others' input and used her own editing skills to improve the letter's diction. She also made the decision, based on her prior experience with business letters, that the letter should be no longer than a page. In some parts of the task, she was using general knowledge from previous experiences, and in other parts she was using context-specific knowledge learned at JRC.

Unlike business letters, the press release was a new genre for Ursula. In her first 3 months on the job, Ursula had to write two press releases. She had never seen a press release, but one in the computer files from her predecessor in the job provided the basic format: the heading, the approximate length (one to three pages), the standard close. Several board members and her boss gave lots of input for the content of her first press release, but she wasn't happy with the result. She drafted the second one on her own. She then sent it to Barbara, the new board member who ran a PR agency, and Barbara revised the draft. Ursula told me:

> She wrote that and then I looked at it, *I've used that as a model,* and she helped me with some little things . . . deciding on who you're gonna send it to . . . try to get a quote from somebody worth quoting. . . . So she's taught me quite a bit. (9/15/92, p. 1, emphasis added)

From July to September Ursula put out three more press releases. Two were low-status texts that she crafted on her own, following Barbara's model. The third, a high-status text announcing Mei's promotion to executive director, Barbara wrote and Ursula edited "a little bit." She noted what Barbara was able to do:

> The quote she made . . . is good. She makes it sound pretty impressive . . . makes it sound like, wow, we work for a place like that. *I learned a lot from that one.* (8/5/93, p. 5, emphasis added)

The genre was still one she was uncomfortable with, and as we'll see in Chapter 5, one requiring many more tries before she began to master it. But even before mastery, she became a coach to another staff member, Sarah:

It's her first press release, and [she] asked me to look it over, so
then I didn't want to change it too much . . . but I wanted to get
a little bit more of that tone . . . the PR tone. See, she's very dry,
there's not a lot of transitions between, and she kind of sticks the
quotes inside; when someone reads the press release they wanna
see who's speaking. (11/3/92, p. 4)

Writing roles were shifting constantly at JRC, in keeping with its nonhier-
archical structure and community values. The learning was spontaneous,
in the midst of other activities, through working out the content and
structure of various pieces with colleagues. At this point Ursula still was
not able to produce a good press release on her own. But the collaborative
session with Birgitte is a good illustration of Vygotsky's (1998) notion of
the zone of proximal development. In this "zone," independent action is
still not quite within reach, but with the help of another, the learner can
stretch to the next stage of development.

The most consistent, ongoing source of learning for Ursula, though,
was Mei's written comments on her drafts. One of the letters she drafted
in that initial 3-month period of the research study was to a local hotel
manager with whom JRC had a business relationship. The purpose of the
letter was to ask the hotel to donate a weekend suite and dinner for two
as a raffle prize for JRC's fund-raising dinner. She drafted the letter and
passed it to Mei with a handwritten note at the top, "Please review."
When it came back, Mei had written in a few changes, the most important
of which was the last line. Ursula had written, "Please call me if you wish
to contribute to our annual dinner." Mei had crossed out that tentative-
sounding sentence and written more positively, "Please call me to make
the arrangement." Asking for things with appropriate business etiquette
was new territory for Ursula, but she understood the significance of
Mei's change:

I'm learning how to ask for money, and how to ask for things. Mei
wrote in, see, little things to make it. . . . "If you wish to contribute," I have. She says, "to make the arrangement," so *she's teaching
me, she's my mentor.* (9/15/92, p. 1, emphasis added)

On a letter to another business partner, asking the partner to come to the
annual dinner to receive an award, Mei crossed out a sentence in the first
paragraph, "We welcome this forum to acknowledge your support," and
added an additional paragraph to Ursula's draft. Mei explained her
changes:

I crossed [that sentence] out because I thought when we honor someone, we want to make the person feel the warmth and a very genuine appreciation. . . . *I think we've gotten to a point she kind of understands a lot of the changes.* (9/24/93, p. 4, emphasis added)

Ursula's comment about this editing session corroborated her understanding of Mei's brief coaching comments, whether oral or written: "She just says a few things, I might write on a pad, or just remember. And she doesn't have to say a lot. You know, 'Slant it towards this'" (9/28/92, p. 3).

Early into her job at JRC, Ursula also observed a high-status writing project that others were working on. She hoped to move into proposal writing, and her boss was already taking steps to prepare her for that task:

> *I've been invited to meetings to hear about proposal writing and how it's done. Pam* . . . her project director conducted a meeting, so *I just sat in and got an idea of how they look at it and how they go about it and the same things about the tone of it,* . . . should it be factual, should it be a little bit sell, so . . . *I've done some revising of some proposals I've seen but I haven't written one yet* and I don't know enough about them yet to take one on. (7/14/92, p. 3, emphasis added)

Observing, ghostwriting, authoring, and coaching became part of a seamless pattern of interaction and learning for Ursula.

Pam's Start at JRC

Pam came to JRC with a variety of experiences with workplace writing from school, summer jobs, and one administrative assistant job after graduate school. In fact, when I asked how she learned to write business letters, she replied:

> Probably in typing class when I was in seventh grade and they just said, "You have to set this kind of tone and it has to look like this and you always address people like this." And it probably stayed with me all this time. I don't know. *You kinda pick it up. I mean, when I was at [previous employer], my boss always typed his own letters . . . so I would see them . . . his were always real short.* (2/3/93, p. 6, emphasis added)

The summer jobs during college were with IBM, and one involved working with a team of technical experts researching the feasibility of em-

ployee suggestions. Pam's job was to translate what they knew into pre-
sentations and memos that others could understand:

> It was very direct and technical . . . and I had to learn what all the
> terms meant. . . . The writing was really easy because the team was
> really easy-going and they all didn't really care about writing. . . .
> You just read a memo and—*I mean if you read one memo, you can
> pretty well figure out how you're supposed to write a memo.* [laughs]
> (5/10/93, pp. 7–8, emphasis added)

She also had to write the rejection letters to the people whose ideas were
turned down. She learned the art of tactfulness:

> They gave me a few samples. And then they said, "Well, you pretty
> much have the rough skeleton of a reject letter." . . . So I had to
> learn how to say, "Well, your idea was really great. Really appreci-
> ate your input and bla bla bla but you know, unfortunately, we
> found that," and then the analyst would just make notes and say,
> "This is why I rejected it," and then I would have to make it sound
> nice. (5/10/93, pp. 7–9)

So far, Pam had learned formulaic types of business writing by example—by just "picking it up." She'd also been introduced to rhetorical
moves such as conveying bad news politely.
    Pam had had one other experience with business writing before com-
ing to JRC—in the marketing department of a computer game company.
Here's her account of writing press releases there:

> Sally was a really fun boss. *I said, "Well, what am I supposed to do?"
> And she said, "Well, you can look at some of these old ones that I've writ-
> ten but just write."* . . . *It was really automatic with her.* She would just
> whip it out, you know. I never felt like I caught on. *I kinda did my
> gut feeling, but I always felt like, "Well, is there something I'm missing?
> . . . Is this right?"* (5/10/93, pp. 3–4, emphasis added)

The press release is a complex genre, so Pam wasn't immediately able to
imitate what the experienced writer, Sally, seemed to do "automatically."
But by the time she came to JRC, Pam had had some experience with
business memos and letters and the more journalistic genres of ad copy
and press releases. She had also had several experiences of plunging into
new territory—in terms of both subject matter and genre—without a lot

of guidance. This experience would serve her well at JRC, for Pam would quickly be challenged again with new writing responsibilities.

Here is a log of some of Pam's writing during the first 3 months I observed her (shortly after she'd joined JRC):

Text	Pam's Role
July	
support letters/federal grant	clerical assistant
federal grant proposal	ghostwriter
job developer memo	co-author/low-status text
city grant proposal	co-author/high-status text
staff workload chart	author/low-status text
memo—staffing need	author/low-status text
August	
letter to city councilman	ghostwriter
thank-you letters to businesses	co-author/low-status text
letter to city bureaucrat	co-author/high-status text
September	
speech for executive director	co-author/low-status text
letter to seminar leader	author/low-status text
letter to potential client	author/low-status text
status report to board	author/low-status text

Like Ursula, Pam assumed multiple writing roles shortly after joining JRC. When Pam transferred to Project Advance just before the beginning of the research study, Mei and Donald were in the midst of writing a federal grant proposal. As we've seen, Mei brought her in on the proposal-writing process, in multiple roles. She was clerical assistant for the process of gathering support letters to send with the proposal, as well as co-author and editor. And she was both participant and observer in the planning meetings. Donald recalled later that Pam gathered data for the needs section and contributed some text to the section on program factors. He edited or rewrote some of her writing, but, he added:

> *She was a very observant participant. She was clearly learning. . . .* I would have loved to have had exposure to that kind of a process. That would have probably saved me a year or two in my own development as a grant writer. (2/25/93, p. 5, emphasis added)

In fact, as we saw in Chapter 3, she moved right into co-authoring a high-status text, a grant proposal to the city, soon after the federal grant proposal was sent off. Mei let Pam take the lead in drafting the narrative portion but guided her on its content, and she handled the budget herself. Pam prepared a draft, drawing heavily from the federal proposal that had just been completed.

I sat in on Pam and Mei's meeting to review Pam's first draft of the proposal. The meeting lasted less than 30 minutes. Mei flipped back and forth between the RFP and Pam's draft, giving her comments rapid-fire; Pam was seated across the desk from Mei, taking notes on a yellow pad. Here is a summary of the points Mei covered:

- which category of funding to apply for (Pam had misinterpreted the RFP)
- the need for an abstract, even though the RFP didn't call for one
- four key points for the abstract
- what content to emphasize, what to downplay
- the need to condense information in the draft—either eliminate redundancies or give less detail
- points to keep hitting that the audience wants to hear
- which paragraphs or statistics to use from other documents
- the need to define terms (can't assume the audience knows them)
- the need to make each section self-contained
- the appropriate length for the narrative (10 pages)

Mei's tone throughout the session was matter-of-fact. She made the writing process sound easy—just do this, add this, take away this—never questioning whether Pam could do the task. Mei said midway through the session, "Fine. Good draft." She closed the meeting with a question: "Should we go over this again tomorrow at 11?"

Mei's comments to Pam reveal many messages about norms of the discourse community (level of audience background knowledge, relative unimportance of the text in the funding process, politically sensitive issues, etc.), as well as information about the subject matter, genre conventions, and rhetorical strategies. This information never was labeled as such, however; explicit instruction focused on completing the task at hand—what to say, in what order, and in which sections of the proposal. The next day at 11 a.m., Pam had another draft ready; the document was close to its final form. Although in retrospect, a year later, Pam felt that she didn't do a really good job on the proposal, it was good enough to secure a grant for $67,000 for JRC.

Another one-on-one conference Pam had with Mei, several months later, concerned the 3-minute speech Pam had to give that night to the Citizens Committee, at City Hall, to ask them to increase the funding level for the proposal to the amount of the original request. This conference was very brief—5 minutes from start to finish. Mei dropped by Pam's cubicle, Pam handed her the three-paragraph draft, and Mei gave her feedback, again in rapid-fire fashion, standing beside Pam's desk. Note the range of topics covered in this brief dialogue.[1]

MEI: Um, I think the first thing, it's good, what we're doing, employment training model, and um, we could say "created the model, working closely with small business and hotels." We don't have to say [inaudible] "labor community." Instead of saying "unemployed immigrant" we should say—um, we should say, ah, "low income."

PAM: So use the language of the
　　　　　　　　　　　　　　　　[
MEI:　　　　　　　　　　　　　　　Yeah, we should use their language=

PAM: =OK.

MEI: ="Low income residents, /mmhm/unemployed individuals, and immigrants"/Mm hmm/ uh=

PAM: =All that? OK [laughs]

MEI: You know, when you speak=

PAM: =Uh huh

MEI: =You don't have to be so coherent on the grammar=

PAM =Yeah, that's true.
　　　　　　[
MEI:　　　　　　　　　　And you want to hit them on these things/ right/'cause, you know, they're going to be listening to a hundred people, so what's going to make you stand out=

PAM: =Right.

MEI: What's going to make you stand out is this grant. I th— we should just say the um, we don't have to say the amount, 'cause they don't/mmhm/they don't care/mmhm/you should say, "The amount that you have recommended for Project Advance um, will not = will not be able to *maximize* our potential"=

PAM: =Oh, OK.
　　　　[
MEI:　　　　　　　Our intake. They don't remember [inaudible]/

PAM: Yeah. Yeah.
                   [
MEI: 'Cause, um, and then you should just say
     that we, "We are requesting that you restore it to our
     original requested
                        [
PAM: Full, original . . .
MEI: amount"/OK/ the reason is, you know, with additional—the
     reason is—obvious. "The additional $30,000/uhuh/ that
     you're going to be restoring"/uhuh/ keep using the word "re-
     storing." We're not asking for more, we're just asking to re-
     store/mmhm /the, "the $30,000 that you'll be restoring in our
     grant/mmhm/ will be able to leverage more than $100,000
     more federal money"/uhuh/ and, you know, you are, "We are
     asking the city to invest $30,000 to bring in *over $100,000* more
                                                                    [
PAM: Oooh,
     that sounds so compelling
                              [
MEI: For the city"/uhuh/so, you know,
     then people can remember you. We're asking for—"Your in-
     vestment in something that's very meaningful," and then with
     $30,000 we'll get over—we should say, you know, "We're lev-
     eraging $150,000 *more* federal money with"—"If you restore"=
PAM: =But it's $430,000.
MEI: Yeah, but that's . . .
PAM: Oh, that we got before=
MEI: =That we got before=
PAM: =Oh, I see.
MEI: So we could say $150 thousand more.
PAM: OK=
MEI: =Federal grant. "Of federal money to benefit—our city."
PAM: OK.
MEI: So I think you should hit them that one point.
PAM: OK. So restore, restore. OK.
MEI: Then I think this, you could um emphasize, you know, ex-
     plain what it is. We have, is a collabora—it's unique—"It's one
     of its kind of collaboration with a community organization,
     small and big businesses as well as labor union. It's the only
     kind of collaboration that will provide job training," and then,
     you know, we're going to shoot for a, um, "We're gonna to
     work towards a guarantee for/mmhm/ all these peo= all

these people. For unemployed individual, low-income resi-
dent, and immigrant/mmhm/ into a *job*/mmhm/ that they
will become self-sufficient/mmhm/It's a progressive," then
you should sum up and say, you know, "This is a unique
model. It's a progressive model/mmhm/ in adult uh edu-
cation."
PAM: Mm hmm.
MEI: "And it's a service that will help people to a self-sufficiency."
PAM: And keep hope alive [laughs].
MEI: Yeah right= [chuckles]
PAM: =OK.
MEI: [inaudible] Yeah. I'll think it'll be fine. I think this is good.
'Cause when you speak, they will just probably remember you
on a very sharp point you say. They won't remember how
much [inaudible]/OK/ that's why I just say
                                                    [
PAM: [sneezes] So give
them sound bites=
MEI: =Yeah. So after that . .
                    [
PAM: You're so good at that. I wish I could
have watched you campaign.
MEI: [laughs] Um, say, "I would like to give you the detailed infor-
mation . . . and I hope that you will," you know, give us your
"most favorable consideration." That's it=
PAM: =OK.
MEI: I think you'll do fine.
PAM: OK.
MEI: You're very good at that. (10/8/92)

This exchange between Mei and Pam typified "editing sessions" at
JRC. Here are some significant elements of the conversation in relation to
Pam's learning to accomplish the writing task at hand:

- The exchange opened and closed with Mei's giving Pam a vote
  of confidence: "It's good," and "You'll do fine, you're very good
  at that." The praise legitimized Pam's writing role (author/low-
  status text).
- Mei's comments, although brief, touched on four issues: (1) diction, (2) context of the communication, (3) persuasive strategies,
  and (4) the logic of the primary argument (the concept of leveraging).

- Twice Pam made connections between what Mei said and what she already knew: "So use their language." She connected what Mei said to the RFP, and on the issue of making a single point in the speech, Pam made two connections—first to the "sound bite" strategy used in electronic news media and then to the same rhetorical strategy as it occurred in political campaign speeches. She was linking new information to background knowledge she already had.
- Pam's interjection of an exaggerated rhetorical statement—"And keep hope alive"—suggested that she could step back and see the rhetorical manipulation involved.
- The latching (contiguous speech) and overlapping that occurred— four instances when Pam overlapped with Mei and 10 instances of Pam's latching onto Mei's speech—indicated her active role in the conversation, even though she was the apprentice. While Mei was doing most of the talking, Pam nonetheless participated actively in moving the conversation forward.

Mei's coaching of Pam was spontaneous, brief, and in the midst of the actual task. And the coaching was multidimensional: Mei drew on discourse community knowledge, content knowledge, genre knowledge, and knowledge of rhetorical issues—all within a 5-minute period.

After Mei left for an appointment with United Way leaders, Pam returned to the computer to turn out another draft of her speech. Within the hour, she printed out three subsequent drafts. The speech expanded to six paragraphs. She asked one of the instructors, Drake, to time her as she read; it was over 3 minutes, so Drake gave some suggestions for shortening it. Pam said, "It's making me crazy. I can't believe this is taking so long." She called downstairs to Birgitte, who also had to give a speech to the Citizens Committee that night for her program. Birgitte came to Pam's office, and they went through their speeches together. Another instructor eating her lunch at her desk listened in and asked a question about the leveraging concept, which didn't quite make sense to her. Birgitte suggested that Pam slow down so it wouldn't sound so much like she was reading, and she urged her to put in a few colorful anecdotes. Pam took a break for lunch at 1:30, commenting to Birgitte, "I think I'll trash this. Just turn it into an outline." At 2:45 p.m. she went to the computer room to work, so she could print out as she wrote. At 3:30 p.m. the outline was done, incorporating most of the suggestions she received throughout the composing process.

Because Pam perceived that no "official" institutional voice dominated at JRC, she elicited input from others besides Mei. Although all offered reasonable and useful input, the task became complicated because that much input was too much for Pam to handle at this stage in her writing development. The next time I saw Pam we had the following exchange:

ANNE: In hindsight, how do you feel about [the speech]?

PAM: My biggest thought is why did I spend all day on that stupid thing. It wasn't worth it.

ANNE: How did you feel about how it went?

PAM: I guess I felt like I got everything said that needed to be said, and then it wasn't so bad. I don't know. I didn't really have too many expectations of it. I didn't even expect people to be listening really. I think it was just like a courtesy thing. [laughs] Oh yeah, the mayor's sitting up there. It's like, "Is he really listening?" Doubtful

ANNE: So what would you do differently, say, next year you have to do the same thing?

PAM: I would like give myself like 45 minutes or an hour before the thing started to just prepare. (10/20/92, p. 1)

Although Mei, Birgitte, and others gave Pam suggestions for the speech in light of the context for the communication, the reality of a packed Board of Supervisors' chamber at City Hall, with one 3-minute speech coming right after another, sank in only when Pam experienced it first hand. Only in hindsight could she appreciate the most critical factor in the communication event: the overall positioning of this one communiqué within a complex web of communications between two discourse communities, JRC and city government.

One final example will illustrate the degree to which learning was folded into doing and the ways in which newcomer and old-timer collaborated. As a result of a phone call from the mayor's Office of Economic Development, JRC suddenly needed to produce a letter regarding the figures in the budget for the Project Advance proposal. Mei alerted Pam to the situation, and Pam started a draft. Here's how she explained the process:

ANNE: So how did you write this?

PAM: [Mei] gave me an outline. She said, "They might question this, this, and this. If they do, our response is this, this, and this."

ANNE: *So did you write a draft and show it to her and she edited it, or . . . ?*

PAM: *Yeah. Or like I'd be writing it, and then she would come in and*

> *she'd go, "Oh and this too." And I would just quickly insert it, you*
> *know? And then she's blip out again.* That was a busy day.
> ANNE: So she would literally edit as you were at the keyboard?
> PAM: Or would add more stuff as I was at the keyboard. And . . .
> so I think I showed it to her once, and then she just went
> through and changed things—'cause we had to fax it to him
> by the end of that day—and *we were both in and out and in and*
> *out.* (8/18/92, pp. 1–2, emphasis added)

We see Pam, just a month after starting her new assignment with Project
Advance, as co-author with her boss on a short-fused, high-status text.
Mei guided the overall plan for the letter's content, Pam studied the budget and questioned Mei about particulars, and together they crafted a response.

A few months later Mei explained her view of her role with newcomers like Pam and Ursula.

> Ursula and Pam are very new, and they are the people that I'm try-
> ing to train in particular. And *I think it comes with experience and it*
> *comes with their own observation.* I generally share my experience
> with them. But at no time will I impose my judgment or my analy-
> sis on them. I will generally tell them, "This is what I think, and
> this is what to look for and this is what direction to go into," from
> the point of view of getting the funds for the agency. *But I like to*
> *give room for people to develop their own skills as well as their own analy-*
> *sis.* (10/20/92, p. 6, emphasis added)

As an old-timer in the organization, Mei was conscious of her coach role
and aware of the tension between too much coaching and not enough.
And on the other side, Pam and Ursula as newcomers were very ame-
nable to being coached, unlike their former colleague, Jenny.

CHARACTERISTICS OF A WRITING APPRENTICESHIP

In general, learning processes at JRC followed the cognitive apprenticeship model of legitimate peripheral participation (LPP) reported elsewhere to describe everyday learning situations (Lave & Wenger, 1991;
Resnick, 1987; Rogoff, 1990). I will indicate here the qualities of LPP that
writers at JRC experienced and some additional qualities of the learning
processes at JRC that may extend a conception of LPP.

- *Writing roles at JRC were assigned according to both the writer's level of expertise and how critical the text was to JRC's survival.* We've seen, for example, in Pam's participation in the federal grant proposal project and in Ursula's participation in handling the printed materials for the annual fund-raising dinner, the ways in which even a novice took part in the important tasks of the organization, handling the piece of a larger whole that was within her capabilities at the time. Old-timers scaffolded tasks, depending on the newcomer's level of expertise and the status of the text. For a high-status text like the letter associated with Project Advance's budget, or the federal grant proposal, Mei provided Pam with a lot of input and feedback. For less important texts such as thank-you letters or the city grant proposal, Mei gave less oversight.

- *Writing roles were shared among members of the community.* Only two roles—the clerical assistant role, which newcomers could assume, and the negotiator role assumed by old-timers—were associated with a single stage of development. Four roles fell across the spectrum from newcomer to old-timer (observer, reader, editor, and co-author/high-status text), and a number of the other roles could be assumed at most stages of assimilation or expertise.

Rogoff (1994) states, "In communities of learners, both mature members of the community and less mature members are conceived as active; no role has all the responsibility for knowing or directing, and no role is by definition passive" (p. 213). In fact, Leong and Mei relied on others' writing skills to a great degree—in part because both were nonnative speakers of English, but also because a strong sense of shared expertise inhered in the discourse community's value system. We also saw how Birgitte, Selma, Ursula, and Pam brainstormed, co-authored, and edited writing projects among themselves and with Leong and Mei.

- *Both teaching and learning occurred informally.* Learning was informal, and teaching occurred within the organization in the context of getting real work done. Pam attended one grant-writing workshop during the year of the research study, and Birgitte attended fiction-writing classes at the university extension, which helped her write proposals at JRC. Such external, formal learning situations were the exception, though. In this environment, top priority went to meeting deadlines and getting work done; learning had to be a part of such activity, not separate.

- *Learning was both assisted and unassisted.* Assisted learning included co-worker feedback (oral and written), experts' feedback (the executive director and board members), and collaborative planning or writing sessions. Unassisted learning included observing others' writing activities, reading sample documents, drafting and revising based on feedback (trial-and-error learning), and self-reflection. The latter often was manifested in my weekly interviews with the writers, but I suspect it was an ongoing process even if not overt. The learner had to figure out at least some portion of any new task on her own, so that being an expert at learning was as important as having a particular writing skill.

• *Assisted learning focused on two of the five knowledge domains for expertise in writing at the institution.* The majority of the assisted learning focused on aiding newcomers with subject matter knowledge or rhetorical knowledge. The other three knowledge domains—discourse community knowledge, genre knowledge, and writing process knowledge—were largely unmentioned in any overt way by experts: Mei, board members, foundation leaders, or government officials the writers interacted with. When Mei was coaching Pam on how to redirect the federal grant proposal toward the city's needs, she did not make explicit that these were in fact norms of a particular discourse community, with different norms for written text for other discourse communities. This knowledge—both for Mei and eventually for Pam—was tacit knowledge, beneath the level of consciousness and never spoken about directly.

Lave and Wenger (1991) argue that knowledge domains or pre-existing structures "may vaguely determine thought, learning, or action, but only in an underspecified, highly schematic way" (p. 17). The data here suggest that the domains of knowledge or any structured way of viewing the writing situation was in fact covert or tacit on the part of Leong, Mei, and the four writers—if it existed at all in the writer's or coach's mind as a schema. However, the schemata of the different knowledge domains do enable the researcher to see what goes on during learning. The question of whether the schemata for domains of writing knowledge, if made overt to learners, would be useful to the learning process, particularly in border crossings between discourse communities, will be addressed in Chapter 7.

• *A continuous cycle of participation and feedback aided the learning process.* We've seen the various forms that participation in writing activity took at JRC. Feedback occurred in internal editing sessions and from the intended audience of a text. Most texts resulted in action, and by the nature of the action writers knew if they'd achieved the intended response—hopefully a grant, a commitment to collaborate on a project, or a favor. Feedback was usually constructive. Even if Mei wanted Pam to make changes in her speech, she validated what was good and built on Pam's text for a better product. If external evaluators commented on a grant proposal, they usually suggested ways the proposal could be strengthened.

When I asked Pam at the end of the research study to reflect on how she had learned to function as a writer at JRC, she said, "I think people learn business writing just by being there and then finding out how people react to your writing" (8/5/93, p. 15). Ursula made a similar comment when I asked her to sum up how she learned to write something she'd never done before: "See how other people have done it. And take advice" (8/5/93, p. 6).

The expression *on-the-job learning* is common parlance in our culture. But the exact nature of that learning—particularly in its informal forms—has been hard to examine precisely, because it is spontaneous, unplanned, and seemingly random. Ursula's and Pam's learning process certainly was influenced by the nature of JRC as an institution: It was a small organization with little stratification between workers and managers. Learning also was shaped by the personalities, internal motivations, and previous experiences of the individuals involved.

For example, the learning processes for Selma and for Birgitte were somewhat different from those for Ursula and Pam. For Selma, the learning process at JRC was more gradual. She spent several years as an administrative assistant, writing memos and letters and editing others' work, before she authored high-status texts. Given her background, she did not see herself as a writer in the same way that Ursula did when she started out at JRC. Birgitte came to JRC with considerable experience as a writer and a program manager, so she began functioning right away in those capacities at JRC. The beginning of her development as a writer in business contexts began in graduate school and in several jobs prior to JRC, where she wrote extensive reports and some grant proposals.

Given the idiosyncrasies, then, of a learning situation, what can be gleaned from this particular setting that may be generally useful in understanding informal workplace learning situations? Or, to return to the questions posed at the beginning of the chapter, how does a writer master the context-specific knowledge and skills of the discourse community, and what hinders or helps that process?

We will see in Chapter 6 that each of the four writers came to JRC out of home and school environments that fostered strong writing skills, explaining, in part, the levels of writing roles and writing projects that each could step into almost immediately at JRC. But more important, each writer was successful at JRC because she deepened her general knowledge in each of the five knowledge domains with knowledge specific to the site of composing and in the process assumed more and varied writing roles.

All four writers were able to articulate their growth as writers at JRC and the important lessons learned in regard to writing in this context. As Ursula summed up her learning strategies, "See what others have done and take advice." In fact, she was an expert situational learner, taking her cues from many signals in the environment: listening closely to how her boss talked, watching other writers she respected in the organization, "snagging" model texts she encountered elsewhere, being a "scavenger of ideas." The other three writers were experts at learning from their surroundings as well. They were self-starters, they constantly scanned their environment for cues about the writing situation's requirements, and they were flexible and willing to assume a variety of writing roles.

We see then the importance not just of acquiring new knowledge and skills but also of knowing *how* to learn in informal settings. If expert writing practice in any given context for learning has a large component of context-specific knowledge, as we have seen in the case of writing at JRC, then writers must be skillful at learning within the particular community of practice. The meaning of the phrase *life-long learning* takes on new urgency as we begin to understand more fully the nature of expert writing performance, entailing the ability to use site-specific tools for learning and to learn through observation, models, and self-reflection. Above all, life-long learning requires the learner to be flexible and open to continued learning; this was a universal characteristic of those who gained writing expertise at JRC. From an institutional standpoint, the manager's willingness to assume a coaching role—and to provide in that role meaningful, progressively increased levels of activity and responsibility—also aided the learning process.

A POSTSCRIPT: INDIVIDUALS VERSUS THE COMMUNITY

We have examined here writing activities as they were staged and orchestrated through institutional forces at JRC. But each of the writers in this study was by no means a clone of the institution. Each came with individual motivations and aspirations and with personalities that affected her response to institutional stimuli. While it would be both beyond the scope of this study and probably impossible to fully plumb the psychological depths of each individual writer, a few observations on this aspect of their behaviors at JRC deserve mention, particularly in light of debates about whether institutional structures or individuals are responsible for learning (Lave, 1993).

We've seen a number of institutional values and processes that fostered learning for newcomers to JRC's writing community. But there were also discernible individual factors as well. First, an important key to the success of the four writers within this institution was their buy-in to the organization's mission. Without this buy-in, it is doubtful that any learning would have taken place or that any texts would have been written successfully. When I asked each of the writers how she saw her personal values fitting with the institution's values, each affirmed a commitment at least to the larger purposes behind JRC's mission—to help others in the community. Ursula told me:

> *I'm proud of where I work now.* If people ask me where I work I'm happy to tell them that I'm working for an organization that helps people ... and has a good record and I know that the people work hard and that ... we're effective, so those are values that I share with JRC (1/12/93, p. 7a, emphasis added)

Pam expressed some frustration when she was in a management position rather than being a direct service provider to JRC's clients, but she recognized the importance of the role she played:

> It fits with my values because it's got a commitment to—how shall we put it? What do we usually say? Disadvantaged communities ... *none of us are real heroes or totally altruistic or anything, but we want to do what we can.* (12/1/92, pp. 6–7, emphasis added)

Selma and Birgitte were perhaps less motivated by altruistic motives, although they definitely felt JRC's mission was worthwhile. When I asked why she came to JRC, Selma said, "I came here because I needed a job. That was the bottom line. And it happened to seem okay. I think my friendship with Leong probably kept me here" (2/16/93, p. 16). And Birgitte offered this perspective: "I think it is largely because I'm sort of doing my own thing.... I like to start new things. I like to have things that I run" (4/20/94, pp. 4–5).

Second, each was able to monitor and successfully handle individual frustrations with the "institutional" way of doing things. There were acts of resistance, but they were small and often humorous, and largely went unnoticed. After a board meeting in which Ursula observed behaviors she found frustrating, she played with the language she used to write up the minutes as a way of venting her frustration. She said:

> I used a lot of big words and I put it very formal but a little sarcasm in it, and I really enjoyed it and I knew nobody would really catch it. (10/27/92, p. 2)

Ursula also related a tale passed on to her by Birgitte, who loved a good joke. The story went that one time Birgitte put a provocative sentence in the midst of a serious letter she was drafting for Leong. She wanted to see if he really read the letter closely. The letter came back signed, the provocative sentence unnoticed, much to Birgitte's glee.

And finally, each of the writers at JRC was motivated to grow and develop her individual talents and saw her job duties in some way supporting that growth. After several stultifying secretarial jobs, Ursula wanted to write as much as possible and in particular to learn grant writing so that she could work in fund raising for nonprofits. Pam was committed to community development as a career and saw the workplace literacy project as one viable program toward entitlement for disenfranchised immigrants and low-income people. Selma was interested in running programs effectively and enjoyed the challenges of learning to develop new programs and write grant proposals to fund those programs. And Birgitte was motivated primarily by the desire to think and write creatively—whether it meant working on a fiction piece in her spare time or working on the concept paper for a new program idea at work.

We move now to a more in-depth look at one of the critical areas of learning for writers new to a particular discourse community: the acquisition of context-specific genre knowledge.

CHAPTER 5

Learning New Genres: The Convergence of Knowledge and Action

I don't think things I've written would fall into a genre.
. . . I wouldn't consider academic writing as a genre . . .
and I wouldn't consider writing proposals a genre, but
I suppose one could. But to me a genre would be more
like classical things that you could group
—Selma, Transcript of Interview

WHAT WRITERS DO and what they say about what they do may be two very different things, particularly when it comes to the issue of genre knowledge. Three out of the four writers I followed at JRC hesitated when I questioned them about the notion of genre in connection with their writing at JRC. They associated genre with belles lettres, fiction, or various types of reading materials, but not with the everyday types of texts they wrote. And yet, as we've seen, no writer can participate in a discourse community without adopting the genres of that community. We've heard Selma, Pam, and Birgitte talk about the genre of grant proposals in connection with their fund-raising efforts with government and private sector discourse communities, and we've heard Ursula talk about the press release, letters of request, and a number of other genres she must write to the larger business community beyond JRC.

The importance of genre acquisition for writers should not be underestimated. As we've seen, the norms of the discourse community are embedded in its genres. But most important, genres *do* the communicative work of the community. Assuming the more advanced writing roles at JRC required mastery of a number of genres significant to that discourse community.

In this chapter, I focus in particular on three genres that writers at JRC needed to learn—the press release, the letter of request, and the grant proposal—not for purposes of informing the reader of the workings of these particular genres, but for purposes of elucidating issues associated with learning any new genre. This close examination of three writers learning genres new to them will help us to see what aspects of a genre are learned most easily and what aspects come within the writer's control only after repeated attempts and continual feedback from the environment in which the genre does its communicative work. Also, since genre knowledge in this instance was acquired through informal learning rather than explicit genre instruction, it will be possible to examine the hypothesis, suggested by Freedman (1993), that genres are acquired best through participation in the discourse community rather than through any explicit teaching of genre conventions.

After several months of collecting data, I questioned the four writers about their understanding of the nature of genres. They articulated the traditional view of genres as being "(a) primarily literary, (b) entirely definable by textual regularities in form and content, (c) fixed and immutable, and (d) classifiable into neat and mutually exclusive categories and subcategories" (Freedman & Medway, 1994a, p. 1). More recent conceptions of genre include everyday genres (in speech and writing) such as conversational greetings, lab reports, or business letters (Bakhtin, 1986). Genres are now viewed as any regularized forms of communication arising in response to recurring situations. They are seen as dynamic, changing as individuals and communities adapt them to particular local conditions, as we've seen in the case of the grant proposal. The importance and very character of genres in the business world are judged not on aesthetic considerations but on the basis of the social action(s) that they accomplish (Bazerman, 1988; Berkenkotter & Huckin, 1993; Miller, 1984). For example, a federal grant proposal will be evaluated not according to general standards of good writing such as conciseness, cohesiveness, and graceful expression, but rather on the basis of whether (1) it conforms to the requirements for structure and content spelled out in the RFP, and, in turn (2) it accomplishes the intended action—to secure financial support for social endeavors. Likewise with a press release: Its intended actions—dissemination of news to a widespread audience and public visibility—are the ultimate criteria for its success or failure.

In addition to the social dimensions of genres, genre knowledge also serves an important cognitive function for the writer in the process of composing. Composition scholars have researched writers (and readers) drawing on representations, or schemata, of "writing plans" (i.e., genres) in generating or interpreting texts (Bereiter & Scardamalia, 1987; Flower

& Hayes, 1981; Flower, Schriver, Carey, Haas, & Hayes, 1989). As Fowler (1982) characterizes the process:

> Far from inhibiting the author, genres are a positive support. They offer room, as one might say, for him to write in—a habitation of mediated definiteness: a proportioned mental space; a literary matrix by which to order [her] experience during composition. (p. 31)

Without these "writing plans," as Flower and Hayes (1981) refer to them, the writer may experience cognitive overload while composing in an unfamiliar genre and resort to handling the most accessible features of the genre or transposing the composing task into a different and more familiar task (Durst, 1984; Eiler, 1989; Flower, 1989).

Studies of children acquiring story grammar or other school genres give some indication of a slow, iterative process for genre acquisition (Freedman, 1987; Langer, 1985). But within the context of this study, the question must be raised: What is the process for acquiring competence in new genres among adult writers at advanced levels of literacy?

Separating discussions of genre from discussions of discourse community is a bit like the chicken and egg problem: Can you have the one without the other? And which comes first? Theoretically and practically, the two concepts are closely intertwined. But for purposes of parsing complex cognitive and social processes associated with writing, I draw the distinction between the two as follows: Genre acquisition involves the writer's pulling together into one artifact—the written text—all of the social and cultural issues of both the sending discourse community and the receiving discourse community, the specific content issues, and the exigencies of the immediate rhetorical situation. Although genres are fluid, this complicated web of information must become, in any particular communiqué, "containered" into a particular structure, in a particular linguistic register, with the particular content unique to this genre. Genre acquisition is the complex activity of learning to combine all of these elements into a cohesive text.

However, because discourse communities shape genres, mastering a genre requires an understanding of the genre's function within the discourse community. In this analysis of several instances of genre acquisition, I will look at the acquisition of the textual features of the genre and the writer's understanding (or lack of understanding) of discourse community values and goals that affect the norms for the genre. At this intersection, where a particular writer and her writing task must interact with a discourse community's genres and norms for communication, genre acquisition is negotiated.

LEARNING THE GENRE OF THE PRESS RELEASE

On the surface, press releases appear simple—they are short (usually one to two pages double-spaced), with a closely prescribed format in terms of structure and layout, and the appropriate content is "whatever newspapers print." Barbara, a professional publicist who was on JRC's board, began a conversation with me about the genre by saying it was a very straightforward genre, yet an hour later we were still discussing its nuances. She talked first about the genre's fundamental content requirement and formatting conventions:

> Well, what's involved, number one, there is a protocol . . . . It goes back to the basic journalism stuff that you learn, who, what, when, where, why, and how, and the *point is that you have to say all of that, ideally in one sentence* in your lead paragraph. . . . The protocol also involves a certain format, that is how it looks on a page. . . . In order to be absolutely correct there has to be a dateline, a location reference, where's the news coming from, it needs to be spaced, usually it's required double-space. (8/20/94, pp. 2–3, emphasis added)

Ursula knew about the format. For her first press release (3/18/92) she went to her predecessor's computer files and found a sample press release. She copied the format but missed an important element—the dateline. But by the third release, she had mastered the format.

Barbara's explanation of the genre continues:

> So you get that kind of information out of the way first, then you come up with a title. Titles, just like headlines in a newspaper or other publication, is its own art and science, and most people . . . don't understand how to craft a good title. And titles are important even for a good press release. . . . It's very short and it's easy to read, it's something that your eye can jump on and even though you may not have necessarily read word by word you understand what the meaning is and it piques your interest to go to the copy itself. (8/20/94, p. 3)

Ursula's title for her first press release was 19 words. Reading it over, Barbara commented, "The title is too long and as a result the meaning doesn't get conveyed."

Nor does the first paragraph of Ursula's release make things any clearer:

[Samuel Ng], recently appointed by [the Mayor] to the influential post of Fire Commissioner, will be honored at a dinner celebration at [New Pacific Restaurant] on Thursday, March 19. Mr. Ng's appointment is in recognition of his outstanding contribution as a political leader and prominent philanthropist.

Barbara commented:

Paragraph one [of Ursula's release] does address this who what when where why stuff but unfortunately it isn't structured in such a way that the journalist really knows what's the most important thing here, 'cause if you look at this we've got two people named. . . . We've got a place named, a restaurant . . . the date of the event, but the idea is we want to talk about why this guy is unique.
The least important thing in this paragraph is that it's taking place at [this] restaurant . . . so a journalist would read this and probably draw the conclusion that . . . they must have bankrolled the whole thing. . . . Why else would you put the name of the restaurant in the first sentence of the press release? . . . *Those are the kinds of little innuendoes and nuances that you have to be constantly mindful of.* (8/20/94, pp. 4–5, emphasis added)

What to put in the press release, and in what sequence, required acute awareness of the rhetorical situation *and* discourse community norms. In the first draft of her 2/17/93 release about a graduation ceremony for JRC students, Ursula structured the information in this sequence:

first paragraph

4 Ws—who, what, where, and when the event takes place
accolades for the theater owner who donated the space for the event
mention of the keynote speaker—a local politician

second paragraph

boilerplate copy about JRC

third paragraph

connection of the graduation event to the state's unemployment
   problem

In the first paragraph she took care of the sponsor's desire for an accolade, but the information of interest to journalists didn't come until the third paragraph. Reporters are on a tight deadline and may receive as many as 100 press releases a day; they judge the release in a quick glance at the headline and maybe the first sentence. The news must be presented in descending order of importance to the primary audience—the journalist—and not according to the sponsor's needs. And yet mention of the sponsor must be subtly and carefully interwoven in the text so as not to be "chopped" off by a quick editorial move on the journalist's part. We begin to see that what looks, on the surface, to be a straightforward genre in fact can present the writer with considerable rhetorical challenges.

What counts as news is also at issue. Barbara explained:

> *It's relative, it's a subjective answer on what is a good story,* there are some places [small towns] where anything constitutes a story just because there's no definition, but the minute you start to move closer to the major media markets then degrees of definition set in. (9/10/94, p. 1, emphasis added)

In general, JRC wanted to reach two different media markets: on the one hand, their news was targeted to the local Asian press because of the strong Asian ties of the organization; on the other hand, JRC needed to position itself in the mainstream newspapers read by funders, potential employers for students, and politicians. The Asian press would print anything pertaining to the Asian community, not strictly on the basis of journalistic value but out of a philosophical commitment to that community. The mainstream press, in the major media market where JRC was located, was a much tougher audience to persuade to run a story. *News* was a relative term with highly localized and temporal meanings.

A look at the events JRC wanted Ursula to publicize over the course of a year reveals how difficult it was for her to "create" news about JRC:

3/18/92   JRC supporters' recognition dinner
6/22/92   job fair for the public
7/10/92   graduation ceremony for JRC students
8/26/92   JRC alumna award
9/22/92   JRC fund raiser
2/17/93   graduation ceremony for JRC students
5/20/93   graduation ceremony for JRC students

The job fair had the greatest potential of matching the journalist's purposes, as it was an event for the general public. The award given to the alumna had potential as a "human interest" story, and a political candidate's speech at the fund raiser might have been of interest if the politician made any important statements at the event. The other events would be of no interest to the journalist unless a news angle were created.

In addition to the issues of conflicting rhetorical aims, the sequencing of information, and the creation of "news," writers also dealt with the issue of *linguistic register,* a term generally construed to mean the particular vocabulary and syntax of a given text (Halliday, 1973). The press release is a genre modeled after the news story, so it must reflect the lexical and syntactical features of the journalistic register: plain language, short clauses, and short paragraphs.[1] This seems straightforward enough, but in fact the contradictory purposes of the genre—to report the news objectively but also to persuade the reader of the importance of the news— make the choice of words challenging for the publicist.

We've heard Ursula express her discomfort with what she labeled the "rah rah" language of the press release. She tried using qualifiers like "outstanding," "prominent," and "most influential" to heighten the newsworthiness of the story about the newly appointed fire commissioner. Her first press release (3/18/92) also contained hyperbole: phrases such as "without question" and "one of the best attended events in recent history." The first draft of her 2/17/93 release, almost a year later, still had some hyperbole; for example, she said, "The use of this beautiful theater . . . was generously donated . . . [and] in light of [the] staggering unemployment rate." Only in her two releases that were feature stories rather than news did the hyperbole vanish and the voice sound more natural. In fact, Ursula commented about one of these human interest releases:

> This one I was pleased enough with, it's the alumna of the year.
> 'Cause she had a good kind of human interest story, so it was easy.
> Immigrating from China, her father died, and then she went to our
> training and got a job and is supporting her family now. . . . I felt
> more comfortable with that than just gloating about how wonderful
> JRC is. (Ursula, 8/5/93, p. 5)

Even after 6 months, with coaching from Barbara and having read others' press releases, Ursula was still learning how to use linguistic and rhetorical moves to achieve the genre's contradictory purposes of telling news and creating goodwill. As Table 5.1 shows, she was not yet able to execute consistently even those genre features she knew. Her release about the political candidate speaking at the fund-raising dinner, on

Table 5.1. Ursula's Growth in Mastering the Press Release

		3/18/92 Public event	6/22/92 Public event	7/10/92 Agency event	8/26/92 Feature story	9/22/92 Public event	2/17/93 Agency event (1st draft)	2/17/93 Agency event (2nd draft)	5/20/93 Agency event
Rhetorical issues	• Appropriate news angle		✓					✓	✓
	• Subtle positioning of sponsor		✓					✓	✓
Content issues	• Headline short and "newsy"				✓			✓	✓
	• 5 Ws, with appropriate emphasis on most important ones			✓	✓			✓	✓
	• Quotes to support message			✓	✓			✓	✓
	• No extraneous information			✓	✓			✓	✓
Structural issues	• Information sequenced in descending order of importance to news media							✓	✓
Linguistic issues	• Simple language and syntax		✓	✓	✓	✓	✓	✓	✓
	• Tone: without hype but compelling			✓	✓	✓	✓	✓	✓
Format issues	• Standard information (release date, place, contact)	✓	✓	✓	✓	✓	✓	✓	✓
	• Standard layout	✓	✓	✓	✓	✓	✓	✓	✓
	• Length: 1–2 pages		✓	✓	✓	✓	✓	✓	✓

Note: Check mark indicates that element was present in writing sample.

9/22/92, for example, did not contain a strong enough news angle to hook the mainstream press, and the title was 17 words long.

Ursula felt she had an "aha" experience with the "100 People Find Jobs" release, in February (2/17/93). She'd been looking at releases Barbara had written or edited, and she was more aware of the requirements for a successful release. But when Mei took Ursula's slant (not news) and transformed it into "news," and when Birgitte leaned over Ursula's shoulder as she was at the keyboard and threw out a rhetorical question to lead off the story, Ursula understood that "creating" news involved manipulating the content and the structure of the genre.

Her initial paragraph read:

> One hundred students will graduate from Job Resource Center (JRC) Friday, February 19, at 6 p. m. with certificates of completion in computer and office training, hotel service industry training, and literacy. The newly renovated [Name] Theater, will be the site of the graduation ceremony. The use of this beautiful theater . . . was generously donated by [sponsor's name].

The revised first paragraph was significantly different:

> This Friday, over one hundred immigrants, refugees and displaced workers will celebrate finding full-time employment. How did they do it? They enrolled in a training program that has consistently beat the odds. JRC, a 27-year-old nonprofit vocational training, literacy education and employment placement organization, has again placed over 90% of its graduating class. In light of [state]'s staggering unemployment rate (nearly 10%), the achievements of JRC and its students are especially significant.

Instead of cramming all of the 5 Ws into the first sentence, Ursula highlighted just the most important one—that in a time of high unemployment in the state, these people had become employed. In the second sentence she grabbed the reader's attention with the rhetorical question. She sequenced information in descending order of importance; JRC got recognition, but it was subordinate to the news. And she shortened her sentences. As Table 5.1 shows, her second draft of the 2/17/93 press release was the first in which she was able to capture all of the genre conventions in the text, and she repeated this performance on her next press release, on 5/20/93.

Understanding the social action the genre represents within the discourse community is also crucial to the press release. On the one hand, the goal is to "place" a story, from the sponsor's point of view—or "find" a story, from the journalist's point of view. On the other hand, the second-ary and more long-term agenda involves maintaining a positive, mutually beneficial working relationship between sponsor and journalist(s). Bar-bara explained that one journalist with whom she had an ongoing rela-tionship by phone and face-to-face would print almost anything she sent: "I don't know why. She seems to think anything I send her is good" (9/ 10/94, field notes). No doubt it was the personal relationship that aided Barbara in placing the stories.

We see then the interplay of oral and written communication be-tween publicist and journalist and the genre's function to meet the goals of overlapping discourse communities. In the year of the study, Ursula was not exposed to or guided toward the other modes of communication (such as phone contacts) needed to support press releases. Her focus was solely on reproducing the genre conventions of the press release. As a re-sult, even though she was learning the genre conventions of the press re-lease, none of her releases was picked up by the mainstream press.

The goal of cultivating one-to-one relationships via print and oral communications also affects the way in which the publicist disseminates the press release. Barbara described two ways of doing so:

> Shotgunning is when you draw up a media list of about 100 or 200 or more and you don't really direct it to anybody and you shoot it out and . . . then you sit back and wait to see if somebody picks it up . . . but *if you're really looking to get a nice story written up that has insight and some imagination attached to it then the worst thing you could do is shotgun it, and then what you need to do is what we call shop-it-around.* So you shop-it-around one by one and I personally prefer to begin with a phone call.
>
>   . . . The time when shotgunning is appropriate is when all you want to do is keep the name of the organization out there in front of journalists, so that when journalists do have to write a story about some aspect that affects our organization they will think to call you, *so you shotgun these press releases not because you expect a story to appear but you just want to keep the journalists reminded that you're there.* (9/10/94, pp. 2–3, emphasis added)

Even the shotgunning approach, which Ursula used for all her re-leases during the year I observed her, has its pitfalls, though. Barbara ex-plained:

There's an upside and a downside, when you have somebody who isn't an experienced press release writer who's just constantly generating documents and sending them out, if they are so convoluted and so hard to read, then no matter how great the frequency, you end up defeating your own purpose. (9/10/94, p. 3)

In my final interview with Ursula, when I asked her to look back over the press releases she'd written in the past 12 months, she said:

Barbara, who edited this one [the job fair release], . . . made it so much better and I learned a lot from that. . . . I learned facts in beginning, background in the middle, quote and who's gonna be there, kinda was how she did it, I think. So I kinda just followed that format and I'm not good at that rah-rah language. (8/5/93, p. 4)

While Ursula progressed in her understanding of the genre and in her ability to write it, her knowledge was still not at the same level as that of Barbara, who had had the advantage of focusing on the genre a great deal more and working with other professional publicists who mentored her. The differences between novice and expert genre knowledge are hard to delineate precisely, but it appears that what Barbara possessed and Ursula was still in the process of learning was (1) an ability to coordinate all aspects of a genre's conventions—rhetorical strategies, choices concerning content, sequencing, and linguistic register—so that they work together, and (2) an understanding of how the genre works within the discourse communities involved, so that the text furthers the goals of the community.

Writing press releases was about 1% of Ursula's job, and as we saw in Chapter 3, press releases fell very low in the hierarchy of texts at JRC. She was beginning to show an understanding of all the formal features of the press release when the research project ended. She mastered the format issues early. Rhetorical, content, and structural issues—as well as the nuances of the journalistic register—were much more difficult to master. The subjectivity of the news and the differing needs of two audiences call for great rhetorical acumen on the writer's part. The coaching Ursula received—at least what she reported to me—did not allow her a deep enough understanding of the rhetorical and discourse community issues. And what she expressed as discomfort with the "rah-rah" language was in reality not understanding how to use persuasion in this genre and discourse community honestly and effectively.

Writing effective press releases also calls for the ability to "think like a journalist," that is, to understand the norms of the discourse community of the news media. Without a full understanding of discourse community issues—values and goals, communication processes, and norms for texts—the formal features of the genre and its communicative function could remain unclear and even illogical. Ursula next needed to learn how to manage the interpersonal relationships accompanying the press release—that is, the full range of communicative practices of the discourse community, of which the press release was only one component. This knowledge no doubt would have furthered her understanding of the textual intricacies of the genre. She also needed to add to her repertoire of genres the tip sheet, the backgrounder, and the pitch letter, often used as alternatives to the press release in working with the media.

THE SUBGENRE OF REQUEST LETTERS

As we saw in Chapter 3, business letters were another genre Ursula needed to master. In July, when we were looking retrospectively at the business letters she had written in the past year, Ursula expanded the list of subgenres of the business letter to include "inviting, asking for money, thanking for money, asking for gifts, rejection letters for people who apply for jobs" (7/20/93, p. 10). The first three kinds of letters could be subsumed under the category of request letters. Throughout the year Ursula reported more struggles with these letters than with any other type. In Chapters 3 and 4, we saw her struggles with balancing between being polite and being assertive in request letters. She had a sense that a certain decorum had to be followed, but clues to that decorum were scant. Whether asking for a raffle prize for an event, for a cash contribution, or for someone to be a keynote speaker, Ursula found how to ask problematic.

When I spoke with Barbara about this type of business letter, she responded immediately, "Letters of request are interesting animals" (9/10/94, field notes). She described her "formula" for these types of letters.

> BARBARA: Normally you wouldn't even write the letter without having a phone conversation or some kind of personal conversation first to tell you whether you can go ahead and write the letter and expect a yes. . . . Don't ask unless you know the answer is yes.
> ANNE: What's the thinking behind that?
> BARBARA: Well, it's a face-saving thing. . . . There's something to be

said for not letting people get used to or just becoming the
least bit comfortable with saying no, there's something to be
said for that philosophically and psychologically. . . .

*Now the letter, even though you know that you're going to get
a positive response, the letter still has to be very strategically written.* . . . They need to show their decision makers to reinforce
why they have already said yes to me. . . .

ANNE: So then . . . what are your guidelines for the actual writing?

BARBARA: Well my guidelines, first of all, my first paragraphs are
always short. I write first paragraphs as if I were writing a
press release. I always start out by saying, "I am writing to request," I don't beat around the bush . . . so by the time they've
read the first sentence of the first paragraph they know what
I'm asking for.

My second paragraph will always go into the reasons
why they should say yes . . . and then the third paragraph is
supporting information and then in the close there has be
this call to action. (Barbara, 9/10/94, field notes, emphasis
added)

Barbara learned the conventions of request letters from a former
boss, a highly successful executive in international trade and diplomacy.
Ursula's coaching in this subgenre of the business letter came from her
boss, Mei, and her letters of request over a year-long period (see Table 5.2)
indicate a gradual movement toward almost all of the norms for the genre
that Barbara spelled out, suggesting the genre's stabilized features within
the larger culture of American business.

The first request letter Ursula showed me (7/7/92)—an invitation to
the Secretary of Labor to speak at JRC's fund raiser—exhibited few of the
features of a good request letter. The initial draft, written by a co-worker,
had the request in the first sentence: "JRC would be honored if you would
be our keynote speaker." Ursula moved the request to the next to the last
sentence of a long introductory paragraph about JRC. But she had mis-
givings:

[The request] seemed too abrupt in the [draft I was given], to be
the first sentence, though probably, practically it should have been
closer to the front just because it's not likely that her assistants are
going to read this whole thing, and it may just look like . . . we're
just sending them information about JRC. So I did think about
that. . . . *If I wasn't going to follow up right away with a phone call, then I
would have put it closer to the beginning.* But I wanted to give her a

Table 5.2. Ursula's Growth in Mastering Request Letters

Element of Mastery	7/7/92 Speaker request	7/31/92 Request to accept award	8/26/92 Raffle prize request	11/16/92 Donor request	3/13/93 Speaker request	3/15/93 Food request	5/6/93 Speaker request
Prewriting: • Phone or face-to-face conditioning to say yes				✓		✓	✓
Writing:							
Rhetorical issues • Clear statement of bottom-line benefit to giver			✓	✓	✓	✓	
Content issues • Direct statement of request	✓	✓		✓	✓	✓	✓
• Supporting information	✓	✓		✓	✓	✓	✓
• Indication of sender's follow-up action					✓		✓
Structural issues • Direct statement of request in first sentence					✓	✓	✓
Linguistic issues • Positive statements (active voice), no conditionals						✓	
Format issues • Concise: 1 page maximum	✓	✓	✓		✓	✓	✓

Notes: Check mark indicates that element was present in phone transcript or writing sample. Requests of Nov. 16, 1992, and May 6, 1993, were made by Mei; request of Mar. 15, 1993, was made by Ursula.

little idea of who we are. (Ursula, 7/28/92, pp. 9–10, emphasis added)

In the second and third paragraphs Ursula's intent was to show the Secretary of Labor how she would benefit from doing the favor. Ursula said, "We know she's a Bush woman, so we'll put in that, you know, that she could talk about Bush's thing and do a little pre-campaign promo for her guy" (Ursula, 7/29/92, p. 10). Although Ursula understood the need for stating the benefit to the speaker, unfortunately she stated the benefits in oblique terms; also, most of this information came after two lengthy paragraphs extolling JRC's achievements, violating a fundamental norm in all business communications: Get to the point quickly.

Writing to a high government official without any insider knowledge of the discourse community in which the communication took place handicapped Ursula. But even in writing to a local hotel manager to request a raffle prize for the fund raiser, she struggled. Here's how the letter began:

On September 23, JRC will celebrate its 26th year at the [restaurant name] in [location]. Our Annual Dinner is an excellent opportunity for JRC to not only raise funds, but to also celebrate our excellent working relationships with our many business partners.

The request was buried in the middle of the last paragraph and was stated in the conditional: "It is our hope that [hotel name] will contribute to our fund-raising efforts by donating a free stay." The letter closed with this statement: "Please call me or my assistant if you wish to contribute to our annual dinner." The letter gave the impression that the writer was uncomfortable making the request. A single edit by Mei to make the last line positive—"Please call to make the arrangements"—clued Ursula that she needed to be more assertive and positive in her requests.

On another occasion, a board member had contacted a business associate who had indicated a willingness to give JRC a large donation toward starting an endowment fund. A letter was required to keep the negotiations moving along. Ursula described the rhetorical challenge of the situation:

We wanted not to be pushy but to . . . thank them for their support, assuming they're gonna give it to us, and here's more information, and it's still being negotiated. . . . *It's like $20,000 pant, pant, pant, and just a casual thing, thanks for your support, look forward to meeting you kind of thing.* (1/19/93, p. 4, emphasis added)

Here's the letter that Ursula drafted for her boss:

> Dear [Name]:
>   Per [Board Member]'s request, I have enclosed a packet of information on JRC. I hope the enclosed will be of help to you in discovering the valuable skills that JRC provides to immigrants, refugees, low-income children, the under-employed and the unemployed.
>   I personally want to thank you for your interest in supporting JRC. With your help we can continue and expand upon our vocational training, literacy education and employment placement programs so that we can better serve the community.
>   If you have any questions or would like to schedule a tour of our facility, please give me a call.
>   Sincerely,

In the second paragraph, Mei crossed out the beginning of the second sentence and inserted "Your support will enable us to," a stronger statement indicating an expectation of a positive response. She also changed the last paragraph: "I look forward to meeting you and to giving you a tour of our facilities. Please give me a call."

Six months later, Ursula was in charge of the job fair and needed to line up speakers and donations. She had worked on the job fair the year before as an assistant, and with that experience and almost 12 months at JRC, she had started to gain a sense of how to approach the request letter. While she was in the middle of writing something for another project, it occurred to her that she had a friend who worked in a bakery chain. She stopped and called him to see if he could arrange a donation of morning pastries. The tone of the letter following up to the phone call differed vastly from her letters 6 months before, and as Table 5.2 shows, she incorporated all but one of the "norms" for a request letter. Here's how the letter begins:

> We are writing to request your store [name], to donate pastries for 400 people on Saturday, June 5. On this day, JRC will host its second annual Career Day conference. The purpose of Career Day is to prepare Asian and Pacific Islander high school students for their entrance into the work force. . . .
>   Career Day promises to be a highly visible event. Congressional representative [name] and [local councilman] are among the invited speakers. As donors to the event, [baking company] would receive acknowledgment on all flyers, programs, press releases and

in our quarterly newsletter which reaches over 2,000 business, political leaders, news reporters and community organizations.
    We look forward to a positive response. . . .

She commented about this letter and the others she wrote for the event.

URSULA: This was a lot easier than the annual dinner.
ANNE: Why were they easier?
URSULA: Most of the people I was writing to I had some kind of
    phone conversations with. They knew me enough. . . . I wasn't
    too intimidated by any of the people I was writing to, I felt
    that they were willing to do it anyway. (7/20/93, p. 10)

For the first time, Ursula took the step of making personal contact with
many of the people she was requesting help from. After she'd established
these relationships and paved the way for a "yes" response, the request
letters became much easier to write. Even in the case of the congressman
with whom she had had no personal contact, she wrote a request letter
(3/13/93) similar to the others; it began: "We are writing to invite you to
deliver the keynote address."
    She still relied on Mei to put in what she called the "schmoozy" stuff.
For example, Mei added a sentence in the letter to the congressman that
read, "You are highly regarded and will serve as a role model for this
generation of youth." Ursula noted one more correction from Mei: "And
then my faux pas of etiquette, that I'll say call us. . . . [Mei] corrected that"
(5/13/93, p. 1).
    After a year of writing more than a dozen different variations of a
request letter, Ursula was clearer on the features of this subgenre. As
Table 5.2 shows, she made progress in incorporating more of the genre's
features over time. But she hadn't quite mastered the genre. The primary
challenge is understanding the rhetorical exigencies of each request-letter
situation: The particulars of the request itself and of the writer–reader
relationship differ in each situation, making each letter unique. Here's a
comment Ursula made on the subject of request letters shortly before our
year together drew to a close:

Mei asked me to write a letter to ask this guy to help us get the Secretary of Labor to speak at our annual dinner. . . . I don't know how
to politely ask someone to go way out of their way to bug the Secretary of Labor for us. I'm very uncomfortable with that kind of writing. . . . I really don't know the etiquette of doing that without being offensive; we could also ruin a good contact. . . . *If I don't say it*

just right it could offend . . . and there aren't words in the dictionary to look up in the thesaurus that would say it just right. (Ursula, 8/5/93, p. 10, emphasis added)

As with the press release, the key to a full understanding of the intricacies of the genre lies not so much in linguistic complexities but rather in the genre's function within a given discourse community and how that function drives a set of complex interrelated linguistic features. We turn now to look at a third genre writers at JRC needed to master, one much more complex than a press release or request letter.

THE GENRE OF FEDERAL GRANT PROPOSALS

A grant proposal written for one of the federal agencies in Washington, D.C., represents a clear example of a genre that is "codified by an individual or body into specific standards designed to regulate the form and substance of communication" (Yates & Orlikowski, 1992, p. 303). Jane, a program officer in the U.S. Department of Education, told me, "We take the law and write the regulations. We repeat back the law rather than clarifying it. The Office of Management and Budget (OMB) sets up the format for the Federal Register. We follow their guidelines" (8/24/94, field notes). In fact, the RFPs they created became the "genre codes" by which writers in agencies such as JRC crafted federal grant proposals. As Pam commented:

> As a genre, I feel like it's more . . . like in high school when they're just trying to teach you essay writing . . . you just parrot whatever that is, I think that's kinda what this [federal grant proposal writing] is except in much greater detail. (8/23/94, p. 3)

When I asked Pam how she approached writing a federal proposal 2 years after her first exposure to the genre, she said:

> *I have a systematic way of going through it* which is I get on the computer and I type out the entire RFP on the computer, like every number, every point, and I type it all in outline form the way it is here. I don't even summarize it, I type the whole thing, exactly as they phrase it and so as I'm doing that I'm getting a sense for how it flows. (8/23/94, p. 1, emphasis added)

Pam typed out the section of the RFP called "Selection Criteria." For the workplace literacy grant, those criteria added up to a list of over 39 points and subpoints to be addressed. And as Pam now knew, the process for grant proposal review involved a panel of readers checking off each of the selection criteria and awarding a score based on the number of possible points for each section. So at the most basic level, writing a federal grant proposal is like making a checklist or, as Pam put it, "parroting back" what they want.

However, as we have seen with other genres and from the comments of professional grant writers like Donald, what may appear simple is in fact only the tip of an iceberg of complicating factors.

In addition to the social factors undergirding the writing of the proposal, the textual features of the genre were in fact quite complicated. A veteran in the U.S. Department of Education, Jane, admitted the RFP did not facilitate a well-written response: "Writing for a federal grant is not like any other kind of writing. Once in a while you see one that's smooth and beautiful, but they're often repetitive and awkward" (10/5/94, field notes). While to the novice the federal grant proposal as outlined in the RFP may look like a straightforward, formulaic genre, in fact, seasoned grant writers talked at length about the complexities beneath the surface features of the genre. I enumerate here some of those textual complexities, as explained to me by professional grant writers, as background for the issue of how a writer masters the genre.

Rhetorical Issues

1. *Demonstrating a strong—but not overwhelming—need.* Tom, the government grant specialist who assisted grant writers and was a reviewer of proposals, explained the contradictory aims:

> The writer has to sort of walk between those extremes and say— not make yourself look so needy that you look incompetent, but not make yourself look so competent that you don't need anything. (3/11/93, pp. 26–27)

2. *Demonstrating agency credibility—the chicken-and-egg problem.* Without a strong track record of running programs like the one applied for, an agency may not be funded. Yet without funding, the agency has limited credibility. Selma faced this dilemma when applying for her first family literacy grant. JRC had a strong track record in running adult literacy programs but no experience with preschool/family literacy programs; it

was turned down in its first two attempts to secure a grant in this program area, no doubt in part because of the credibility issue.

    3. *Anticipating/predicting the unexpected.* A grant proposal is a blueprint for a plan of action, and yet most government proposals are for new research or new programs. As Carol, a linguist who had written numerous grant proposals, said:

> The thing that I find most difficult about it is that a standard grant proposal asks me to tell them what I'm going to find out. And I don't know what I'm going to find out. If I were to have written an absolutely honest grant proposal I would have said, "Look, the situation you want me to investigate is completely fascinating. I'm a smart person, as you know from my track record. I find out interesting things. You put the two together and I cannot fail to find out something interesting, and possibly useful." Now you don't write a grant that way. You absolutely cannot write a grant that way. I mean at the heart of the discourse problem is that . . . a grant proposal is an intrinsic lie because it claims that you know what you're going to find out. (1/19/94, pp. 7–8)

In the case of JRC, Pam must write expected outcomes (for example, changes in pretest and posttest scores) for a new workplace literacy program that has never been tried before. The writer must convey a sense of certainty and at the same time try to create room for the program to unfold and evolve.

Content Issues

    1. *Demonstrating that the project is unique—but reliable.* As Anna said, "Try and tie your project to trends, [but] well-established trends, not emerging trends" (1/19/93, p. 6). Government agencies often provide seed money for new projects, but at the same time they are looking for model projects that are sure to succeed and can be replicated.

    2. *Fitting government requirements, yet meeting local conditions.* As Maggie explained from her agency's perspective,

> You can't just say what you need and how much it's going to cost and who needs it. The last government proposal I did . . . was specifically for a group of men with real special needs in terms of psychological services 'cause they've been living basically in concentration camps for the last 10 years. And the gray area between physical health and mental health is made by the government into

a 10-foot-high concrete fence. . . . The government's much more
rigid in terms of how you describe things. (11/10/92, p. 4)

In other words, Maggie had to finesse the distinction the RFP made between physical and mental problems in proposing the kind of program
she felt would work. For Pam, this problem came up when she had to
write about ways of institutionalizing the workplace literacy program in
small business settings. The government's definition of "institutionalize"
was not going to fit the realities of small businesses; she had to find creative ways to plan for and write about this criterion.

3. *Providing required details but keeping the overall focus clear.* The level
of detail required in a federal proposal is substantial—usually a proposal
narrative will run 40 to 50 pages. As Donald said, given these constraints,
"An awful lot of good ideas don't get funded because of these layers of
stuff that mediate against the actual grain of the idea floating to the surface" (2/25/93, p. 11). As Pam described it,

> In a proposal you always want to figure out what your themes are
> going to be or what you want them to always keep remembering,
> so then I go through and sort of make sure that those themes are
> highlighted. (8/23/94, p. 2)

Structural Issues

1. *Understanding and utilizing each section of the RFP to advance the argument.* At first glance, the sections of a federal RFP may look discrete (or
unconnected) and even redundant. For example, as Donald explained,

> *If you look at that RFP, I mean what's the difference between . . . program
> factors and program plan? Give me a break. I don't know. I . . . finally*
> figured out what that was by looking at what other people had
> written. (2/25/93, p. 24, emphasis added)

So the writer must first figure out the differences among the sections in
terms of content and then find a way to build cohesiveness. This requires
getting to what Donald called "the deep structure," or the level of discourse function. He said:

> I've had to really analyze and think about it, and it seems to me
> that in every grant that I've ever seen or ever written . . . it can be
> boiled down to maybe a half a dozen critical functions . . . that
> need to be accomplished. (Donald, 2/25/93, p. 6)

Freed and Roberts (1989) argue that in spite of the lack of concurrence over the nature of the proposal genre in over 40 business writing textbooks, in fact the genre has six core content elements that advance the argument.

The federal RFP for workplace literacy programs contained all six of these elements, without, however, a one-to-one correspondence between Freed and Roberts's list and the seven major sections of the RFP. Donald summed up what he and Pam and other successful government grant writers had to learn about structure: "You have to latch on to what's the story you're trying to tell here. . . . You have to control the structure, not have it control you" (2/25/93, p. 13). Although following the format of the RFP was unavoidable, the grant writers learned to use that format to convey their "stories."

2. *Handling overlaps in RFP sections.* The RFP has clear redundancies. For example, in the RFP, under Plan of Operation, 2. i. asks the writer to "Describe roles of members of partnership." Under point 4 in the same section it asks for "Quality of plan to use resources and personnel." Another section, "Applicant's experience and quality of key personnel," contains three points: "1) extent of experience providing these services, 2) quality of key personnel, and 3) determine personnel qualifications." Pam came to view these redundancies and the job of the writer in this way:

> They all overlap, and . . . you just repeat it . . . [Donald] finds a way to say it that's a little bit different but doesn't stray too much 'cause you don't want them to think it's a completely new idea. So [Donald] used a lot of devices like, "To reiterate" bla, bla, bla. (8/23/94, p. 7)

The skilled grant writer must balance the need for repetition and cohesiveness without losing the forward momentum of the story being told.

Linguistic Issues

1. *Using a voice that is both objective and persuasive.* Government bureaucrats are looking for reasonableness, for objectifiable measures of success, so the writer must choose language that conveys what Maggie referred to as "the appropriate narrative distance." She said:

> It's how close or how far away does the authorial voice sound to the reader and how close or how far away does it need to sound for that particular piece to have the desired impact. . .
>
> I think there's a real grandiosity that new grant writers get . . .—at least I did. . . . I said to myself, "I could get $100,000 to do

what I want to do, so I have to make it incredibly grandiose in terms of being the only and most important human need in the whole world." And I think that just, in retrospect, pushes all the funders' Beware of Zealot buttons. (Maggie, 11/10/92, pp. 5–7)

McIsaac and Aschauer (1990) corroborate Maggie's point: "[The grant proposal] language should be positive and persuasive, but never exaggerated" (p. 538). Or as Myers (1985) says, "It should persuade without seeming to persuade" (p. 220).

Trying to start on another proposal toward the end of her first year of grant writing, Pam wrote a descriptive, impassioned introduction to get going. She said:

I started going wild with my imagination and trying to figure out why I would want ownership over this kind of idea or this model. . . . The first paragraph . . . it was to help me picture what this program would look like. (Pam, 5/18/93, p. 4)

The revised first paragraph of her final draft contains only the last two sentences from the original draft. She replaced narrative description with facts, selecting only the facts most relevant to her proposed program. As the writer, she was taking a backseat to the facts rather than presenting an eyewitness account—in effect achieving the appropriate narrative distance Maggie referred to.

2. *Language and formatting that are clear, yet appropriately technical.* As Donald put it, "You have to layer this bureaucratese on it to give it credibility" (2/25/93, p. 22). The writer needs to use technical language familiar to the grant review committee in order to demonstrate competency in the field. Pam gave an example from her experience with the workplace literacy proposal:

If they ask you for individualized educational plans, it doesn't matter if to you that just means I meet with students regularly and we have teacher-counselors for student interviews. It doesn't matter whatever you call it, you gotta call it what they call it in here otherwise they're gonna think you're not doing it. (8/23/94, p. 7)

Another kind of credibility is achieved through formatting. Donald talked about using charts to give what he called face validity: "It makes it look more official and technocratic and 'Gee, these people really know how to plan stuff 'cause they know how to make all these charts'" (2/25/93, p. 19).

In sum, the federal grant proposal is a genre with a number of intricacies and paradoxes inherent in its seemingly straightforward form—more so than grant proposals to local government agencies or to foundations. Donald summed up the federal proposal this way: "There's all these factors weighing against clarity and good writing. And yet, if you can manage to write well and clearly, you're going to be head and shoulders ahead of everybody else just because somebody might actually understand what you're talking about" (2/25/93, p. 11).

Selma's Learning Process

Two of the four writers at JRC, Selma and Pam, were learning to write federal grant proposals during the year of my observations at JRC. I've discussed in Chapters 3 and 4 some aspects of the learning process that these new genres required, but here I account for the process in detail.

At the time that my research project began, Selma had been writing city grant proposals for about a year. She told me how she began writing these proposals:

> We had somebody on the staff who was a good writer . . . and those are probably the first proposals that I looked at or read or fixed or helped with. . . . When Jane left is probably when I started actually writing, and *the first few I probably borrowed heavily from some of her previous ones.* (Selma, 7/21/92, pp. 10–11, emphasis added)

These proposals were mostly a cut-and-paste operation from the previous year's proposal. But she did make some small changes to the previous Private Industry Council (PIC) proposals when she wrote one that July. She said:

> The more you write, the more you get an idea of what's going to work and what's going to sound better. And I also didn't have as much experience running the program at that point. I have a better idea now what it needs and what we can do. (Selma, 8/18/92, p. 4)

It is telling that she made a strong connection between participating in the activity that drove the genre and knowing how to handle the genre.

In contrast to writing the PIC proposals, which became easy for Selma, writing the first family literacy proposal for a state agency (which channeled federal funds) presented several challenges. She had to conceptualize a totally new program geared to preschool children and their parents—a population JRC had not served previously. As we saw in

Chapter 4, this first family literacy proposal was conceived with only a few weeks' worth of information gathering. And the RFP confused Selma. She said:

> I kinda bogged down at first by the form of what they were asking, and I just found myself repeating myself over and over again . . . so I talked to somebody [in the state office]. . . . The person just told me you don't have to follow the outline. Just get the information in somewhere and they'll find it. So I did. (Selma, 7/28/92, p. 10)

The narrative portion of her proposal was 23 pages—two under the limit. On the surface, it appeared Selma had constructed a proposal with the necessary components. But a number of warning signs just in terms of content and structure indicated that the proposal would not be successful:

- Section headings did not follow the outline given in the RFP.
- Several sections required by the RFP were left unmentioned.
- A number of elements of the program design were treated in very general terms.
- Some statements were contradictory. On page 7 a statement said that the program would be modeled after "Type 1 Model: Direct Adult–Direct Child," and on page 9 a statement said that "classes and activities will be structured similar to the Kenan Family Literacy Program Model."
- The six objectives on page 12 did not correlate with the five goals listed on page 3.
- A separate section after the Plan of Operation, "Response to Selection Criteria," was largely a repetition of the Plan of Operation.

This proposal represented a significant departure from what Selma had written up to this point. For the first time, she was required to conceptualize a new program, and the contradictory nature of the RFP offered her little guidance about the type of program the government was looking for. The inconsistencies and vagueness in the content and lack of any clear, cohesive line of argument from section to section of her proposal resulted from insufficient subject matter knowledge and from unfamiliarity with the discourse community norms for rhetorical and linguistic features that made the federal discourse community's grant proposal different from the city's. Given the 3 weeks she had available to tackle this new genre, with all of its associated actions, and the minimal coaching from any insider to the receiving discourse community, the result was not surprising: Two months later Selma learned that the proposal had been turned down.

But funding was available directly from the Department of Education in Washington, D.C., for the same type of family literacy program. Even before she began writing the proposal, Selma told me:

> I think we'll put in a good proposal. I think it'll have all the right terms and the concepts in there (p. 1). . . . There's some things that I've read that have given me a better understanding of the way a program should run, so I can put more specifics into it than I put in the first one. . . . I also have a copy of [agency name]'s winning proposal, which I have read pretty thoroughly. I'll probably adapt some of the things that are in there. (10/27/92, pp. 5–6)

She also said that she planned to mention the professor from a nearby college whom she'd consulted to "give it some clout and some credibility" (10/27/92, p. 4). About the writing itself, she said:

> In the needs section I had to write more persuasively. I think in the program design I had to write more creatively . . . which is not my strongest area. . . . It means more . . . kind of imagining how the program will look. And trying to get it on paper. (Selma, 11/24/92, pp. 10–11)

The resulting 41-page narrative proposal showed a marked difference from the earlier family literacy proposal. The thoroughness of the proposal, the level of detail, the references to other experts, and the clear tracking with the specifications in the RFP all suggested a writer who was now in command of the writing situation and who had begun to understand the genre's requirements—particularly the content and structural requirements. And Selma understood that the federal government was a discourse community with different expectations from city government. Four months later, the news that the proposal had been accepted brought much jubilation to the office.

Here is a portion of my conversation with Selma during our last interview before she left JRC for another job:

> ANNE: So what are some of the challenges in writing a grant proposal?
> SELMA: *Figuring out what will work from the guidelines that you're given.* Figuring out how far the money will go. Figuring out

what the people need and how much time it will take, how
much energy.

ANNE: What about the writing itself?

SELMA: *The writing itself takes some planning, which I don't always do*
very well.

ANNE: Planning in what sense?

SELMA: Well, you know, are you going to approach it section by
section? Are you going to do the abstract first and then do the
other pieces? Is somebody going to write some of the other
parts?   Looking at the rules . . . do you need facts and fig
ures or do you need charts? Do you need resumes? Do you
need timelines? . . . Are there other programs, existing programs, that you can adapt? (5/4/93, pp. 2–3, emphasis added)

The two elements of genre acquisition uppermost in Selma's mind during
this conversation were creating content (i.e., the program design) and
managing the writing process for this lengthy, complicated document.
While Selma did not articulate some of the rhetorical, structural, and linguistic complexities of the genre, which I've enumerated, she nonetheless
produced a text for the Department of Education that contained a number of those features, in marked contrast to the first family literacy proposal. She had succeeded in climbing a steep learning curve in a relatively short period of time.

Pam's Learning Process

Pam's exposure to grant writing was more accelerated than Selma's. We
saw in Chapters 3 and 4 the first stages of Pam's learning to write city
and federal grant proposals: her watching Mei and the outside grant
writer tackle a large federal proposal and her taking on small pieces of
the task. Along with smaller roles on other city and federal proposals,
Pam wrote a 30-page final report to the Department of Education on a
program previously funded. Compiling this report allowed her to think
about the grant-making process from beginning to end, including some
of the rhetorical challenges. One such challenge had to do with how facts
were reported. She told me:

We have these statistics that we have to massage to make it into
the government's format, and so that doesn't really reflect what we
think is the reality. . . . Sometimes it's hard because people want
certain things measured that you can't measure very well. (Pam,
10/27/92, pp. 5–6)

The reports to city agencies created a similar dilemma of wanting to give an accurate picture of reality, and yet "if we give them what we think is the accurate picture, then they might think that our program isn't as successful . . . so there's all these mixed motives, you know?" (10/27/92, p. 8). Persuasion, in the grant proposal, requires a delicate balance of different requirements of the genre and of the discourse community: Being accurate and being positive can be hard to achieve within one set of data.

At the end of a year in the job, Pam assumed the lead role on a new federal proposal.[2] At this point she faced the biggest challenge of all, conceptualizing a whole new program. With her co-worker Penelope, she began to work on a grant proposal that built on earlier successes but took into account and tried to rectify problem areas. Here are some of their tasks, all of which are part of the inventor role, in which the writer is creating new material to write about:

- assess flaws in current program models to be improved upon in the new plan
- solicit input and negotiate roles with six high-tech corporations that would participate in the training
- conduct needs assessment meetings with corporate trainers at each of the business locations, survey employees, and tour assembly lines to determine language levels and skill gaps in the work force
- continue to build buy-in and partnership with the six businesses through ongoing meetings and phone communication
- initiate and promote discussions with a local university extension program to develop a partnership for developing and disseminating curriculum materials—a priority in the government's guidelines that year
- solicit curriculum materials from other ESL and workplace programs to gather program ideas
- think on paper, generating numerous lists, flowcharts, and diagrams to map out the components of the program

Pam also had a procedural schema for breaking down the writing task into manageable chunks. Her first document was a four-page proposal abstract that she shared with potential business partners during initial meetings to provide an overview and get input. She also input the RFP into the computer as her outline for the proposal and labeled a file folder for each section of the RFP so that she could collect and organize background information. Then she started working on the needs section, which she felt was less intimidating than other sections. As she finished one section, she looked for another section she could hook it to and started on that. Pam was very conscious of how the sections needed to connect to each other: "When I write a proposal I like to do it so that I'll stack up a bunch of pins that each correspond with a need and then by the end of the plan of operation all the pins should be knocked down" (8/23/94, p. 2). She developed a system to help her remember all the needs that she had to address in a proposal.

Describing how she viewed the discourse function of each of the proposal sections after 2 years' exposure to grant writing, Pam articulated a much different understanding of the genre that she first thought would allow paragraphs to be "slapped in anywhere."

> ANNE: I'd like you to explain to me the linkages between the sec-
> tions, you know, program factors, extent of need.
> PAM: I'll write the program factors first 'cause that's sort of like a
> skeleton of the whole project   then the extent of need for the
> project is to really set up the reader to feel like, "Wow, some-
> body's got to get in there and help." . . . Quality of training and
> the plan of operation sort of get written at the same time
> 'cause the training is the heart of your plan. . . .
> ANNE: I guess I don't really understand the quality of training
> section. . . .
> PAM: It's almost like they took out a piece of the plan of operation
> and really expanded it, 'cause that's the part they really care
> about is the quality of training, and then afterwards they want
> to make sure you're actually going to be able to implement it
> in a reasonable way. . . . The quality of training is a separate sec-
> tion conceptually too, 'cause there you're really talking about
> learning theories and curriculum. . . . The plan is just like,
> "This is our schedule, this is the timetable, so-and-so's going
> to do this.". . . Then applicant's experience, that's pretty much
> boilerplate stuff. . . .
> ANNE: It was not clear to me that program factors were in essence
> a summary of the whole thing.
> PAM: The thing that sort of tips you off is that these questions are
> . . . almost like rhetorical questions . . . but then you look and
> it's like 20 points for this section, for these really simple,
> straightforward questions. So that's when you know they want
> you to . . . hit them with the . . . star points of your proposal.
> (8/23/94, pp. 3–7)

Pam had at this point grasped what Donald referred to as "the deep structure" of the genre and was using signals such as the number of points awarded to a section as a guide to the readers' priorities.

An early draft of the proposal showed a number of promising qualities, too. For example, the following paragraph gives a strong close to a section describing the specific training needs of the targeted business partners:

> The [company name] manager's private lament echoes the thoughts of many managers who realize that their companies have shot themselves in the foot. Over the past twenty years, the high tech manufacturing industry has relied upon immigrant labor to achieve the high standards of productivity, quality, and cost-effectiveness which have been foundational to this industry's success. Now, the majority of the skilled labor force upon which these companies have relied is unable to master the core English literacy competencies being instituted.

Here is another paragraph that rings with candor, a tone of authority, and a strong commitment to the project:

> Having run three workplace literacy demonstration projects, we have moved beyond merely providing the service and "learning the ropes" of effective workplace literacy. We realize that we need to press on and answer questions with which experienced practitioners wrestle. We have also developed some very carefully thought-out theories of our own, which we would like to share. Thus, we have chosen to address all three phases in workplace literacy evolution in this project design.

The indication of insider knowledge and experience comes through strongly in this early draft. There is evidence of extensive research and a vision of what the program will look like. Pam used almost no boilerplate in the draft; even in the section addressing JRC's qualifications to run the program, she put in new and current information on the agency's successes and rephrased traditional verbiage.

Circumstances beyond Pam's control led to a final product that she no longer felt ownership over, and the submitted proposal was turned down. But in spite of this unhappy ending to a long writing project, the data spanning 2 years of Pam's experience working with federal proposals indicate marked changes in her understanding of this complex genre. She talked about "Mei being the idea generator and me just being the mouthpiece" when she began learning to write the federal grant proposal in July 1992. A year later, in thinking about her upcoming federal proposal, she said, "Some day I'd like to get at that stage when I'm not just taking other people's ideas and having to make them my own" (8/5/93, p. 5). By the time she finished the federal proposal in the spring of 1994, she had moved from observer and ghostwriter (her first roles on a federal grant proposal) to inventor.

Ironically, when I asked Pam to recall her first impressions of federal grant proposals 2 years earlier, she told me:

> I don't think the writing daunted me at all about these things 'cause it's easy to just write something but the hard part is coming up with the plan to write about, . . . the writing is pretty straightforward, just answer each question. (8/23/94, p. 6)

The data reported in earlier chapters, in fact, show something different. Coming up with the program design for a federal proposal is indeed paramount and requires a great deal of background knowledge, conceptual ability, and marshaling of resources. But the genre was also challenging rhetorically, structurally, and linguistically in the early stages of learning, appearing less daunting only after it was mastered.

GENRE ACQUISITION AT ADVANCED LEVELS OF WRITING LITERACY

As I pointed out in the beginning of this chapter, recent studies of writers' handling of genres in academic and workplace settings have moved in the direction of an examination of the social contexts shaping the genres and the social actions genres enable. This movement sharply contrasts with earlier studies, which focused solely on analysis of the writer's acquisition of the text's formal features (Freedman, 1987; Langer, 1985). Here I have taken as broad a view as I could, considering discourse community issues as they affect genre acquisition as well as rhetorical and content issues in the learning processes of these writers over the time span of the study.

What do the data show us? Were there patterns to these writers' processes for learning new genres? What were some of the differences between novice and expert production of genres? And what aided the learning process for mastering a given genre? Was immersion in the community of practice a sufficient means for acquiring mastery of a genre? Here are the patterns that emerged in the data:

• *The major elements of the genre had to be reckoned with, how-ever minimally, from the outset.* Unlike other skills, which can be acquired building-block fashion or a step at a time, genres can't be approached piecemeal. While Ursula focused in early attempts on the genre's super-ficial features, she still had to deal with rhetorical, content, structural, and linguistic issues. One of the challenges of teaching genres is that they provide no clear starting point. Once written, they can be dissected piece by piece, but the creator of a text has to attempt to handle all features of the genre.

• *Given the holistic nature of genre acquisition, the learning was iterative rather than sequential.* No doubt the limitations of short-term memory forced the writer learning the genre to focus attention on only a few ele-ments at a time, as suggested by Pam's comment that she "threw every-thing in" to her first draft of a grant proposal, relying on the more sea-soned writers to eliminate or structure elements as necessary. Any genre provides more complexities than a writer can focus on at one time. Only as certain aspects of genre writing, such as choosing appropriate content or sequencing information, became "automatic" can a writer then focus on the more situation-specific aspects of the communiqué (Himley, 1986).

Another way to describe the iterative process for learning new genres evidenced in this study would be to say that learning declarative knowl-edge went hand in hand with learning procedural knowledge. Berken-kotter, Huckin, and Ackerman's (1988) study of Nate, a graduate student learning the genre of social science research, indicates that his declarative knowledge (subject matter knowledge about social science) grew much faster than his procedural knowledge (knowledge of how to write in the social science genres). In the case of the writers I followed at JRC, their growth in specific content knowledge (such as an understanding of fam-ily literacy or workplace literacy) often grew while they were writing the community's genres. Learning both types of knowledge appeared to be concurrent, even requisite, to writing in a genre.

• *What changed over time was the depth of understanding of each aspect of the genre and of the interrelatedness of all aspects.* Not only did the growth in understanding occur in relation to each aspect of a genre, but this understanding became more complicated and layered with subtleties. In cognitive terms, texts produced and writers' retrospective accounts indi-cated that the cognitive "problem space" for the writer's task expanded over time to encompass an increasing array of elements in producing a given genre.[3] For example, Pam understood she needed to "spew out language" from JRC's "well-oiled machine" in her early attempts at writ-ing sections of a grant proposal, but she had little understanding of how the different parts of the proposal functioned rhetorically and structur-

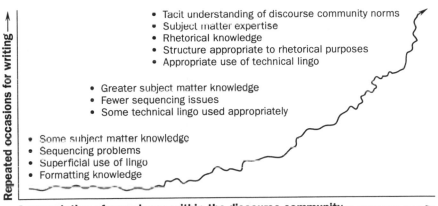

Figure 5.1. The learning curve for genre acquisition. Understanding of the intertwined elements of a genre increases with repeated occasions for writing and with discourse community knowledge.

ally. Two years later, her explication of the federal grant proposal was a much fuller representation of the genre and she could articulate the role the genre played within the discourse community that "owned" it. Figure 5.1 is a simplified, two-dimensional representation of the spiraling, iterative process of genre acquisition.

•   *Genre knowledge was incomplete if divorced from full knowledge of the discourse community in which it functioned.* Conversely, mastery of a genre was gained through full participation in the discourse community in which it was used. More experienced writers of grant proposals, press releases, or letters of request whom I interviewed had personal involvement with the discourse communities they were interacting with, through face-to-face or phone conversations, or even collaborative efforts on a given project. The combination of oral and written communication increased exposure to other discourse communities and enabled an understanding of community values and goals—what cognitive scientists would label *local knowledge.* That knowledge in turn enabled the writer to manipulate the textual aspects of the genre to achieve the desired rhetorical effect.

For example, Pam's in-depth understanding, that the "program factors" section of the proposal was a skeleton of the whole project and that "quality of training" entailed explaining the relation of curriculum to learning theories, did not come from reading a how-to manual. Rather, her conceptual understanding of the genre features came from a trip to

Washington, D.C., where she talked with the authors of the RFPs and with other experts in the discourse community of workplace literacy programs. She got an insider's view of the values and goals that in turn drove the communicative processes and shaped the genres. To give another example, Ursula's realization of the need to list the benefits of a gift or of being a keynote speaker came from her understanding of the intricate network of support that business and political leaders gave each other. She gradually shortened her introductions and the overall length of request letters because of her own experience at JRC with the overwhelming pressure to work through an in-basket overflowing with mail—a reality in almost all workplace settings.

• *Immersion in the discourse community in which a genre was used did not immediately or automatically give a writer an understanding of or control over its production.* All of the informants in the study were learning new genres "on-the-job," but as the data show, mastery of the genre did not come automatically or quickly through immersion in the discourse communities in which the texts were produced. Even though model texts were available, the rhetorical situation was tangible and immediate, and the tasks were "authentic," Ursula had not "mastered" the press release after a year of producing them. Pam was immersed in the grant-writing process from the very start of her new job in an apprentice-like role (assisting Donald and Mei), yet when she attended the grant-writing workshop and received "formal" instruction in the genre, her understanding of the relationship between structure, rhetorical context, and content grew. Immersion in the discourse community certainly motivated and aided learning of the genre, but immersion did not automatically produce expert grant or PR writers. These data cast doubt on Freedman's (1993) hypothesis that "explicit teaching [of genres] is unnecessary" (p. 226). The data here suggest, rather, that a combination of coaching and immersion in the social context is the optimal condition for learning a new genre.

• *Writers could articulate genre knowledge when asked, but the knowledge was otherwise largely tacit.* None of my informants mentioned the concept of "genre" until I brought up the term midway through the year. As Ursula said when I first raised the question of genres, "Genre's too good a word for business writing." Rather, the focus was either on the task or on general standards for good writing. In part, since genres are in very real ways the containers for action in the workplace, they become invisible to writers in their day-to-day tasks. But when asked, the four informants also could articulate what they knew, suggesting that genre knowledge may not be at the forefront of a writer's thinking as she writes, but may be characterized as "tacit knowledge" (Polanyi, 1966) or stored in long-term memory as schemata to be drawn upon "unconsciously" during the composing process (Flower & Hayes, 1981).

Further implications of the data for teaching of genres in formal and informal learning situations will be addressed in Chapter 7. I turn now to the final piece of the story for Ursula, Birgitte, Selma, and Pam. Having looked at three overlapping issues in connection with their learning to write in the workplace—the issue of learning the norms and intricacies of several discourse communities and the issues of what expert knowledge consists of and the learning processes to gain that knowledge—I move to earlier times. What home and school experiences with literacy may have helped or hindered these four women in bringing their writing skills to the workplace? And how useful were the writing skills they gained in academia, when they moved to workplace contexts for writing?

CHAPTER 6

Earlier Literacies: Antecedents to Workplace Writing

Saw a cat hunting in a field as I drove the little boy in to school this morning and thought how devious and long is the preparation before the son of man can go out and get his own dinner. Even when a scholar has the multiplication table at his tongue's end, it is a long way to the first field mouse.

E. B. White, *One Man's Meat*

WE HAVE SEEN Birgitte, Ursula, Selma, and Pam learning about writing in the workplace—both at JRC and in earlier jobs in the business world. Now I back up to their academic training in writing. All but Selma could retrieve, in fact volunteered to retrieve, schoolwork stored away at home; they were as curious as I to look at these writings, filed away years earlier, the artifacts of other lives as writers. Witness Birgitte, in the midst of a hectic workday at JRC, showing me two thick file folders of papers she wrote in high school, college, and graduate school. Or Ursula, talking with excitement about her first 30-page paper in the last semester of junior college—an analysis of Tennessee Williams's view of southern women—in the midst of phones ringing and conversations in nearby cubicles about budgets, proposal deadlines, and the annual fund-raising dinner. Although hardly a complete or systematic data set, the school papers and memories of school writing these writers shared offer a glimpse into their developmental processes from the earliest stages of literacy through college or graduate school.

Even if the data set were complete and a true longitudinal study of the four women had been conducted, tracing the developmental process of their writing abilities would be problematic. The few longitudinal studies of writing development that have been reported focus primarily on measures of linguistic or cognitive ability as evidenced in the written product.[1] But as this ethnography demonstrates, a text, and hence a writer's effectiveness, cannot be measured apart from the rhetorical situation.

Only in recent years have researchers focused on academic writing as a unique, socially embedded writing practice distinct from other cultural instances of writing (Heath, 1981; Perelman, 1986; Scribner & Cole, 1981). These data suggest the complexity of school cultures for the student writer in terms of negotiating among differing expectations for writing within particular classrooms or academic disciplines. What would the developmental process look like for someone moving from outsider to insider in a school discourse community? How exactly could insider status be measured? Tracing the development of writers from elementary school through graduate school in relation to degrees of social participation through writing must necessarily be imprecise given the scope and complexities of such analysis.

Even tracing one aspect of writing development, linguistic skills, is problematic. Composition researchers (Hunt, 1965; Loban, 1976) have suggested that increased length of syntactic measures such as T-units (a main clause and any subordinate clauses attached to or embedded within it) in samples of older students' writing, compared with that of younger students, indicates growth in the ability to express concisely (through the use of embedded clauses and modifiers) more complex relationships between ideas. But, as Faigley (1980), Witte & Davis (1983), and others have shown, these indices vary in relation to genre and audience and come laden with cultural values. Freedman (1984) and Haswell (1991), in fact, provide empirical evidence of the subjectivity of what counts as "mature" writing by demonstrating the disjuncture between English teachers' expectations for "good writing" and the work of competent writers in workplace settings. And as Brown and Herndl (1986) demonstrate, stylistic patterns in individuals' writing may result from social pressures rather than linguistic abilities. Furthermore, students have been shown to regress in writing performance at the level of sentence grammar when first attempting more complex cognitive and rhetorical tasks (Haswell, 1991; Kitzhaber, 1963), making a neat, linear progression of linguistic skills unlikely. Rather, writers' growth in linguistic abilities is likely to resemble a spiraling process that allows for regression and plateaus in learning as well as forward progress (Haswell, 1991).

Writing development also has been defined in relation to general cognitive development. Since writing and thinking are closely intertwined, it is appropriate to examine these two aspects of growth side by side. Cognitive psychologists have posited the notion of a linear progression from concrete to more abstract thinking (Piaget, 1970; Vygotsky, 1978), or from dualistic (either/or) to relativistic thinking (Perry, 1968), and, in general, empirical findings support such a progression as evidenced in students' writing over time (Freedman & Pringle, 1980; Haswell, 1991; Hays, 1983). However, a precise scale for measuring levels of abstraction would be difficult to construct.[2]

These are just some of the problems in any attempt to analyze a series of performances of a single writer, encompassing the full range of writing dimensions. Nonetheless, I present three of the writers' accounts of writing experiences, from earliest memories to the completion of formal education, and a brief analysis of the data from multiple developmental perspectives: syntactic development, cognitive development, and movement toward legitimate participation in a given discourse community. A sense of the journey toward expert writing performance will be evident. And for purposes of this study, these data offer a comparison of academic contexts for writing and the context for writing at JRC as three of the four women experienced them.

EARLY EXPERIENCES WITH LITERACY

Birgitte grew up in a multilingual environment. Originally from a northern European country, she studied English, French, and Spanish in addition to her native tongue, beginning in elementary school. Her earliest and fondest memories of writing were letter writing.

> BIRGITTE: I wrote letters when I was really young, to this guy in my father's office. I remember writing those letters. Every week we exchanged letters, since I was like 4 or 5 years old.
>
> ANNE: Why did you write to this man?
>
> BIRGITTE: For some reason, I really liked him. And he had a cat, and I was really sort of interested in his cat.
>
> ANNE: So you'd write him letters.
>
> BIRGITTE: Yeah.
>
> ANNE: Did he write back?
>
> BIRGITTE: . . . Yeah. That's the first thing I remember writing. I can't remember what else I wrote. I don't think I wrote stories. I read an awful lot when I was a kid. But it's mostly letters that I wrote.
>
> ANNE: *What was instruction like in school for writing?*

BIRGITTE: *It was no free writing at all, or fiction writing. It was all assignments on special topics.* (9/15/92, pp. 11–12, emphasis added)

Birgitte's mother liked to write and would even write some of Birgitte's school compositions during her high school years, just for fun. Birgitte said, "She liked to get the comments back. And she liked the research. . . . It would be like a comment on what has television done for contemporary culture" (9/15/92, p. 12). Birgitte's grandfather also wrote—beginning at age 82—and published two books. Birgitte had strong role models at home for literate practices.

For Ursula, her earliest memories of writing centered around a diary her father gave her at age 6:

URSULA: I personalized everything, so my diary had a personality too. . . . And if I didn't write in my diary every day, it felt neglected. And so it was part 'cause I enjoyed doing it, and it was part because I had this obligation to this thing with a personality. So a lot of my entries are, "I'm sorry I didn't write in you yesterday, but I was at Laurie's house."
ANNE: *What prompted you to start this diary?*
URSULA: *Well, my father gave it to me because I was always writing and drawing. . . . I'd write, you know, cards and notes to my parents. I had a little symbol that I put on the back, like a Hallmark card, but it was an Ursula card. . . .*
ANNE: So what do you think the diary did for you?
URSULA: It was my confidante, and I put all my feelings in there and I don't think I talked about the God thing with anybody but this stupid diary. . . .
ANNE: *Was writing a struggle at first, or you didn't worry about spelling or . . .*
URSULA: No, I wrote backwards. I have a little bit of dyslexia I think 'cause if you hold it up to a mirror you can read it, but it was all backwards. (7/28/92, pp. 14–16, emphasis added)

And like Birgitte, Ursula loved to read. She said:

I've always read a lot. When I was young, I remember being so desperate to read that I'd take things out of the fridge to read the ingredients. I read because I could (a major accomplishment, I remember), my parents encouraged me, and because it gave me even more food for my already stuffed imagination. When I ran out of books to read, I'd write them, illustrations and all, bind them together and send them to my Aunt Helene. (personal correspondence, 12/2/94, emphasis added)

Pam grew up in a bilingual home. Her mother, a librarian and former elementary school teacher, read to her in both Mandarin and English. But reading and writing came first in English; Pam rebuffed her mother's attempts to teach her Chinese characters and did not learn to read Chinese until college.

Early memories of writing centered around stories and plays she and her friends made up:

> I had a lot of really creative friends who would . . . just get together to do the typical things that kids do, make up little neighborhood plays and write—we'd make those big diorama things, where you have a big roll of butcher paper, and you paint pictures along it. (7/20/92, p. 8)

She also recalled having pen pals from about second or third grade on—writing copious letters—and starting a journal in fifth grade.

Elementary school also offered many opportunities for creative writing:

> I always went to those schools that—they publish little booklets of what their kids write, so every year all the kids wrote little haiku and little poems and short stories and stuff. (7/20/92, pp. 7–8)

Pam also reported on a typical sixth-grade research assignment:

> *I would say, "Mom, can you look this up in the encyclopedia for me?"* and then she would haul out anything that was relevant, she was a librarian. Like I would just go to V for Venezuela and then she'd go, "Oh they have a thing about the Orinoco River, you should do this too." *So she would basically do all my research for me and stack it all up and say, "Read all of these things,"* and then I would just copy sentences *from the encyclopedia. . . .* Like this [reads from paper], "Huge deposits of iron ore are in the northern edge of the Guana Highlands." (11/11/94, p. 1, emphasis added)

And like the other three women in this study, Pam read constantly when she was young. She remembered weekly trips to the library to take out 12 books at a time—the limit—to be read and returned for a new stack the next week. In fourth or fifth grade, she was put in a special program for elementary-age children reading at the high school level.

We see then that the three writers under consideration had a strong predilection from an early age toward the printed page—as readers and writers. Many children read avidly during elementary school, but these three women also found strong personal reasons for writing: communicating with real and imagined friends and family through stories and letters. School writing tasks took a backseat to memories of personal writing. It is also interesting that two of the three women were exposed in their early years to more than one language.[3]

HIGH SCHOOL EXPERIENCES

For each of the women, first memories of formal writing instruction popped up in accounts of high school years. As we've heard, Birgitte's mother wrote "maybe a paper a month" for Birgitte in her last 2 years of high school. But, Birgitte added, "We worked pretty hard. . . . We had lots and lots of papers" (9/15/92, p. 13). Her papers in English focused on literature. She brought me two papers, one on *The Graduate* and the other on a short story by Somerset Maugham, "The Kite." Here were her comments, reading the papers with me:

> BIRGITTE: They are very forced. . . . It was clearly a struggle to write English. You can tell that I'd been using the dictionary to look up words, and I sometimes find an inappropriate word.
> ANNE: So what tells you it's very forced?
> BIRGITTE: "The principal character is Benjamin." Period. "In chapter two we meet him on his 21st birthday" There's like very truncated . . . very short sentences. They don't really hook up very much. *It's really trying to show the teacher that I read the book, and I'm really trying hard to find examples and quotations.* (2/2/93, p. 8, emphasis added)

In fact, the paper on *The Graduate* (handwritten, eight pages, 848 words total) consisted of five paragraphs, arbitrarily constructed (with no topic sentence or paragraph cohesion), and a mixture of short sentences without any connectives and a few long sentences with garbled syntax. Here is a sentence that got away from the writer:

> When, later in the book, Ben falls in love with Elaine, Mrs. Robinson does everything she can do to spoil the connection between

the two young people, partly because she is jealous of Elaine, but mainly, I suppose, because she is afraid of losing Elaine's love and respect, if Elaine finds out that she had had an affair with Ben.

The first paragraph of the paper (21 sentences long) indicates Birgitte's unfamiliarity (and probably discomfort) with the genre of the academic essay and its requisite hierarchical structure. The paragraph states the novel's theme—Ben's search for identity—and begins to analyze Ben and Ben's relationship with his father. The focus shifts from one topic to another without warning and with only partial treatment of each topic. The only transitional device is the word *anyway*, which is commonly used in oral storytelling.

Aside from structural problems in the paragraph, there is also evidence of a writer not yet familiar with the genre conventions of literary analysis. She uses the technical term *leitmotif* to refer to the book's theme, but as is typical of writers unskilled in literary analysis, the analysis is superficial and supporting evidence takes the form of a plot summary (Durst, 1984; Eiler, 1989). Birgitte told me her task was to indicate to the teacher that she had read the book. She also knew she should include some supporting quotations from the text, and she gave three in the paper, but she didn't yet know how to integrate the literary text into her own; she said, "He expresses himself on page 66, saying . . . . " But in spite of these signs of inexperience with the genre of literary analysis, awkward sentence constructions, and little cohesion between sentences and paragraphs, Birgitte's English compositions in high school are remarkable as a nonnative speaker's considerable progress toward written fluency.

Ursula's high school experience included some traditional writing instruction and some nontraditional instruction. She remembered two English teachers in particular:

> Mr. Peters . . . used to jump on the table and say, "I am ON the desk!" Jump in the trash can. "I am IN the trash can. . . . " I remember *Lord of the Flies* and being really impressed with that story. . . . I don't remember ever having original ideas about that. *He brought up the pretty standard stuff . . . you're supposed to get from English literature stuff, and then we'd just sort of reiterate it in a paper and give it back to him. So I don't remember having to think too hard.* (10/6/92, p. 5, emphasis added)

She also read *Gulliver's Travels* in Mr. Peters's class. Here are the first three paragraphs of her five-paragraph, 320-word essay about the book:

> In my opinion, Gulliver is not the voice of Jonathan Swift but the tool used cleverly by Swift to present his satire.
>
> In Part I, Swift uses allegory in order to satirize the court of George I. The Big-Endians represent the Roman Catholics and the Little-Endians represent the Protestants. The differences between these two seem insignificant, yet the consequences of their differences are tremendous. Gulliver at this point in the novel seems to be kind, maybe naive. He learns, however, that the Lilliputians are as small in mind as in stature. Swift, not Gulliver, seems to be saying people are petty, pretentious and vain.
>
> Gulliver seems different in Part II. He now represents the arrogant attitude of the English of his time. He continually makes a fool of himself with his efforts to be considered an equal even though he is thought of as a minuscule freak. The giants of Brobdingnag appear grotesque to Gulliver but they are refined and good people. Thus, causing more injury to Gulliver's pride to find that these people are superior to him in very way. Here Swift is mocking foolish, ignorant pride.

She received an A- on the essay, and at the top of the paper, in bold handwriting covering Ursula's own text, Mr. Peters had written: "Extremely well done—a tad brief and some excerpts from book not covered. Thanks."

Reflecting on the essay later, Ursula said:

> URSULA: We saw the movie and then I read *Cliff Notes* probably to get this stuff. And I didn't really think. You know, it wasn't part of my idea to have to strain myself. . . .
>
> ANNE: Anything else in terms of the writing that jumps out at you, looking back now at high school?
>
> URSULA: I do remember learning some good words at this point, like "purveys," "implying," "suggests." *I learned those kind of words, that I can say something without committing myself to it, and I was starting to learn the language of writing a literature paper.* (10/20/94, p. 18, emphasis added)

Looking at Ursula's essay from the standpoint of the genre of literary analysis, we see not a plot summary, as in Birgitte's essay on *The Graduate*, but rather a high level of generalization without any development of key points or substantiation from the literary text. Paragraph structure is also weak: The first paragraph hints at two issues—the novel's purpose (political satire) and the shifting points of view in the novel—without any apparent linking or distinguishing between them. But overall, the essay follows the five-paragraph form precisely.

However, it is noteworthy that Ursula was attempting to distinguish between two different points of view in the text—the main character's and the author's—a complicated issue in works of fiction. We don't know if this issue was one she discerned on her own, with the aid of *Cliff Notes*, or from her teacher's comments in class. And as she indicated, she made an effort to adopt the appropriate academic stance of hedging her opinion through her use of the verb *seems*. On another occasion, Ursula told me, "I've always been obsessive about words . . . people's verbal habits, I'm always aware of them" (8/5/93, p. 14). In fact, even in high school she made a dictionary of unfamiliar words, and then she and her friends would write letters using their new vocabulary words: "*Procure* would be the word. 'Let us have Amy procure some beautiful boys so we can. . . . ' It was always high school talk but with these big words" (8/5/93, p. 15). But the vocabulary in the essay on *Gulliver's Travels* is not the specialized vocabulary of literary criticism.

Ursula remembered one other English teacher in high school who stood in sharp contrast to Mr. Peters—Mrs. Byrd:

> She had us write journal entries and personal stories. . . . She was very encouraging, and had good ideas, interesting ideas. . . . We'd do our writing, and then we'd read each other's journals and critique them. . . . I don't remember the criteria exactly, but she had an interesting way of having us look at each other's stuff. (10/6/92, pp. 2–3, 7)

Here is the first paragraph of one of Ursula's descriptive papers for Mrs. Byrd:

> I gathered all the necessary artillery, a sponge, a bucket of water, "Pinesol," a bottle of furniture polish, a vacuum, a rake, flashlight, compass, and "De-Bondo." The time had come, three weeks of sleeping on the couch had passed. It was time to clean my room.

Sensory detail abounds, but the exaggerated tone indicates a writer trying to impress upon the reader the importance of her words. She is probably not sure of her purpose in writing the piece or of the genre's requirements, making a decision about tone problematic. Nonetheless, unlike

Birgitte, whose high school writing seemed restricted to the "school essay," Ursula was able to experiment at least in one class with several genres, trying out diction, tone, and content for each.

Mr. Peters and Mrs. Byrd represent two very different approaches to writing instruction, Mr. Peters typifying the current-traditional paradigm for instruction and Mrs. Byrd typifying the expressivist approach (Berlin, 1987). We also see two different approaches to socializing students into the discourse community of academic writing. Given Mr. Peters's expectations that students repeat back to him his expert knowledge, Ursula had little real work to do. We might label her participation in this discourse community "mock participation"; it was superficial and did not move her very deeply into the discourse of literary analysis, although she did start to pick up some of the specialized vocabulary of the community.

Mrs. Byrd, like Mr. Peters, was in the gatekeeper role—she had her red pen and her grade book—but her invitation to revise a paper suggested a willingness to help Ursula move into the discourse community of literary scholars. At this stage, though, Ursula was not interested; she was planning to attend secretarial school after high school and did not see the point of any serious attention to writing.

Pam entered high school with a full arsenal of tools to excel at writing— excellent grades all the way through elementary and middle school, parents with advanced degrees who supported her reading and writing efforts, and many positive experiences with writing. Like Ursula, Pam remembered two English teachers most vividly—her eighth-grade teacher and her ninth-grade teacher. Recalling her eighth-grade teacher, she said:

> He was helping to write a grammar textbook, and so *he would have us critique the writing of the textbook.* . . . He really drew us out about, "Well, do you understand this sentence?" And then we would have to admit, "Well, no," and then we'd have to figure out why we didn't understand it. *He made us think that it was okay to not understand a sentence because sometimes it is written poorly. Even those written by a grown up.* (Pam, 7/20/92, pp. 9–10, emphasis added)

Her ninth-grade teacher, Mr. Harley, was also memorable:

> I didn't really get any hard writing instruction until [ninth] grade. I had this teacher who gave us all Ds on our first assignments. . . . And so on our first essays that we turned in, he passed them all back . . . and he said, "Oh you guys are kinda quiet. Well, I just wanted to let you know that I'm going to be using college-level cri-

teria to be grading you on your papers, and junior high level is not going to cut it. "... I think we really felt like *somebody was teaching us something, had some standards. Things like how to take criticisms, how do you ask other people for help on your writing.* (7/20/92, pp. 9–10, emphasis added)

Mr. Harley also emphasized grammar, as did her teacher the year before. Pam said:

> *I think we knew the grammar beforehand, but I didn't really know why it was useful.* He would make comments on the paper, saying, "Well, why don't you use another construction?" Or, "You're using all these passives here." "What kind of sense do you think that conveys?" And *so he really made me see the connection between grammar and intent.* (7/20/92, pp. 9–10, emphasis added)

Mr. Harley also made his students do a lot of drafts. Pam said, "I think that was the first time any of us had realized that we have to write many, many drafts. We just thought, 'Eh, write it, turn it in,' but he was never satisfied with that" (7/20/92, p. 10).

One of Pam's papers for Mr. Harley's class in the spring of ninth grade reveals considerable skill in handling the genre of the academic essay and the critical thinking required for literary analysis. Here are the first two paragraphs of a seven-paragraph, 589-word essay on James Thurber:

> Readers of James Thurber have always looked forward to a chuckle when reading his stories or essays. Thurber opened up the readers' eyes about something they would never usually give a second thought to. He would put down on paper the curious thoughts and peculiarities that everybody thinks but no one dares admit. This understanding of the little frustrations and anxieties that we all face was the main appeal of his humor. Thurber's characters touched the reader in a special way with their funny little predicaments. Somehow, they always managed to magnify the trivial, inconsequential complexities of life.
>
>   Some were caught in hilarious and ludicrous situations. A prime example is the couple in "The Topaz Cufflinks Mystery," betting on the issue of whether a man's eyes would shine like a cat's under certain conditions, which the man promptly tried to recreate. Most people would let it pass, but not Thurber's characters. They stubbornly pursued the issue, and the story becomes quite farcical.

The bibliography at the end of the essay lists over 50 stories from *Thurber's Carnival*, which Pam read for the paper. Pam discusses 11 of the stories in her essay to illustrate the common foibles of the main characters or the typical situations that result in Thurber's unique style of humor. The degree of critical analysis in the essay surpasses Birgitte's essay on *The Graduate* or Ursula's on *Gulliver's Travels*. The essay has a beginning and a concluding paragraph, and each paragraph in the body of the essay has a clear topic sentence. Paragraphs are unified, each contributing supporting evidence to the controlling idea of the essay, stated at the end of the first paragraph. Her conclusion restates the opening thesis, but in a new way: "Readers will delight in . . . these lessons on how to make mountains out of molehills." The essay is unmarked by Mr. Harley except for a comment at the end of the first paragraph, "Good intro," and a single sentence on the cover page: "You use abundant examples to excellent effect. A/A"

Pam's other significant writing experience in high school was her work on the school newspaper, as a staff writer, then editor, which presented an opportunity for a different type of writing. In the requisite journalism class, she learned "how to write under deadline and how not to care so much about whether it's perfect, and how to write in a more catchy way" (11/11/94, p. 4). As editor, she also learned about changing the style of writing to fit the content: "I had to be able to switch into sports writing, and then switch into gossip column or, whatever, *so you sorta had to be flexible like that*" (5/10/93, p. 13, emphasis added). The newspaper represented an altogether different discourse community, too:

> We all had standards for each other about writing clearly and writing well but . . . *it wasn't the same kind of pressure as if you were writing essays for your teacher. . . . We were writing for each other, we could throw in little snide comments and inside jokes and slang.* (Pam, 11/11/94, p. 4, emphasis added)

She compared this experience with the writing in her academic classes:

> *I think a lot of us padded our essays with extraneous information. . . . We just had this idea that for an academic class the longer it is the better, so we would just pad it with redundancies and stupid things that didn't really move your point along,* but for [journalism] you could just get to the point. . . . And it was also fun 'cause this was a class where we got to read each other's writing, and work on writing together as a group and we just didn't do that for our other classes, . . . and those classes were all very competitive, too, all these college-bound

people, so people were very self-conscious about sharing their writing with other people, (11/11/94, p. 4, emphasis added)

As Pam depicted it, the newspaper staff looked like a community of writers at work. The writing served a social purpose and was held to a different set of standards from the writing for classes.

For Birgitte, writing instruction in her high school English class in her native country probably focused on fluency and correct expression, with little attention to genre or rhetorical concerns. Ursula and Pam moved beyond the merely personal and creative types of writing they enjoyed as children and into the beginning forms of academic writing. In a few instances (Mrs. Byrd's class for Ursula and Mr. Harley's class for Pam), some attention was given to the writing process, but a heavy emphasis on grammar and the conventions of the academic essay prevailed.

These three writers appear to have been at different levels of overall writing maturity at the end of high school. An analysis of cohesiveness at the paragraph and whole-text levels reveals differences. Birgitte's writing (in English) was the least developed, as might be expected of a writer working in a second language (see Table 6.1). Both Ursula and Pam showed evidence that they'd begun to understand the structural features of the "school essay." In addition to structural differences, Pam's essay on Thurber exhibits greater depth of analysis of literary elements than Ursula's or Birgitte's and greater use of textual evidence to support her thesis statement—a sign that critical thinking was a part of her writing process at this stage. Both Birgitte's account of the task in writing on *The Graduate* (to show the teacher she'd read the book) and Ursula's comment about her essay on *Gulliver's Travels* for Mr. Peters ("I don't remember having to think too hard"), as well as the texts themselves, suggest only minimal analytical thinking in connection with the writing tasks.

WRITING IN COLLEGE

For Birgitte, the mention of college writing evoked strong memories of learning to think in English (she came to the United States for college) and to simplify the long, convoluted syntax of her native language. Here is her response when I asked her to take a look at one of the college papers she'd given me.

> BIRGITTE: I was . . . trying to repeat what this TA . . . wanted me to write. It's so yuck. "The most compelling independent variable

Table 6.1. Analysis of Text Cohesiveness

	High School Paper	College Paper	Graduate Thesis
Birgitte			
Paragraph coherence	Weak	Weak	Strong
Thesis statement	No	No	Yes
Supporting evidence	Weak	Weak	Strong
Opening and conclusion	No	No	Yes
Pam			
Paragraph coherence	Strong	Strong	Strong
Thesis statement	Yes	No	Yes
Supporting evidence	Strong	Weak	Strong
Opening and conclusion	Yes	Yes	Yes
Ursula			
Paragraph coherence	Weak	Strong	
Thesis statement	No	Yes	
Supporting evidence	Weak	Strong	
Opening and conclusion	No	Yes	

Notes: Analysis of writing samples of three of the writers from high school through college (Ursula) and graduate school (Birgitte and Pam) gives some indication of a developmental path. Cohesiveness at the paragraph and text levels is one measure of both genre acquisition and ability to control a line of argument. A thesis statement, supporting evidence, and an opening and conclusion are hallmarks of the academic essay. The high school papers were essays on the film *The Graduate* (Birgitte), James Thurber (Pam), and *Gulliver's Travels* (Ursula); the college papers were on Plato's *Protagoras* (Birgitte), linguistics (Pam), and *Gulliver's Travels* (Ursula).

that explains the delayed U.S. responses to the 1948 Berlin blockade and the 1961 Cuban missile crisis is the bureaucratic pluralism inherent in the U.S. political system." *It sounds stupid and pretentious. It's a ridiculous way of writing. And I'm trying to show off. It's really not working.*

ANNE: Why do you think you were trying to show off?

BIRGITTE: ... it's just not me writing. *It's me trying to write in the way that I think somebody else wants me to write.* . . .

ANNE: You say it wasn't altogether clear what they expected?

BIRGITTE: *Oh, it was totally clear what they expected. . . . It was trying to sound fairly sophisticated, really clearly showing you'd read all the books* and . . . their interpretation of the outcome is the one that you would be holding up as the right way of explaining things. (2/2/93, pp. 10–11, emphasis added)

This paper, written early in college, does start out with a thesis statement, standing alone as a paragraph, followed by two more single-sentence introductory paragraphs. But the paper does not present the arguments and supporting evidence in a clear, linear sequence. Here are the first three paragraphs:

> The most compelling independent variable that explains the delayed U.S. responses to the 1948 Berlin blockade and the 1961 Cuban missile crisis is the bureaucratic pluralism inherent in the U.S. political system.
>
> The "middle-of-the-road" response to both crises is a result of the balancing out of "Hawk" and "Dove" perceptions of the Russian challenge of upsetting the status quo (breaking down the deterrence) and the following difference in perceptions of alternative ways of responding to the conflicts.
>
> The most significant independent variable therefore becomes a systematic political argument on the second level of analysis.

In the margin, her professor had bracketed the three paragraphs and written, "All one paragraph." Throughout the essay, paragraph structure still does not follow the norms for academic writing. For example, another paragraph in the same essay begins:

> (1) In both crises the Presidents (JFK and Truman) were late and ill informed due to internal power struggles between two departments. (2) The reason for the acuteness of the 1961 crisis was the late discovery of the missiles.

The topic shifts between (1) and (2), leaving the reader to figure out the connection. The concluding paragraph of the essay states the thesis ("The thesis is that. . . "), but the point is different from the one in the essay's opening. The writer was not yet in control of her thinking or of the structural conventions of the genre—both of which are necessary for successfully executing the writing task.

Analysis of an essay Birgitte wrote in her political theory class in her senior year reveals a continuation of the problems in the earlier paper. To a reader unfamiliar with the works Birgitte is referring to, the essay is probably unintelligible. Here is a sample paragraph:

> (1) The dynamic of the Protagorasian society can only preserve a consensus as long as its external boundaries are relatively stable. (2) Socrates' attack of the Protagorasian method of ensuring stability reflects a promethera [sic] of the later demolish of Pericles' Golden Society. (3) Socrates perceives that a society in which justice is but a hierarchically super-imposed, diffuse concept of how one

should act in a number of situations will be incapable of preserving stability. (4) The inherent centrifugal dynamic of a society that is ruled according to these principles will inevitably lead to its own disintegration.

The paragraph has multiple problems at the sentence and paragraph levels: In sentence (1) the subject *dynamic* and the verb *preserve* confuse rather than clarify the intended meaning; in sentence (2) the verb *demolish* is used instead of the gerund *demolishing*, and new information—the linkage to Pericles' Golden Society—is introduced with no explanation; in sentence (3) the long string of modifiers between the subject *society* and the verb *will be* creates confusion; and in sentence (4) the meaning of *centrifugal dynamic* is unclear. The vocabulary and syntax are very complex, as if she overcorrected the simpler prose of her high school papers. At the end of the paper the professor wrote the following list of comments: "1) chaotic, 2) intelligent, 3) watch your sentence structure and usage."

In Birgitte's senior year, one professor worked with her at length on her writing; this is what she remembered:

> BIRGITTE: *He made me think of [writing] very structurally. . . .* One of the best things he made me do was to be a teaching assistant for a political science writing class. And I really learned a lot from seeing other people's bad writing.
> ANNE: What specifically [did he teach] about structure?
> BIRGITTE: Just that you have to present things in a logical manner. *And I also think he helped me stop writing Germanic style. Like in long sentences.*
> ANNE: But still pretentious?
> BIRGITTE: Yeah. . . . (2/2/93, pp. 13–14, emphasis added)

The pretentious tone stood out most to her as she reread her college work. At another point in the conversation she said:

> [It's] sort of the feeling that I'm not writing—it's almost like somebody else holding the pen. And writing to please somebody else, . . . —not just in terms of what I'm saying, but also how I'm saying it. *I have this image that the more difficult it is to understand it, the better.* (2/2/93, p. 14, emphasis added)

From her own reports, by the end of college Birgitte knew the structure of an academic essay, but she was not yet able to apply this knowl-

edge to her own writing. She said, "I wrote really clumsily in college. . . .
I think I learned a lot that didn't really appear until I got to graduate
school" (11/24/92, p. 3). She also did not feel free to express her own
views in her college essays, although her professor commented that the
political philosophy paper was "intelligent." She felt her professors in her
chosen major, political science, although helpful, patronized her. We do
not see a writer participating in any genuine way in a discourse community of other writers and readers.

For Ursula, junior college came as a great relief from the boredom of
secretarial work, and with the initial step toward a higher degree she
immediately set her sights on the state's most prestigious public university and began taking her academic writing seriously. She vividly recalled
her first English class, with Mrs. Macky:

> *I got much more conscious of style in this class.* . . . She taught building
> up style. She had us reading all kinds of interesting things with dif-
> ferent styles . . . just simple things, *I mean starting with a clause . . .*
> *and building up to my thesis rather than saying it right there in the begin-*
> *ning.* . . . I'm really much more interested in language. . . . That's
> when I got my thesaurus. (Ursula, 10/20/92, p. 20, emphasis
> added)

Several papers from Mrs. Macky's class indicate that Ursula had mastered the five-paragraph essay. The length of the essays is usually two-
and-a-half pages (typed, double-spaced), and topics range from a commentary on AIDS awareness to an application of ideas in Machiavelli's
The Prince to contemporary social/moral issues. Each essay has a thesis
statement at the end of the first paragraph, three paragraphs of development, and a concluding paragraph. In the margins of Ursula's papers,
Mrs. Macky noted fine points such as transitional words between sentences and paragraphs, an occasional subject–verb agreement problem, or
an inappropriate sentence fragment. The only comments on content are
very general: "Excellent job of analysis," for example. Ursula's arguments,
usually based on a reading of some supporting text, are not developed
to any depth. In the essay on *The Prince,* in the space of four paragraphs
she talks about the Iran-Contra scandal, Jesus, Gandhi, and Martin Luther
King to support her thesis: "Therefore, I contend that unworthy means
ultimately dissolve honor and trust and cannot be justified by the end
result." In looking over the essays, Ursula commented:

> *At that point, it was easier for me to write these because, you know, I*
> *thought I knew everything. . . . I would never write like this again. . . .* I'm
> so much more aware of my audience now than I was then. I mean
> I was just so arrogant that . . . I just assumed that they were going
> to believe me at that point. (11/10/92, p. 1, emphasis added)

Here's her account of her last English class at the junior college level:

> I wrote—I think it was seven or eight, 8-page papers, and a 30-
> page paper at the end, a research paper . . . and *she was telling us,*
> *"I'm preparing you for college,"* because it was the highest English
> class at this junior college. And so that class helped me a lot. She
> had us write about ideas. We'd read essays then write eight-page
> papers on what the ideas were in the essay. And she was very
> picky. . . . *Any inconsistency, any fact that didn't fit in . . . any sloppy*
> *thing to back it up she wouldn't take.* (Ursula, 7/28/92, p. 6, emphasis
> added)

To do the research paper (an analysis of the women in three of Tennessee
Williams's plays), Ursula had to learn to use the library; her boyfriend
came to the rescue:

> What I would do before he taught me was find the section, and just
> look at all the books. I didn't know, you know, magazines and . . .
> how do you find . . . the microfiche. (11/10/92, pp. 2–3)

The instructor did walk the students through the research process,
though, showing them how to use note cards for taking down and organizing information from references. At the end of Ursula's draft of the
introduction, the instructor wrote, "Gr-r-r! Snarl! I was just beginning to
enjoy it," suggesting a reader who was actually enjoying the student's
text and reading for more than evaluative purposes.

About the paper itself, Ursula said:

> I loved writing this paper, and I really was proud of this paper. . . .
> I liked my thesis, and I could prove it through the books. . . . I
> loved writing these kind of papers. . . . *And I felt ready. When I fin-*
> *ished this, I felt ready for [the university].* (11/10/92, pp. 3–4, emphasis
> added)

Nonetheless, when Ursula transferred to the university for her junior
year, writing her first paper at the university was traumatic:

> I wanted to get an original thesis. . . . I had done some research and I knew the kinds of things that I could write about *Gulliver's Travels,* and I didn't want to do something typical. So . . . that idea came to me, you know, something obscure. Oh, he's consistent? Oh, that's what I'll do. It didn't quite work for Part III, so I'll make that really small. And I just hoped she wouldn't notice, but she did. . . . And I'd . . . try to make . . . each paragraph, a little work of its own, and getting the transitions and all of that stuff. (7/28/92, p. 5)

The paper on *Gulliver's Travels* from her junior year of college is in marked contrast to the high school version. This paper, five-and-a-half pages (typed, double-spaced), shows not only originality, but also a clear, linear unfolding of ideas and the use of numerous direct quotations from the text to support the line of argument. Compare the opening of the high school paper, shown earlier in the chapter, with that of the college paper, below:

> Seemingly, Lemuel Gulliver, the narrator of Jonathan Swift's *Gulliver's Travels,* is a contradictory character. In the first part of the book, Gulliver appears to be a good, reasonable, and moral man. Yet, in Part II, Gulliver is decidedly petty and foolish. Although Gulliver is used by Swift primarily as a satiric device, Gulliver's characterological development through his travels is in accordance with his basic personality. For example, it is clear from the onset of his narration that Gulliver is fond of details and factual data. His punctiliousness demonstrates Gulliver's pride in what he considers to be his purely rational mind. The changes that occur in Gulliver's personality are due to injuries to this pride and his inability to acknowledge that he is merely, in Swift's words, "rationis capax."

In the margin beside the first paragraph of the college paper, the professor wrote, "Excellent opening paragraph. Clearly and elegantly stated thesis." Ursula is still writing the same genre she was taught in high school—the academic essay—but instead of focusing primarily on the form, she is now much more focused on content and rhetorical strategies: how to interpret the text originally, with textual evidence as support. In the first paragraph we see the use of "big" words: *characterological development, punctiliousness,* and the rubber-glove word (as Peter Elbow, 1991, would call it), *seemingly,* which indicates the author is downplaying her assertion so as to appear properly tentative and humble to her audience of literary scholars. *Seemingly* is a much more subtle rhetorical stance than the opening to her high school paper on *Gulliver's Travels:* "In my opinion. . . . " Even in the first paragraph, the invocation of text (*in Swift's words, "rationis capax"*) lends support to personal opinion, and the connectives at the beginnings of sentences (*yet, although, for example*) mark the logical progression of the argument. The professor comments at the end of the paper:

> This is a splendid essay—elegantly written, well-structured, convincingly argued, and copiously supported.

Ursula's joy in receiving this feedback was immense—enough to warrant a phone call home to read the professor's comments to her mother.

But other literature classes presented new writing challenges for Ursula. Even though the genre was always the same—the academic essay—differing perspectives of professors within the discourse community of literary scholars started to affect a paper's success—or lack of success. One of four White women in an African American literature class, Ursula felt "really judged. . . . There was a lot of really major stuff coming down in that class between the White women and the Black women" (11/3/92, p. 10). Here are her comments on the Alice Walker paper for that class:

> ANNE: What made it hard to write?
> URSULA: *'Cause I didn't feel . . . that I had the authority, and I didn't feel that the teacher felt I had the authority to write anything interpretive about it.*
> ANNE: Because you weren't Black?
> URSULA: Right . . . literature is literature. But . . . after taking that class, *I realized how much of this is experience-based, and it's a different culture than the one that I know and the one that I read from mostly.* (11/10/92, pp. 910, emphasis added)

And of a paper she wrote for a deconstructionist professor, she said:

> *I didn't feel comfortable with that paper at all because I was just trying to please this weird agenda* that I'd never even heard of before until I walked into that room. You know, the signifier, the signified, and all of that, and I just didn't know what it was. *If she ever tried to explain it, it just went right over my head. . . . This is just me pounding on the computer keyboard.* (11/3/92, p. 12, emphasis added)

In some classes she did feel a growing sense of authority. In one Shakespeare class, she came very close to participating legitimately in a community of scholars:

This class, all we did was perform *Henry VIII* and then at the end
we had to write how performing the play helped us understand the
play. . . . We really learned and worked and talked about Shakespeare. (11/3/92, p. 9)

That class inspired a strong feeling of community and participation.
Here's an account of what happened in another literature class:

When my teacher gave me the bad grade on that, I brought in
[*Franny and Zooey*], my Buddhism book, and little Post-its and
showed him. . . . *I was very good at writing what the teacher wanted, and
I could have written what he wanted, and I didn't want [to].* . . . That was
actually the scariest confrontation I ever had with a professor. I was
nice, but . . . *I didn't care if he was going to give me an A or not. I just . . .
really wanted to try to see if he could understand what I was trying to say.*
(8/2/92, pp. 9–10, emphasis added)

The professor reread her paper and raised the grade from B- to B, but in
a note on the last page, he said, "On second reading I still find your
terms 'ego,' 'ego gratification' confusing mainly because 'phony' seems
to Holden to refer to excessive attention paid to other people, to confor-
mity, etc." Ursula and the professor had reached an impasse. From a social viewpoint, the professor, acting as "gatekeeper" to the inner circle of
literary scholars, did not appear willing to find a way to assist Ursula in
deepening her understanding of the text or in participating as a legitimate
member of the discourse community.

By the end of college, Ursula felt comfortable, in general, writing
literary analysis, following an expanded version of the five-paragraph
essay:

When I first started going to [the university], . . . I would rewrite, rewrite, be very worried about everything, and it took me a long time
to write a paper, and I'd spend so much time on it, and then *towards the end it got a lot easier, I almost had a formula. That's when I
started to get worried that I wasn't learning anymore* (7/21/92, p. 2, emphasis added)

In spite of writing mostly in a single genre, almost formulaically,
Ursula occasionally departed from the normal academic essay: beginning
a romance novel with a friend from a Shakespeare class, ghostwriting
compositions for an ESL student, and writing a "creative" paper in her
autobiography class. Her description of ghostwriting for the ESL student

shows her propensity to pick up on another's speech and thought patterns, which she then mimicked in writing:

> I had to get into Will's mind. His answers were very black and white, so I thought I'd make his papers that way, and also I made his sentences really long, 'cause that's how he spoke. (10/20/92, p. 5)

For the autobiography paper, she had to struggle with the fine line between writing for school and writing for oneself. She said:

> That was . . . confusing . . . the line between writing a scholastic paper and a sort of creative paper. (7/28/92, pp. 1–2)

The ghostwriting and autobiographical writing were steps in her development of writing versatility. She was adept at the genre of the academic essay and had a heightened consciousness about the manipulation of words to achieve a desired effect. And the content of her papers from her junior and senior years evidenced an ability to think analytically and to synthesize ideas from multiple sources.

With a good record in advanced placement (AP) English at the end of high school, Pam was exempt from the first-year writing program at the private university she attended. She began her freshman year with a fairly strong sense of herself as a writer, only to find that the writing demands in college were different and unclear:

> *In high school they really . . . just baby you.* "Well, this is the conflict you're going to write about, it's man against man . . . now support this statement. . . . " *But in college the way to own it was to come up with it yourself and then make that as clear as possible through your language,* and that made it difficult for me. (11/11/94, p. 7, **emphasis** added)

Her professors' feedback on her papers was limited:

> *Freshman–sophomore year, probably a lot of junior year, I had no models or guidelines, so I just kept on and took stabs in the dark and tried to figure out what was really different about college writing and how could I make it better. They don't really tell you what's the difference between the A they gave you on the paper and the B or C.* I never really had a sense of whether it was just the writing itself, like it's not organized, or the

thoughts weren't coherent, or whether it was the content. . . . It was always this mystery. (11/11/94, p. 8, emphasis added)

The papers she showed me from college, limited to samples from her sophomore year, consisted of a series of two-page papers for a linguistics class and two longer research papers, one for a speech therapy class and one for a sociology course. Other than a few stylistic notations, the only comment on a paper for a sociolinguistics course corrected her use of the term *apathy* to characterize her parents' linguistic mistakes to the more technically correct term *interference* or *transfer*; she received a B on the paper. In the revised version, she used the term *interference* twice—once appropriately, and once inappropriately—and added another paragraph to illustrate her point.

Compared with the high school essay on Thurber, paragraph coherence remains strong, but the thesis of the essay and the conclusion are not substantive, either in the first or second draft. The statement at the end of the second paragraph seems to be her main point, and the conclusion is a weak generalization: "As long as we all can communicate, the situation remains acceptable." The essay is drawn solely from personal experience without generalizing beyond differences in pronoun usage in the two languages she's observed. In fact, the professor noted at the end of the paper, "More can be said here. Many American children insist on correcting certain errors in their immigrant parents' English, but apparently Chinese-American children don't. You might ask Persian Americans (or Turkish or Hungarian, etc.)." Pam's own evaluation, as she reread this paper and several others from the same class, is telling: "I wish I knew what I wrote these papers for; they seem to have no point" (11/11/94, p. 8).

Pam apparently was in much the same situation as the first-year writer described in Bartholomae's (1985) "Inventing the University":

The student has to appropriate (or be appropriated by) a specialized discourse, and he has to do this as though he were a member of the academy . . . ; he has to invent the university by assembling and mimicking its language while finding some compromise between idiosyncrasy, a personal history, on the one hand, and the requirements of convention, the history of a discipline, on the other. (p. 135)

She was a novice in the discourse community of linguistics, trying to speak its language and define topics appropriate for a dialogue with her professor, but without clear guidelines for the writing or the background knowledge that would have helped her shape the content. Although she received an A on the rewrite, she said, "I didn't know how to write to the professor . . . and I just felt like I was in this fog, so, when you don't have a point to make it kind of makes it difficult to write" (11/11/94, p. 6).

The 17-page research paper written her sophomore year for a requisite sociology class, Community Services for Seniors, lists as references four primary source documents, six interviews, and three periodicals. It reads well; paragraphs are linked, it has a clear opening and conclusion, data sources are integrated into text, and it is well researched and documented. If the paper has any fault, it is perhaps its scope: The conclusion—that the elderly are in need of more services—says nothing new, and there is little evidence of the writer wrestling with thinking. The introductory profile of a senior citizen she interviewed, though, is captivating: "Birdie Sherman is friendly and talkative. She has been sitting here at the Senior Center for three hours waiting to get her tax forms filled out by a trained volunteer." By this time, Pam was also skilled in selecting the telling details and painting a scene vividly.

As with the three women's high school writing experiences, college writing experiences varied, even though all went to good schools and were B+ or A students. They held some experiences in common: for example, all found college writing challenging. Writing was always for the purpose of being evaluated, with little overt writing instruction beyond freshman English, with the exception of Birgitte's tutorials with one professor in her senior year. (For an analysis of the evaluative function of the academic essay in higher education, see Heath, 1993.) Discourse community norms were not made clear, nor did professors attempt (perhaps with the exception of Ursula's Shakespeare professor) to treat students as "legitimate" participants in the discourse community of scholars, instead assigning limited and often marginalized writing roles. Although Ursula strove for original interpretations of literary texts (within the bounds she felt the professors set), Pam and Birgitte were more concerned with appropriating the professors' views, in terms of both language and thoughts. Ursula felt by the end of college that she had a clear picture of the requirements of the academic essay, at least when the content was literary analysis; the others' comments suggest less certainty about the requirements for a successful essay in their disciplines.

Birgitte's, Ursula's, and Pam's linguistic, rhetorical, and cognitive growth during their college years is difficult to measure with any precision. For Birgitte, college in the United States was an uphill battle to master academic writing in a second language. As she said, she was operating under the assumption that the more complex something sounded, the better. Birgitte also had not yet mastered paragraph structure or the overall structure of the academic essay. Given these linguistic and rhetorical barriers, evidence of her cognitive progress in analytical thinking is difficult to see. Certainly the subject matter was more challenging than in high school, and at least one professor commented that her thinking was "intelligent" and worthy of an A in spite of her difficulties with style and organization.

Ursula's samples suggest she had greater control of sentence-level issues and greater mastery of cohesion at the whole-text level. Her college papers also reveal more sentence variety than her high school samples, a richer vocabulary, and increasingly complex, sustained arguments. Pam's sophomore-year work, while adequate to meet her professors' expectations, represented her struggle to master the content of disciplines new to her, and as a result her essays do not show any great depth of analytical thinking. On the other hand, during Ursula's college years, she steadily deepened her knowledge of the types of argumentation possible in literary analysis and by the end of college could think about literary texts more analytically.

GRADUATE SCHOOL

Two of the four writers—Birgitte and Pam—went on after college for master's degrees, and both found writing in graduate school markedly different from undergraduate writing experiences.

Birgitte studied public policy in graduate school. All the genres she was asked to write were business genres: memos, executive summaries, and reports. And during the first year, as a part of the school's professional training, she met weekly with a writing tutor, a professional writer from a major metropolitan newspaper. She didn't remember specifically how the tutor coached her, but what did stand out was the amount of writing required:

> We had to write papers every single day, and I think you learn something from doing that. . . . *It was basically writing how you write in the real world instead of writing a paper that you know what your professor wants to hear, and you know what his ideology is.* (11/24/92, pp. 4–5, emphasis added)

Professors were helpful in grad school. Looking at an article one professor had written, she said:

He started out with, "The purpose of [inaudible] is twofold." I
thought, "That's great." And from then I started every single paper
with, "The purpose of the following analysis is twofold." Or three-
fold, or whatever. (12/2/93, p. 13)

Another professor was helpful in suggesting where to look for data for
her thesis and in defining the focus of the thesis.

Looking over her college and graduate school papers, she noticed
some changes.

BIRGITTE: Some of *it's less pretentious.*
ANNE: In terms of—
BIRGITTE: Well, not completely. "Indeed it appears." *It flows better. I*
think that the things we wrote about in graduate school are more inter-
esting. Well, no, I wouldn't say more interesting, but they were
more pertinent than what we were writing about in college.
ANNE: More pertinent to what?
BIRGITTE: To life and like the world around us. . . .
ANNE: Just take a look at this second grad school paper. . . .
BIRGITTE: This one I wrote very quickly. . . . *It's still sort of unneces-*
sarily complicated. And I think it's really one thing that I finally
learned. . . . The more simplistic you can express yourself, the better.
(?/?/93, pp. 13–14, emphasis added)

Birgitte's master's thesis, 42 pages of text and 17 pages of tables and
background information, looks at problems of hyperurbanization in the
Tabasco region in Mexico. Gathering the data was hard, requiring correspondence and interviews with Mexican government officials as well as
library research; she thus ended up with only 3 weeks to write the thesis—by hand, without word processing. She remembered sitting in the library, every day for 3 weeks, "writing and writing and writing. Driven by
fear" (2/16/93, p. 3).

The two-page executive summary reads clearly, with a voice of authority absent from her college essays. Here is the first paragraph:

(1) Tabasco's problems of unemployment, underemployment, inflation, agricultural stagnation, hyper-urbanization, and social tension
are not unique. (2) Every state in Mexico suffers from these economic, political, and social illnesses. (3) But the advent of petro-
leum industrialization and the ensuing transformation of Tabasco's
rural economy into the center of the oil boom has had the effect of
greatly exacerbating the aforementioned problems in this state. (4)

Whereas one out of every two Mexicans is under employed or unemployed, the corresponding figure in Tabasco is two out of every
three. (5) Tabasco's inflation rages at a rate that exceeds the national
average by more than one third, and the state's capital and largest
city, Villahermosa, suffers the nation's highest inflation rate. (6) The
annual population increase in Villahermosa at 8% is more than
twice as great as the national average. (7) *The clash between new and
old appears especially harsh in Tabasco, and the asymmetrical growth of economic sectors has created more severe discrepancies here than in the rest of
the country.* (emphasis added)

Unlike the paragraph on Protagorasian society in an undergraduate paper, this paragraph has cohesiveness in the overarching thesis statement
in sentence (7) and in the use of connectives such as *but* and *whereas* between sentences. Details are marshaled to lead up to the concluding sentence of the paragraph. The tone is detached and objective, but the writer
no longer is trying to obfuscate.

The first half of the thesis describes the problem; the second half
explores two policy options that could remedy the problem, and makes
a final recommendation. The thesis proceeds methodically and persua-
sively, and although it was an academic exercise, it had a secondary purpose: to articulate an existing economic problem in Tabasco for the re-
gional officials. In fact, based on the thesis, Birgitte obtained a grant for
a month of follow-up fieldwork in Mexico. Summing up graduate work,
Birgitte said, "I clearly knew how to write a paper at this point" (2/2/93,
p. 14). She also had a better command of syntax, had begun to learn
several genres besides the academic essay, and was treated as a legitimate
member of the discourse community in her discipline.

Pam started graduate school in anthropology directly after college and
then took 2 years off before going back to complete the MA. Memories
of writing in her second year in graduate school were most vivid, contrasting sharply to undergraduate writing experiences. She said:

> *Before in school I would always criticize the text, but it was only based on,
> "Well, the lecture said this, and the text said this" . . . but when I came
> back to school after 2 years, I was at the point where I was like, "Hey, I
> have definite opinions, and I think they're valid,* and I'm not going to
> just read the text and try to figure out how it fits in the wider con-
> text of other texts and what other people think, but I'm going to
> compare it to me." (10/6/92, p. 1, emphasis added)

She also changed her views on her task in writing academic essays, in a seminar on forms of social oppression team-taught by a law school professor and an anthropology professor. She said:

> The first reflection paper. . . . It was a lot more textbookish. I mean I tried to use bigger words, or I tried to sound more academic. And then after that I thought, "This isn't me. I hate this. I don't have to be like this." . . . Not so much, "Oh, how can I impress the professor and get all the points on the paper?" (10/6/92, p. 2)

The 16-page final paper she wrote for the seminar combined a critique of other authors' views of how to deal with society's oppressed members with a passionate statement of her own view—worked out from the standpoint of ethnographer working in oppressed cultures and from her own spiritual vision. Her handwritten cover note to her professor conveys the conviction with which she wrote.

> Here I am trying to transform my visceral sentiments into a polished message. I harry these unruly emotions. I corral them into structure, clarity, an outline. They must be backed up by the text, validation from other authors who have thought similarly, but in clearer words. It has to be this way in school because no one easily listens to the inarticulate sobs of anger, neediness, tenderness, hope, sadness. So the message is cloaked in dispassionate words, but the real power is in the feelings motivating them. (12/18/90, p. 5)

She had already begun her ethnographic work for her thesis while writing this paper, adding to the authority with which she wrote. At one point in the paper, objecting to the views of an author read in the seminar, she firmly asserted her opinion: "I object to this oversimplification not only because I am an anthropologist trying to substantiate my academic turf, but because it retards rather than propels the process of ending subordination." Her professor's end comment was, "This is a moving paper. . . . It touches feelings, feels Utopian, and yet contains a positive and strong vision for change. . . . Good paper!"

The issue of putting oneself in the academic text is not easy to handle, however. In her thesis, Pam would struggle with how much of her own voice to allow. She said:

> I don't like the way it sounds in your paper if you use too many *I*s, like, "I think this and I"—you know, I just, I go, "Gosh, whoever's reading this is going to think this is such an egocentric paper. So

... I guess I just tried to find a middle ground, you know, like, like not beating people over the head by saying, "This is what I think," but not hiding it either. (10/6/92, p. 4)

The opening paragraph of her thesis is written from personal experience. By the fourth paragraph of the 48-page thesis, she shifts into third person, giving facts and figures that objectify the personal and ethnographic detail of the opening paragraphs. She closes the introduction with this statement:

This paper is both a description of life for the new Asian Americans in [city] and a mouthpiece for the stories people tell as they long to express who they are and what they are becoming. Bringing my experiences to the discussion of the formation of American identity, will, I hope, give real faces to these groups of which we theorize

Most of the thesis is written in the third person, but the reader is made aware of the writer's presence throughout. She writes as participant-observer, taking the reader on her journey of collecting the data and also on her intellectual journey of trying out different theories of cultural assimilation for their "fit" with the data.

The process of writing the thesis differed from writing processes in undergraduate work, too. Here's Pam's description of the graduate seminar supporting the master's students with their writing:

We had a Ph.D. student lead us. . . . We all came and moaned every week and read each other's stuff, and you know . . . it was excellent practice for us because we really learned to be critical of each other's writing and not take it personally. . . . He had a good blend of understanding, you know, how hard it is to be writing, and also at the same time being able to goad you into doing it and say, "Well, this is what people are looking for. . . . I don't care what your style is, change this." . . .

It was like boot camp for writers. . . . A lot of us had to be weaned off the regurgitating what everyone else says. And you know, it's something that you should grow out of in high school when you stop copying out of the encyclopedia for your book reports but . . . there's a little insecurity about am I, do I have the right spin on this person's theory. (8/4/92, pp. 2–3)

In addition to the thesis-writing seminar, Pam had one-on-one talks with her thesis advisor that helped shape her as a writer and move her closer to real participation in the discourse community of anthropology. Here's her account of her advisor's role:

> Ron was great. . . . He was advising me on different things he wanted me to try out. So one of them was how do you integrate the ethnographic detail into the theory in your writing, so he said, "Well, you should—you should play with these methods in your papers. It would be a good chance for you to experiment. . . . " I *mean he couldn't give me any concrete ways to write it*, like he never gave me any mechanical things like, "Use this kind of word, or use this sort of transition," *but he gave me more of a sort of philosophical way to approach things.* (10/6/92, pp. 1–2, emphasis added)

These graduate school writing experiences suggest the beginnings of a shift from a writer who appeals to others' authority, to a writer making her own claims, building on others' work—a sign that she was moving from outsider to insider in the community.

Part of being "legitimate" had to do with establishing her identity, not apart from others in the discourse community, but within it. "Writing whatever you feel like" in reality occurred after Pam had absorbed a lot of the subject matter knowledge and norms for writing in anthropology.

For both Birgitte and Pam graduate school was a major turning point in developing writing skills. Free of technical errors, their writing was cohesive and clear at the sentence-, paragraph-, and whole-text levels. Schooled by their mentors in the particulars of the genres they were writing in—the specialized vocabularies, stylistic choices, and means of argumentation—Birgitte and Pam could use established discourse conventions. Both experienced a certain "coming into their own" in terms of expressing themselves in their chosen fields, Birgitte in public policy and Pam in anthropology. They were able to write in the specialized genres of their respective fields, with more independence in their thinking and writing and less of a feeling, as Birgitte put it, of "people looking over my shoulder" (2/2/93, p 14)

THE LONG ROAD TO MASTERY

Without poring through reams of data or counting the length of T-units, E. B. White (1938) could correctly surmise the truth: ". . . it is a long way to the first field mouse" (p. 81). Getting from the earliest, rudimentary stories to polished, sophisticated prose was indeed a slow maturational process that included assistance from many helpful guides, reading many books, and writing many papers. Here I summarize patterns emerging from these women's stories and their writing samples that may add to our knowledge of school writing and the developmental processes in achieving writing literacy.

- *Strong support for literate behaviors at an early age set the stage for ongoing literacy development.* Others' research corroborates this finding (Bissex, 1980; Heath, 1983; Kirsch & Jungeblut, 1992).[4] The three writers were encouraged early—primarily by parents—to read and write for personal enjoyment. During formal schooling, writing and reading remained strong interests outside required school exercises, and Ursula, Pam, and Birgitte continue to write letters, fiction, or journals outside of their professional writing responsibilities.
- *Even in the college years, these writers had to devote attention to mastery of fundamentals of standard written English.* The writers' samples from college, compared with high school, show that all three grew in writing fundamentals: correct grammar, sentence variety, and appropriate diction. This growth suggests the complexity of the skills and the lengthy amount of time required even for "good" writers to achieve mastery of foundational writing skills.
- *Development of writing skill involved working on multiple subskills simultaneously.* Early attempts at the genre of literary analysis, such as Birgitte's paper on *The Graduate* and Ursula's high school paper on *Gulliver's Travels*, exemplify through their weaknesses the elements a writer must try to handle simultaneously: vocabulary, sentence syntax, subject matter knowledge, genre knowledge, rhetorical knowledge, and, ultimately, the larger aims and values of a given discourse community.
- *The writer's ability to increase complexity of content and incorporate more linguistic and rhetorical standards of the discourse community had to be balanced with the need to communicate clearly, even simply.* Any holistic scale for measuring Ursula's two essays on *Gulliver's Travels*, one as a junior in high school and the other as a junior at the university, would have to register the expansion of the "problem space" the writer represented to herself in connection with the writing task. But witness too the increased clarity of Birgitte's master's thesis on Tabasco's complex economic problems in relation to her complex, but linguistically and rhetorically muddled, analysis of political philosophy in her senior year of college. Or compare Pam's attempt at a sociological paper on problems of the elderly in her sophomore year of college and her master's thesis on assimilation problems of Asian Americans in an urban setting: All measures of writing

ability I've outlined in this chapter show increasing complexity, but at the same time an increase in clarity of expression.

• *Growth spurts occurred at different times for these three writers.* Based on an analysis of these women's writing from junior high through college and graduate school, each writer apparently experienced a spurt in writing skill development at different times. For Birgitte, who was writing in a second language, an approximation of expert writing performance didn't happen until graduate school, when she suddenly seemed in command of written English in the genres required in her work on a master's in public policy. Pam's writing skills in several genres in high school (the academic essay and several journalistic forms) were considerable. In college, by her own reports, she felt lost as to the new standards for expert writing performance in various academic subjects, including her major, linguistics. In graduate school, having chosen to focus on anthropology, she gained considerable fluency and self-assurance in critical analyses of others' work and her own ethnographic reports. Ursula's high school writing, although acceptable to her teachers, did not display as much competence as Pam's high school samples. But unlike Pam, Ursula showed steady improvement and increasing self-assurance during college in writing in her major, literature. Although personal factors no doubt played a part in the variations in growth periods, the degree of support and coaching at a given stage correlated with growth spurts as well. Ursula received the strongest coaching in junior college; for Birgitte, strong coaching came at the end of college and in graduate school; and Pam had her strongest coaching in high school and then in graduate school.

• *The social purpose for writing in school, namely, to please the teacher, earn a satisfactory grade, and accumulate academic credits, was an element of performance each writer attended to.* All three writers talked about the need to understand the teacher's biases and to write accordingly or else risk a lower grade. Teachers' agendas included the acceptable paper length, genre, and in some cases content and rhetorical stance. Although the notion of discourse community was unfamiliar on a conscious level, unconsciously the three writers were "reading" the expectations for joining a given teacher's representation of an academic discourse community.

• *Both the level of participation in the academic discourse community and the socialization process into that community were limited for these student writers.* Birgitte, Ursula, and Pam experienced mostly "outsider" status in academic discourse communities during high school and college. The papers they wrote for classes did not count as anything more than practice exercises in the discourse community, with the exception of Pam's experiences with the English teacher who involved his eighth graders in the writing of a grammar textbook and her experience with the high school newspaper. Graduate school, on the other hand, was transitional for Pam and Birgitte: Their professors fostered "authentic" writing tasks in relation to the disciplinary work of their fields.

On all counts, then—acquisition of foundation skills in writing literacy (fluency and correctness), the acquisition of higher-order analytical skills, and initiation into academic discourse communities—the developmental processes for these writers were long and slow. And these data indicate the necessity to consider competencies in social aspects of writing performance in addition to textual and cognitive aspects.

Some have speculated that a slow socialization process into the discourse communities of academia results from an intentional gatekeeping function of educational institutions. Geisler's (1994) study of writing performances in a college-level class corroborates my informants' difficulties with writing. But Geisler draws the conclusion that education has two contradictory missions: on the one hand, to impart expertise; on the other hand, to serve a gatekeeping function so that only some can move to advanced levels of schooling and enter the professions. Geisler argues that schools manage these conflicting goals by imparting domain content expertise in K–12 and college, and imparting rhetorical process expertise only at the graduate school level (see also Bizzell, 1992; Heath, 1993; Miller, 1991). However, in light of the data we've examined in this chapter, I would argue differently. In several instances reported in the data, teachers did seem to perform a negative gatekeeping role, keeping the aspiring writer from being "in the know" (the college literature professor, for example, who was not willing to engage Ursula in a dialogue about her interpretation of *Catcher in the Rye*), but other teachers invited students to see/do/experience authentic writing tasks (such as Pam's teacher who read sentences from his writing project to his junior high students and asked for their critique). I would argue on the basis of the data here that the issues in achieving expert writing performance are both developmental and curricular. However, these matters will be explored more fully in the next chapter, where I consider the differences between academic and workplace writing and summarize the multiple lenses through which expert writing performance must be considered.

CHAPTER 7

Bridging the Gap: From Classroom to Boardroom

The overall education level of Americans has increased
in terms of schooling and even in fundamental literacy.
But the demands of the workplace simultaneously have
vastly increased. We simply are not keeping pace with
the kinds of skills required in today's economy
— Madeleine Hunin, Deputy Secretary
of Education

THIS ETHNOGRAPHY UNFOLDED as the result of a research methodology, some theoretical hunches, and the process of writing itself, in which, as Bereiter and Scardamalia (1987) point out, knowledge is transformed. The information presented here is situated in time and space, "one more county heard from" (Fishman, 1988, p. 212). Although JRC still carries forth its mission as I write this chapter, those described in this study have left JRC for other pursuits.

A tale of four individuals has emerged here, all of them strong writers, learning to perform expertly at new writing tasks in an environment that differed greatly from school. Written communication, in the workplace setting examined here, is both a call for action and action itself. Written text works for the common good rather than individual accomplishment and is shaped by internal and external discourse communities.

This study examines the complexities of expert writing performances from a social perspective and attempts to understand why writing literacy is not a fixed, finite set of skills but rather an ever-shifting set of demands. Although writing fundamentals—vocabulary, spelling, syntax, diction, and mechanics—must be mastered along the way to writing literacy, as we saw in Chapter 6, this study's primary focus is on context-specific variables in expert writing performances. And, although hardly exhaustive, the study attempts an examination of a continuum of writing situations in school and beyond because, as Geisler (1994) states, "[t]hose concerned with schooling often lack an understanding of mature practice, and it becomes all too easy for K–12 educators to think of the analytic essay as a final achievement rather than a special genre of schooled literacy" (p. 243). I would extend her observation to postsecondary educators as well.

Originally, my intentions for this study were to examine issues that could possibly lead to implications for postsecondary curricula. I discovered en route that looking at expert writing performances as defined by communities of practice, not by standardized tests or even portfolio assessments, led to a different way of theorizing writing expertise. The five context-specific subsets of writing skills and knowledge identified at the site of this study add to current conceptions of writing expertise and help to provide a framework for looking at transfer of learning issues. In the remainder of this chapter, I return to the three central questions raised in Chapter 1 to recast the particulars of the individual chapters against the larger issues those questions raise.

KNOWLEDGE DOMAINS OF EXPERT WRITERS

What are the distinct and overlapping knowledge domains an expert writer draws upon in a given writing situation? And what does a fuller explication of these knowledge domains add to theories of composing?

For a variety of writing tasks, each writer at JRC had to acquire context-specific expertise in five areas: discourse community knowledge, subject matter knowledge, genre knowledge, rhetorical knowledge, and writing process knowledge. All five were interrelated and yet, in this study, were distinct enough to warrant separate analysis and theorizing. This distinctiveness does not imply an attempt at yet another rigid sociocultural taxonomy of writing that would, as Dyson (1993) says, "keep all of us, children and adults, trapped." Rather, to borrow Marilyn Cooper's (1986) suggestion of an ecological metaphor for the social dimensions of writing, each category is integrally connected to the others in a web-like arrangement: When one changes, the other areas change as well. And, as Cooper says, the categories are not fixed, but instead are "made and remade by writers in the act of writing" (p. 368).

Discourse community knowledge is the knowledge domain within which the other four areas are subsumed. The data suggest that a fully articulated notion of discourse community has considerable explanatory power: To understand discourse community knowledge is to understand how the community's communicative practices—including communication channels, norms for genres, and writers' roles—all flow from long-term, overarching goals and values. Unlike rhetorical knowledge, which focuses on the immediate task and a specific audience, such as writing a letter on the occasion of a Chinese association's anniversary, discourse community knowledge illuminates the larger institutional issue at stake in the communicative event: to pay respect to a cultural tradition and a long-term business relationship. Equally important is an understanding of the interplay of oral communications (face-to-face or phone contact) with written texts. Without a notion of discourse community as used in this study, it would have been difficult to explain a number of phenomena observed: hierarchical treatment of texts; gradations of expertise in relation to writing roles; the interrelationship of oral and written discourse and of silence rather than communication on some topics, the practical and symbolic purposes of texts; the differentiations in form, function, and features of the same genre as used in different communities of practice; or the long-term, overarching purposes that various forms of communication served beyond the immediate rhetorical situation.

To come to a full understanding of a discourse community requires awareness that is part anthropological, part sociological, part linguistic, and part psychological. Gaining this knowledge at JRC required being in contact with at least one member of the discourse community being addressed and understanding a whole web of social and political issues with which that community was concerned—almost as if the writer herself had to become a linguistic anthropologist gaining entrance to the community being addressed in order to understand the dynamic nature of its discourse. Over the course of this study, all four women learned a great deal about the different discourse communities external to JRC with whom they communicated. We also saw in the retrospective accounts of school contexts for writing the gradual building of discourse community knowledge in specific academic discourse communities during college and graduate school: literature (Ursula), public policy (Birgitte), and anthropology (Pam). This knowledge led to more expert writing performances.

The other four knowledge areas are also complex. Subject matter knowledge is a requisite component of expert writing performance usually overlooked in most discussions of formal writing instruction (Jolliffe, 1995). At JRC we saw Ursula, with excellent general linguistic abilities, unable to edit the organization's PR materials effectively until she had been at the site for almost a year, by which time she had a deep enough understanding of the agency's programs to bring her editing skills to bear on the institution's texts. Indeed, all four writers spent much time gathering and absorbing information that would be the foundation for their writing tasks.

Likewise, the school writing samples of Birgitte, Ursula, and Pam showed a noticeable relationship between the knowledge base of the writer and overall fluency in the writing. A number of subskills were critical to gaining subject matter knowledge: the ability to research information through a variety of channels, the ability to understand detailed and often technical material (such as a federal RFP) and to learn about completely new topics (e.g., Selma's researching of family literacy programs), and the ability to synthesize quantities of information. In academic contexts, we saw that early instances of writing consisted of repeating subject matter knowledge owned by the teacher, not the pupil, as in Ursula's first essay on *Gulliver's Travels* and Birgitte's first attempts at writing in political science. As each was able to gain a body of subject matter knowledge after a series of courses, she was able to use that knowledge base to grasp more of the subject matter (Ursula's college paper on *Gulliver's Travels* or Birgitte's analysis of state capitalism in graduate school) and thereby to "join the conversation" of others in the disciplines (Bruffee, 1984). Depth of subject matter knowledge, coupled with critical thinking skills, allowed these writers to move from knowledge-telling to knowledge-transforming writing (Bereiter & Scardamalia, 1987).

Genre knowledge, the third knowledge domain, at once constituting both textual and social dimensions, was operationalized here as distinct from, yet integrally connected with, discourse community knowledge and subject matter knowledge. The cases in this report demonstrate that expert use of genre knowledge requires the writer to understand not just the genre's pragmatic purpose, content, structure, and linguistic features, but also how these elements combine in a single text. In addition, the writer must have a deep-level understanding of ways in which the genre's formal features are determined by its role in a given discourse community. Not until graduate school did Pam and Birgitte see the ways in which genres specific to their academic disciplines actually furthered the work of those disciplines. In the workplace, Selma and Pam were successful in writing grant proposals to city agencies after contact with those discourse communities; as Freedman and Medway (1994b) state, "Achieving an effective text involves innumerable local decisions for which decontextualized, formal rules will provide no guidance" (p. 11).

Rhetorical knowledge is perhaps the most fully contextualized aspect of expert writing performance. Beyond issues of discourse community knowledge, subject matter knowledge, or genre knowledge, writers at JRC had to determine the purpose of a specific text and the needs of that text's specific readers. If the letter was to the Secretary of Labor in Washington, D.C., Mei sought out someone locally who had connections with the Secretary's office to review and edit the letter so it appealed to the Secretary's interests. In the case of academic writing, we saw Ursula learning to adapt her textual analyses in deconstructionist or postcolonial seminars according to the professors' criteria and values. Likewise with Birgitte: She knew which political arguments or means of analysis would win a favorable grade from individual professors.

Yet another aspect of rhetorical knowledge relates to particular lines of argument, acceptable evidence, and structural or linguistic features that lend face validity to the text in a particular rhetorical context—all of which would contribute to the text's persuasiveness. For example, Pam's realization that charts or bulleted items seemed to give readers in the U.S. Department of Education reassurance about her program's credibility was a form of rhetorical knowledge. This knowledge came slowly, over time, as a complex web of personal and institutional relations became apparent to the writers in school contexts and in the workplace.

Finally, while Flower and Hayes's (1981) problem-solving heuristic in general outlines the strategic problem-solving process of good writers, in most instances of writing observed in this study, the writers also gained context-specific or genre-specific ways to approach the writing tasks that greatly aided productivity. Certain aspects of writing process knowledge were adaptations to the material conditions of composing (dealing with ringing phones, etc.). In other instances (e.g., the form letter, the federal grant proposal, or the research paper), writing process knowledge was genre-specific. Pam's realization that typing out the language of the RFP as a preliminary outline would help her internalize what the text must address and Ursula's system in college of using Post-its to mark places in a text or 3 × 5 cards to organize evidence for her argument were other forms of procedural knowledge that these writers drew on to accomplish writing tasks. These data lend support to others' claims (Applebee, 1986; Chin, 1994) that process knowledge is situation-specific as well as general.

In sum, the five knowledge domains delineated in this study suggest a composite and complex view of the social dimensions of writing expertise. This schema complicates the current-traditional view (Berlin, 1987), with its emphasis on correctness of form and standard usage, and extends more recent theories of writing: expressivist theories (Elbow, 1981; Murray, 1980) and information-processing theories (Flower & Hayes, 1981) that emphasize general aspects of writing process knowledge; Flowers's (1994) sociocognitive theory and dialogic conceptions of composing (Bakhtin, 1986; Nystrand, 1990; Prior, 1995), both of which emphasize rhetorical problem solving; genre-based theories of writing, which empha-size the marriage of form and function of texts (Berkenkotter & Huckin, 1993; Miller, 1984); and postmodern literary theories of construction—or deconstruction—of existing cultural structures that constrain form and content of writing (Derrida, 1980; Fish, 1980; Foucault, 1977; Jameson, 1981).

Analyzing Local Conditions for Writing

What might be the significance of this schema for the context-specific aspects of composing? First, such a schema offers a more comprehensive frame for analysis of local conditions for writing. For example, since the early 1980s composition researchers have been interested in studying bus-iness contexts for writing in order to make comparisons with academic writing and to prepare students for future jobs. Researchers typically have focused their studies on one or two of the knowledge domains identified in this study: broad norms for texts (Faigley & Miller, 1982; Freedman et al., 1994; Haswell, 1991; Hutson, 1987; Rivers, 1989; Woolever, 1989); spe-cific genre features (Freed & Roberts, 1989; Yates & Orlikowski, 1992); rhetorical issues (Freedman et al., 1994; Odell, Goswami, & Quick, 1983); writing process issues (Ede & Lunsford, 1990; Faigley & Miller, 1982; Hut-son, 1987); or discourse community issues (Doheny-Farina, 1989; Freed & Broadhead, 1987; McIsaac & Aschauer, 1990; Stratman & Duffy, 1990). But comprehending what is going on at one site of composing in relation to another site requires a view of local conditions for writing with sufficient scope and definition to capture the range of factors entailed in the social context under consideration.

Implications for Theories of Composing

Interrelationships of these five areas of domain knowledge help us fur-ther theorize acts of composing. As genre theory has expanded to include the genre's social functions and culture-laden norms, it has become a strong analytical tool for understanding local conditions for composing. Rhetorical theory also has been stretched beyond its traditional bounds to account for more variables. But separating and distinguishing among these interrelated concepts offers greater possibility for parsing the differ-ent levels of "social" or "contextual" knowledge for greater clarity and precision of definition. Such parsing also enables an examination of the hierarchical and reciprocal relations among these domains.

Some no doubt will argue that the five-part schema I laid out here for domains of writing knowledge either includes the wrong domains or, like any schema, compartmentalizes and ossifies what in reality is fluid and changeable. However, as I have emphasized repeatedly, all five domains are both symbiotically related and nested one within another like a set of Russian dolls.

In addition, we saw that these five areas of knowledge represented a spectrum, from the most general information (what is the format of a business letter?) to the most context-specific (how do you ask the Secretary of Labor to speak at your fundraiser?), and that the greater the expertise, the greater the degree of context-specific knowledge. These data confirm theories in cognitive psychology (deGroot, 1965; Dreyfus & Dreyfus, 1986; Perkins & Salomon, 1989a) and composition studies (Carter, 1990; Foertsch, 1995; Smagorinsky & Smith, 1992; Teich, 1987) that increasing levels of expertise require greater context-specific knowledge.

Chess players have hundreds of moves embedded in memory from repeated experiences with the game (deGroot, 1965). Likewise, Flower (1989) argues that, with experience, about 50% of writing tasks can be handled almost automatically—by slotting information into well-worn writing plans (i.e., genres). We saw Ursula's formula for an academic essay, which evolved over a 16-year span of formal schooling, and Barbara's formula for the press release and letter of request.

But in addition to having schemata for "formulaic" writing performances, expert writers have a fuller understanding of the complexities of a given writing situation or, to speak in cognitive terms, the mental representation of the problem to be solved is more detailed. Writers I interviewed about workplace writing who were more seasoned than my four informants described even fuller schemata for writing tasks in the workplace: Recall Donald, for example, explaining the "deep rhetorical purposes" of the sections of an RFP; Barbara describing the reasons for her formulaic approach to press releases and letters of request; and Anna's account of the complex relationship between a foundation's staff and grant seekers.

These accounts corroborate the findings reported in expert–novice studies that experts "chunk" large quantities of information into meaningful patterns. Or to put it another way, experts know how to acquire more knowledge and know what to do with it (Mikulecky, Albers, & Peers, 1994). Their mental schemata for particular writing situations, over time, become more complex and specific—signs of growing expertise. We saw the writers at JRC also gaining deepening understanding in all five dimensions of writing knowledge in relation to specific writing tasks over the course of the data-collection period.

Implications for Developmental Theory

Data gleaned in this study on the local aspects of writing performance also have ramifications for developmental theories of writing, which, for the most part, have been cast in terms of sentence- and text-level development (Faigley, 1980; Freedman, 1987; Freedman & Pringle, 1980; Haswell, 1991; Hunt, 1965; Langer, 1985; Witte & Davis, 1983) or cognitive processing issues (Bereiter & Scardamalia, 1987; Daiute, 1989; Flower, 1989; Flower et al., 1989; Sommers, 1980). The longitudinal data here suggest that in early literacy development, in school, and ultimately in the workplace, tacit learning was taking place in each of the five socially situated knowledge domains, with little conscious attention to them either by the informants or by their mentors. As children, the informants could handle multiple contexts for writing, all of which entailed decisions about content, genre, rhetorical situations, and composing processes: writing letters to friends (real or imagined), writing (or copying) reports for school, and using language to play games. This view of expert writing performance complicates earlier views that developmental processes in relation to writing happen first in the arena of cognitive growth and textual knowledge and only later in the realm of social knowledge (Bereiter & Scardamalia, 1987; Geisler, 1994; Moffett, 1983; Smagorinsky & Smith, 1992). Rather, the data here suggest that literacy development in both areas occurs simultaneously, confirming other research reports (Dyson, 1988, 1993; Florio & Clark, 1982; Heath, 1983; Vygotsky, 1978; Wertsch, 1991) that have documented the early development of social dimensions of writing literacy. Collectively, this research calls into question the theoretical soundness of any writing curriculum that focuses solely on general, context-neutral principles for writing, given the evidence that all literacy learning is fully contextualized. Furthermore, the curriculum espoused by Moffett (1983), based on Piaget's theory that a child's thinking evolves from the concrete to the abstract, is contrary to cognitive theories of expertise and the data in this study, both of which suggest that learning is more general at early stages and more concrete as further experience is gained.

Also absent from the literature on writing development is any continuum depicting growth in the social dimensions of writing knowledge. This study presents a beginning outline of such a continuum. Rudimentary forms of discourse community knowledge can be seen in Ursula's knowing, intuitively, to "regurgitate" the tenth-grade teacher's lecture on *Gulliver's Travels*. We saw subject matter knowledge (Ursula's two analyses of *Gulliver's Travels* 4 years apart) and procedural knowledge (Pam's method of drafting federal proposals) become increasingly complex and specific over time. Early knowledge in the discourse modes (stories, essays, argument), the terms in which the informants discussed school writing, can be seen as the precursor to the more specific genre knowledge they acquired in graduate school and in the workplace. And rhetorical knowledge, first understood as a general schema of writing purposes (to get a grade or to get money) and audience needs (Birgitte's dutiful acquiescence to her professors' political biases), became highly situation specific and more carefully finessed as these writers became more deeply involved in a discourse community's practices.

Furthermore, the evidence here of the importance of localized writing knowledge heightens the urgency for educators and training specialists to delve further into *how* writers learn skills for new occasions of writing. Whatever learning has gone before is not likely to be sufficient when there is a new occasion for writing, whether the new situation is a level of academic study (postsecondary or graduate level), a field of study, or a job situation. The phrase "lifelong learning" takes on new meaning in relation to writing skill, both in considering learning in formal English classes and learning writing skills informally in writing-intensive disciplinary courses or in out-of-school settings. The context-specific nature of experts' writing knowledge leads to the question of transfer of learning and a re-examination of the data in this study from the perspective of the informants' experiences in boundary crossing from one context for writing to another.

FOSTERING TRANSFER OF LEARNING

How can transfer of learning be fostered to give writers flexibility and versatility in handling a variety of occasions for writing? What can aid writers in grasping local conditions for writing?

The heavily contextualized or localized elements of writing expertise detailed thus far would seem to add fuel to the argument of some in composition studies (Freedman, 1993; Petraglia, 1995) that general writing courses, beyond those that teach writing fundamentals, serve little purpose. Petraglia points out that a physical education curriculum has no "ball-handling" courses. Extending the analogy, he questions the validity of first-year composition in the college curriculum and advocates writing courses in the disciplines instead, but this is a shortsighted solution. Expertise in disciplinary writing is a valid goal only for academicians. Pam learned to write ethnography, and Birgitte learned the theoretical frames and genres for public policy analysis. But like many students at the undergraduate and graduate levels, they were simply passing

through the disciplines as a sort of mental boot camp for the general goal
of a liberal arts education. As Ursula commented, "Here I am, typing
away. But . . . I don't think any of that had anything to do with anything
I'm doing now" (11/10/92, p. 1).

Freedman, Adam, and Smart (1994) found that even a university
course that emphasized real-world writing assignments in fact still led
to texts with the earmarks of school writing rather than workplace writing. And Knoblauch (1989) points to the contrast between texts about
professional writing, with their emphasis on formats and uncontextu-
alized skills and strategies, and business writers' dependence on "tacit
knowledge of the business's operating circumstances and expectations"
(p. 256). It would seem then that educators are faced with an impossible
conundrum: No classroom learning can take the place of immersion in the
specific context for composing. Professional writing courses, discipline-
specific courses, and community service writing within a generic writing
course all have value (Carter, 1990), but they may not take the student
far enough to facilitate ready entrance to discourse communities beyond
school. But these findings do not eliminate the responsibility of educators
and training specialists to make informed decisions about writing curricula. In fact, I argue elsewhere that teaching conscious awareness of the
writing process, teaching multiple genres, and teaching the concept of
"reading" a social context for its communicative norms are both feasible
and appropriate (Beaufort, 1998).

Furthermore, an immersion approach to learning writing skills alone
is not likely to accomplish all that is necessary to gain the versatility in
writing literacy so typical of modern societies. The literature on expert
versus novice performance all points to expertise as comprising two opposite and complementary abilities: on the one hand, to draw from long-
term memory those particular experiences that "match" the current situation; on the other hand, to use mid-level abstractions as mental grippers
for problem solving in novel situations. I turn now to this second component of expertise in relation to the findings in this study and its implications for writing curricula and pedagogy.

Matching Versus Bridging Strategies

The expert writing performances in school and workplace settings documented here appear to have been largely the result of repeated instances
of writing in the same genre, in very similar contexts, with multiple models, and with continuous feedback from the environment—what cognitive psychologists call "matching" strategies. For example, as Ursula
gained the local knowledge for the genre of request letters, she gradually

constructed a mental model, or schema, of "request letter" as a subgenre of the genre of business letters. She created a separate file on her computer labeled "request letters" so that she could draw upon a model text to compose new request letters. She wrote request letters, got feedback from the discourse communities about the success of her text, and thereby increased her expertise and participation in the discourse communities involved. Such instances of expert performance would be considered low-road transfer tasks—writing in response to the same occasions, in the same genres and discourse communities—through repeated practice, or what Perkins and Salomon (1989b) refer to as "hugging."

But learning by the immersion method has limitations, namely, (1) lack of preparation for handling novel situations requiring high-road transfer; (2) the possibility of negative transfer (i.e., learning from one situation inappropriately applied to a new situation); and (3) the slowness of the process, as Chapter 5 demonstrated. This points to the need for the other element of expertise, what Perkins and Salomon (1989b) call bridging. As Carter (1990) points out, "Expertise . . . demands a greater flexibility than strict reliance on local knowledge" (p. 274).

In workplace settings, the necessity for bridging from one genre or one rhetorical occasion to another was only too evident in the data. Maggie, a seasoned writer at another nonprofit agency, said, "Everybody switches hats in their communication style at least 20 times a day" (11/10/92, p. 10). Each of the writers at IRC had to write at least 3 or 4 genres to do her job, and within those main genres, subgenres were more specifically tailored to certain types of communication events. In fact, for the 4 informants, a key difference between school and workplace settings for writing was the multiplicity of writing situations encountered in the workplace. With the exception of Pam, whose high school newspaper experience broadened her range of genres and styles, the other 3 women graduated from college basically knowing one genre: the academic essay. Birgitte said, "I got out of college without an inkling of how you write a memo, what a memo is, for example, or how you write a business letter. I had no idea" (4/20/93, p. 11). And Ursula said, "With school papers, I learned the 5 paragraph thing. . . . But with business writing I don't know it as well" (8/5/93, p. 11). While the range of genres, rhetorical situations, and discourse community norms that a professional needs to handle may vary from context to context, a single formula like the one Ursula learned in school for the academic essay is unlikely to suffice in real-world writing situations.

Experts in many different areas of practice have been shown to apply general knowledge, skillfully, in instances where they encounter novelty, necessitating high-road transfer. The situation at hand looks significantly different from anything encountered before and requires problem-solving abilities not required in low-road transfer—the ability to abstract general principles from the particulars of a known situation and the ability to either apply those abstract principles to the new situation or restructure existing information in such a way that new principles can be derived and applied. These mid-level abstractions of general concepts or principles serve as "mental grippers" (Perkins & Salomon, 1989a) for finding a way to read the local conditions for performance. This also is confirmed in Singley and Anderson's (1989) studies on transfer tasks in mathematical problem solving, deductive logic, and statistical reasoning, which led them to conclude, "Within a domain, certain ideas may have broader applications than others, and it may be possible to package these ideas and present them to students" (p. 238).

Toward the end of the year of data collection at JRC, curious to see what my informants perceived as similarities between academic and workplace writing, or how they might have abstracted from the one experience to facilitate coping in the new situation, I asked each what she had learned in school about writing that she found useful in completing writing tasks at JRC. Here are their answers, in abbreviated form:

> *Certainly the skills like being able to summarize something, or write an opinion about agreeing or disagreeing with something.* Those things transferred. You know, history classes, you have to do a lot of interpreting an event, and analyzing and sometimes predicting. . . . Those things helped. (Selma, 5/4/93, p. 6, emphasis added)

> I learned *how to think structurally about writing . . . presenting an argument in a logical fashion.* (Birgitte, 4/20/93, pp. 11–12, emphasis added)

> *You're writing for an audience, as opposed to journal writing. And you want something from that audience.* I want an A. I want you to donate money. You want them to read in both cases and be interested in it and to, only in the case of business writing I guess, take some action on it. And the action I would want them to take on my papers was to give me an A. (Ursula, 8/5/93, pp. 7–8)

> I spent a lot of time at school formulating ideas that have no relevance to anything I'm doing now . . . but I had so much fun taking my little cards and writing my ideas and putting them in order, and connecting them, and making my thesis. . . . *The critical thinking thing did help me bring ideas together.* (Ursula, 8/5/93, p. 12, emphasis added)

> The more you write and the more *you learn how to organize your thoughts in different contexts,* you can pretty much apply that to anything. . . . The purpose of some of these papers is *you try to come up with a real strong idea, and then you convey it and support it. If you can do that, I think you can pretty much write anything.* (Pam, 8/5/93, pp. 12–13, emphasis added)

These women all conveyed that the primary benefit of writing assignments in school in relation to work-related writing was the training in analytical thinking: seeing new, logical connections between ideas and information, making claims based on facts and reasoning, creating a linear order to thoughts on paper. But beyond gaining general analytical thinking skills and some awareness of rhetorical situations, the informants saw little connection between the school and workplace writing situations, nor did they seem to have a ready language for making extensive comparisons of the two contexts for composing.

At the midpoint of the study, after getting a sense of ways that the four women talked about the texts they were writing (usually in terms of purposes, deadlines, content, or rhetorical issues), I asked each to give me a definition of the concept of genre and to name as many genres as she could think of. All four writers defined *genre* as a category of writing, but they tended to associate the term primarily with "literature" or fiction. They exhibited a great deal of fuzziness as to the criteria by which a genre was defined: What was its purpose (e.g., to inspire, for profit, for personal use)? historical time period (e.g., the epic, postmodern writing)? geographical influence (e.g., Latin American magical realism)? Most important, none associated the concept of genre with business writing until prompted to do so by my questioning. And likewise with other dimensions of writing knowledge: The informants did not convey any sense of how or what to abstract from one writing situation that would be useful in another beyond very general matters of logic, structure, and supporting of ideas. Missing was that mid-level of abstraction (the five knowledge domains identified in this study) that researchers argue is most useful in high-road transfer.

Instances of Negative Transfer

I also observed cases of negative transfer in which norms of one discourse community were inappropriately transferred to a very different context for writing. Table 7.1 is a comparison of the variations in literacy practice in two discourse communities—academia (generalized, of course) and the world of one nonprofit agency, JRC. This table reveals some of the

Table 7.1. Comparison of School and Workplace Discourse Communities

	Goals and Values	Communication Channels	Role of Written Text	Norms for Genres	Writer's Roles
Academic discourse community	• Critique of others' ideas • "Objective" truth • Truth for truth's sake • Display of knowledge • Gatekeeping function based on intellectual prowess	• Mostly through text: e-mail, published articles, or written comment on text • Limited oral communication • Three key genres: research report, essay, conference paper	• Stands on its own apart from other forms of communication • Often used for evaluative purposes: grades, promotions, etc.	• Originality is essential • Dense content and syntax • Sophisticated vocabulary • Technical mistakes (grammar, spelling) accepted at novice levels	• Critical thinking and analysis • Linking ideas to previous work of others • Perfecting a few genres • Research skills (library, field, or laboratory)
Job Resource Center (JRC)	• Service to others, altruism • Consensus building with business partners and funding sources • Pragmatic action • Positive public image	• Oral preferred to written • Highly interactive between sender and receiver • Text usually accompanies oral dialogue (telephone, face-to-face) • Many genres and subgenres used	• Text supported by oral communication • Often serves a symbolic function rather than actually accomplishing work • Face validity may be more important than content	• Boilerplate is acceptable—expediency more important than originality • Text should be very clear, easy to read quickly • Manipulation of facts for persuasive purposes is acceptable, even expected	• Strategic thinking • Using text to negotiate relationships • Handling multiple genres • Research skills include extensive social networking

Note: There are many different discourse communities within academia and the workplace. This chart shows some of the differences encountered by the writers in this study.

fundamental adjustments a writer would be required to make in moving between these two cultures. For example, Ursula's comments that she was uncomfortable with the "rah-rah" tone of PR texts reflected her conditioned belief in the norms of the academic community: norms of understatement, objectivity, and persuasion by means of rational argument and marshaled facts. She was uncomfortable with the forms of persuasion in business and on several occasions wished out loud she could "just present the facts." Another academic norm—that the majority of a text be original material—led her to speak of using boilerplate copy from other texts at JRC as "plagiarizing." Pam was conditioned to "just tell everything," so that readers could make up their minds with *all* the evidence in hand—another norm for texts in the academic community. Getting to the point quickly, without disclosure of all the facts, and thereby adapting to the business community norm of quick, efficient (i.e., short) communication was a hard adjustment for Pam. Likewise Selma, schooled in the supposed "objectivity" of academic discourse, found herself hard pressed to write something more blatantly persuasive. Textual values and norms transferred from other discourse communities interfered with appropriating the norms and values of new sites of composing.

Using Mid-Level Organizing Schemata

Could these women have benefited from possessing a more fully articulated set of mental schemata—specifically, a schema for each of the five knowledge domains identified here in connection with expert writing performances? One piece of evidence suggesting the usefulness of mid-level abstract organizing concepts came near the completion of this document, when I spoke with Pam about the new job she had accepted recently at another nonprofit agency, which required her to write marketing proposals and promotional materials. She said to me, "At first I was freaking out, thinking, 'How do I write this stuff?' Then I remembered the stuff I read in your dissertation about discourse community and genres and I realized that's what I needed to think about" (personal communication, 2/5/95). Or reconsider Ursula's comment about business letters as genres:

> It's funny. . . . I said sort of kiddingly, "[Genre] seems like too good a word for [business writing]." This business category I wouldn't even include if I didn't have this job. . . . I would never think of that as a style of writing but now I know that it is. (12/8/92, p. 1)

Also, had they been able to apply the notion of discourse community to the new situations at JRC and juxtaposed those writing situations in more concrete ways with situations familiar from school contexts for writing, would negative transfer have been minimized? Studies have shown that the way in which information is abstracted and encoded influences retrieval (Brooks & Dansereau, 1987; Gick & Holyak, 1987) and that experts have a more fully developed hierarchy of knowledge (Sternberg & Frensch, 1993; Voss, 1989). Numerous heuristics for understanding the writing process and for analysis of rhetorical situations are evidenced in composition texts, but in spite of recent work in genre and discourse community knowledge in writing research and theorizing, composition texts contain relatively few references to these schemata. Further research must determine if overt framing of these mid-level abstractions by instructors would facilitate more flexibility and versatility of writing performance for students and workers in moving from one context for writing to another.

Research shows that opportunities to apply general concepts in multiple instances are also important, so that ways in which the general can illuminate the specific (Perkins & Salomon, 1989a) become apparent. Some recent composition texts also are beginning to broaden the kinds of writing tasks suggested in general writing courses, facilitating understanding of how general principles apply in a range of writing situations. Such an approach would also mitigate concerns (Cooper, 1989; Freedman, 1993) that too many rules for writing, or even too formulaic an approach to conveying genre knowledge, could lead to mechanistic approaches to writing tasks and obliterate the creative and contextual aspects of composing.

The Role of Metacognition

Research studies on novice versus expert behaviors report one other critical feature of expert performance: the practice of mindfulness (Flower, 1994; Flower & Hayes, 1981; Perkins & Salomon, 1989a). Salomon and Globerson (1987) refer to mindfulness as "a state of mind that is defined as the volitional, metacognitively guided employment of non-automatic, usually effort-demanding processes" (p. 625). Specifically, mindfulness involves deriving from materials essential features that are on a more abstract level than the material itself (Salomon & Globerson, 1987) and being aware of the problem-solving process—a sort of executive monitoring function of the mind watching itself work and deciding: What am I doing now? Is it getting me anywhere? What else could I be doing instead? (Perkins & Salomon, 1989a). Without this sort of mindfulness, particularly in complex tasks such as writing, performers can get bogged down in surface-level issues, such as getting the right lingo or simplifying the task to more manageable or familiar processes, overlooking other requirements of the writing situation.

As with all cognitive acts, mindfulness is hard to observe, but during the course of this study, several spontaneous comments from my informants suggested that in fact the very process of participating in the research project was creating a heightened consciousness about their writing. In October, 4 months into the fieldwork and in the midst of a conversation I was having with Pam about the issue of authorial stance in her master's thesis, she said:

> You are going to change the situation just by being there, poking your nose in and asking all these questions. I mean, *do you think Ursula and Birgitte and I write the same as we would if you weren't asking us all these questions? No. Our consciousness is raised, and we're thinking about things in a different way.* (10/6/92, pp. 4a–5a, emphasis added)

In May of the following year, after almost 12 months of fieldwork at JRC, Pam handed me a copy of a memo she had written to Ursula the previous week. The content was personal, and she had added the following P. S. in a type font called "Child's Play":

> p.s. to anne beaufort: I had a dream about writing the other night. I was at a conference of endless writing seminars. One seminar I remember vividly was really weird. We each had to lay a match on the very edge of a table with the head just peeking over the edge. Then we laid paper on top of the matches. The instructor came around and dropped oil on the paper, sometimes in random patterns and sometimes making pictures like Mickey Mouse or clowns faces. Then we lit the match heads and only the oily parts of the papers caught on fire. They burned cleanly, leaving holes in patterns on the papers. The instructor then went around and wrote lists of "genres" on each paper, and we had to fill in words on whatever paper was left to convey the different kinds of genres. The point was to write in interrupted fragments and still get the same gist across. Add that to your thesis! (excerpt from 5/21/93 memo)

While a dream analyst might have an altogether different interpretation of this narrative, Pam's interpretation, elicited a month later, went as follows:

ANNE: So what do you think the paranoia is?
PAM: I don't know. I think it was—Ursula thinks that it's because

> you're making us think in such a meta- meta-writing way
> about how we write, why we write and all that stuff. (7/6/93,
> pp. 7–8)

Sometimes while answering a question, one of the other informants would reveal that the question itself had prompted new thinking. For example, I asked Ursula on what basis she'd decided to change her approach to speechwriting for her boss, and she said, "You ask a question, I don't even think about how [I learned until you ask]" (7/6/96, p. 3).

What I observed at the research site, however, was virtually no explicit focus on the writing itself; writing was simply a means to an end. Attention focused on the action desired from a given writing task, for example, faxing the letter immediately so that a key individual would take the desired action before the city council meeting that night or before the JRC board meeting next Tuesday. If a grant proposal was successful or unsuccessful, no postmortem evaluation of the proposal document's strengths and weaknesses occurred; instead, the focus was usually on what political factors could have influenced the outcome.

Only when I asked the four writers to evaluate their texts in hindsight did they discover weaknesses in the text that may have influenced the outcome. Witness, for example, Birgitte telling me that learning to write grant proposals when she first came to JRC presented no special problem. But when I asked her to look at the first grant proposals she'd written at JRC some 2 years earlier, she said, "It's boring. It's really boring. . . . There's a lot of information, but if I were a program officer and I read it, this wouldn't move me in any way" (1/19/93, pp. 2–3). At JRC, writing knowledge *was* gained experientially and became a form of tacit knowing beneath the level of conscious thinking. However, I suspect that more reflective practice, either reflection-in-action, as Schön (1983) calls it, or metacognitive monitoring of the writing process (Flower, 1994), could have increased each writer's growth and learning.

Other research on the complex mental processes in such diverse tasks as medical diagnosis, architecture, and psychoanalysis (Schön, 1983) also demonstrates that metacognitive thinking, or mindfulness, can greatly aid the accomplishment of complex activities. But JRC is probably typical of most businesses in its lack of any particular focus on writing processes or on the craft of writing. Only in one research report of workplace writing practices (McIsaac & Aschauer, 1990) have I found focused attention on the relationship between writing and end product—the desired action.

But in this study, little apparent transfer of learning took place between academic contexts for writing and the writing done at JRC beyond the level of writing fundamentals. Schemata for understanding common elements across a variety of writing tasks were largely absent. And yet learning did take place, even if it entailed only low-road transfer. These points lead to the final question of this study.

FOSTERING SITE-SPECIFIC LEARNING

What are the individual traits and environmental conditions that foster ongoing development of writing skills in informal and formal settings for learning? What helps or hinders achieving expert writing performance in new discourse communities?

Each of the informants in this study had had success in postsecondary education, if success can be measured by earning entrance to top schools and achieving good grades. Although the particulars of each writer's ways of learning in school are barely sketched here, it is evident from the outcomes that each found ways to succeed in school writing tasks. In college all four majored in academic disciplines that required a lot of writing. Two chose language-related majors, and three discovered in college or beyond the pleasures of writing for personal reasons and aspired to publishing their work.

It is not surprising, then, that they were successful writers in the workplace. But the occasions of writing were vastly different in the two contexts, and others have reported instances of writers being less successful in adapting to new learning situations (Anson & Forsberg, 1990; Doheny-Farina, 1989; Freedman, 1994). Freedman's study is of particular interest. In the case of student interns learning to write in business settings, "[I]t is sometimes unclear to newcomers that they must learn, let alone what and how they must learn, and whom they will learn from" (p. 14). It is thus important to note what writerly behaviors made these women what Resnick (1987) calls "good adaptive learners."

Behaviors of Adaptive Learners

Selma, Birgitte, Ursula, and Pam picked up on, or sought out, means within the environment that would aid them in moving from outsider to insider, from novice to expert in the discourse community of JRC. As was demonstrated in Chapter 4, success in writing projects demanded unassisted learning. Each of the women identified an expert writer who could provide information and models to learn from; each was good at a continual process of reading, listening, and seeking out new information (Ursula's "snagged program" file and Pam's file folders to organize new information for the next grant proposal). Or, to put it another way, each was good at observational learning.

One day I was viewing some of Ursula's handwritten notes from a board meeting and I noticed a vertical line drawn down the page, about 4 inches from the left-hand margin. This was typically the way I would line off my fieldnote pages. So I asked, "When did you start formatting—"

URSULA: I learned this from you.
ANNE: Oh you did?
URSULA: I noticed it's the first thing you did and I thought, "Hey, I'm going to try it the Anne Beaufort way." It works! 'Cause I can work little asides in here [referring to the space in the left-hand column]. (1/26/93, pp. 8–9)

In addition to closely observing her environment to gain new information, each was willing to take the risk of trying something new—a new writing role or genre—in order to further learning; each was aware to some degree of her strengths and weaknesses as a writer and sought—and provided—assistance where needed. Ursula could tighten up Pam's too-wordy prose; Pam could straighten out the logic and sequencing of ideas in Selma's proposal; Selma could catch a grammatical error in the others' writing; Birgitte could add "color" and emotional appeal to Selma's matter-of-fact writing style. Rather than just mentor–apprentice dyads, a rich set of relationships supported development of writing proficiency at JRC.

Here's another example of a writer constantly learning from her environment: Toward the end of the research study, Ursula and I were talking about a speech she wrote for Mei to give at a JRC public event. Peering over the shoulder of another speaker, she had observed his notes in bullet form and decided her next speech for Mei should be done that way, too. She was, as she put it, a "scavenger of ideas." She learned how to learn in the context of JRC, using all of its resources—computer files, paper files, co-workers' expertise, her boss's input, ideas from board members and community leaders. She learned by doing the real work at hand, by observing others, and by teaching others at the same time that she was learning. And, as noted in Chapter 5, Ursula's skill as a learner, and also Pam's, was corroborated by their mentors.

The Social Element in Apprenticeships

It is not accidental that those positive occasions for writing in school that the participants reported all involved either (1) a positive mentoring relationship and/or positive peer relationships or (2) writing tasks that served a purpose to the author besides grades. Ursula's favorite English teachers were Mrs. Byrd in high school, who made writing fun and got the students to engage one another as writers; Mrs. Macky in junior college, who challenged and stretched her critical thinking and linguistic skills; and Professor Kingsley, who invited full participation in the world of Shakespearean drama. Birgitte learned the most about writing from the college professor who tutored her and secured a job for her tutoring younger writers so she could further practice her writing skills. And Pam was captivated by those teachers in high school and then in graduate school who also invited full, authentic participation in communities of writers—the English teacher who brought his students in on editing his book, the advisor who gave freedom to the high school newspaper staff, and the writing coaches in graduate school who worked in class and one-on-one with her on her thesis. Other reports of meaningful experiences of writing in school contexts (Greenwood, 1994; Heath, 1983; Heath & Branscombe, 1985; Kirtley, 1994) also evidence the same elements: authentic tasks and/or positive mentoring relationships—not coincidentally, elements of the social apprenticeship model of learning.

Less-than-positive experiences with writing in school are all too familiar and plentiful. The 1994 National Assessment of Educational Practices reports that 56% of twelfth graders "strongly agreed" or "agreed" that they liked to write, whereas 72% of fourth graders responded that way (Applebee et al., 1994). It appears that some school situations have a negative impact on students' motivation to develop writing literacy. Recall Ursula describing with disdain the ease of obtaining As in Mr. Peters's high school English class by regurgitating his words, and the college professor who refused to acknowledge her attempts at originality in her writing. Or recall Pam's comment that she never did know the difference between a C paper and an A paper in college, or Birgitte's feeling in college that someone else (namely, her professor or the textbook author) was holding the pen writing her papers.

Figure 7.1 depicts the shifting roles and writing activities these four writers reported from high school, college, graduate school, and professional arenas for writing. They experienced a limited range of writing activities in high school and college, and learning activities and classroom communities for the most part did not invite the kinds of authentic tasks or legitimate peripheral participation of the workplace. Other studies corroborate these findings (Hunt, 1994; Walvoord & McCarthy, 1990).

In contrast to school environments that did not foster writing growth, JRC provided the four women with numerous opportunities to participate meaningfully in writing projects. Mei sensed the need to show the

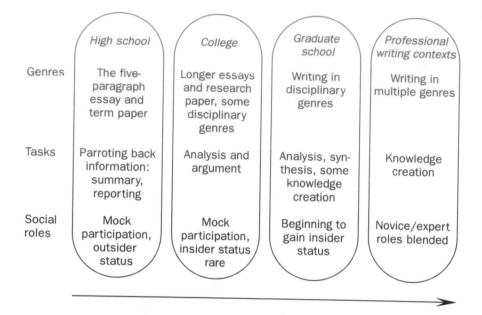

Figure 7.1. Until graduate school and professional-level jobs, the four writers studied here experienced limited opportunities for authentic participation in communities of practice.

novice the whole process even before the novice was capable of handling all aspects. She had good intuition about how much support and guidance to provide and when to allow the learner to try something on her own, and she also had faith in her staff's abilities: She believed them capable of stretching and growing and entrusted them with increasing responsibility and autonomy. Expert and novice, old-timer and newcomer alike contributed to a positive learning environment much like the effective cognitive apprenticeships Lave and Wenger (1991) report from their research. Learning was rooted in practice and in relationships. Legitimate peripheral participation became the norm for new writers in the organization, and stages of apprenticeship ranged from observer or copy editor, to ghostwriter, to author/inventor of high-status texts.

Table 7.2 lays out the essential differences between school models for learning as my informants characterized them and the apprenticeship model for learning at JRC. The purpose of learning new writing skills in the workplace was to take action, whereas in school settings, the purpose of learning to write was to be evaluated. The learning process differed dramatically as well. Learning about writing at JRC was embedded in a

Table 7.2. Teacher/Learner Relationships in Two Models for Learning

	School Model	Apprenticeship Model
Teacher	Gatekeeper/evaluation	Mentor/coach for authentic tasks
	Enforces hierarchy of power	Creates community of learners as collaborators
	Focuses on surface knowledge	Makes insider knowledge explicit
	One-way communication: teacher to learner	Facilitates multiple inputs for learning and feedback
Learner	Mock participation	Authentic tasks
	Has limited status	Participates as valued contributor from the start
	Sees only narrow set of skills	Sees whole process—all aspects

system of relationships, and the learner had the opportunity to observe the workings of the entire enterprise being undertaken. In school contexts, learning either took place in isolation by the individual learner or in a teacher–student dyad. The learner was led step by step but seldom had an opportunity to see "the big picture" until he or she had mastered a series of skills.

The content of the writing instruction imparted in either setting also displayed some broad distinguishing differences. In the workplace setting learners were involved in situation-specific competencies, and their writing activities were authentic from the start, rather than practice drills. In school, my informants were taught generalized rules for writing, to be applied to "practice" situations. And finally, the status of the learner and the learner–teacher relationships were configured very differently: At JRC, membership in the community of practice was conferred on the learner at the outset, and learning was an evolving form of membership. In academic settings, learning was a condition for membership, and the learner was granted little status at the outset. These differences in the learning environment corroborate the findings and thinking of others who have looked broadly at the range of learning experiences in schools and at work sites (Doheny-Farina, 1989; Ede & Lunsford, 1990; Elbow, 1991; Florio & Clark, 1982; Freedman et al., 1994; Geisler, 1994; Kaufer & Young, 1993; Lave, Murtaugh, & de la Rocha, 1984; McCarthy, 1987; Odell & Goswami, 1985; Resnick, 1987).

While some argue that teachers will never be able to simulate real-world contexts for writing in the classroom (Hill & Resnick, 1995), the current emphasis in teacher training programs in the United States on more participatory learning is a step in the right direction. The standard for writing pedagogy in the United States is to use small-group work for a variety of writing process activities, to engage groups in writing projects instead of endless drills on isolated skills, and to coach students in individual conferences. In the process of changing their pedagogy, writing teachers also have created a different role for themselves and a different power structure in the classroom. No longer is the teacher the sole authority; rather, in the case of composition classes, the community also becomes an authority on good writing. And while the teachers are still the "experts," their task has shifted from assigning work and then judging its acceptability, to generating writing with students and coaching the students, throughout all stages of the writing process, toward more expert performances. Rather than operating under the old paradigm of keeping out all but a select few (Geisler, 1994; Miller, 1991), teachers in this apprenticeship-like model invite students to participate in discourse communities they themselves participate in; they share their insider knowledge; they share works in progress with their students and invite students' critiques.

This is not to paint writing instruction in U.S. schools as having achieved a pinnacle of success; if that were the case this study would have been unnecessary. The data in this study suggest that teachers—and teacher trainers—must continue to work at two issues in order to create more apprenticeship-like learning communities in their classes. The first is how to make curriculum/writing assignments rich in social meaning for students, or, to state it another way, how to make the communicative work of the writing project of greater importance to students than grades. A number of approaches have been developed to provide meaningful subject matter for composition classes—at the very least, acknowledging and making explicit to students the social context of school writing (Hill & Resnick, 1995; Lave & Wenger, 1991); engaging students in genuine academic endeavors, such as creating a theory of adolescence (Bartholomae & Petrosky, 1986) or exploring subversive uses of language; creating school-to-work projects under the auspices of service learning programs (Greenwood, 1994; Kirtley, 1994; Watters & Ford, 1995); or creating locally inspired projects, such as organizing writing teams to compile a student's guide to the Metro system in Washington, D.C., documenting a profile of the class of 2000 from multiple perspectives, researching campus problems and proposing (in writing) solutions to appropriate campus authorities, or asking students to study the writing underlife on campus (Anderson et al., 1990). Also, as both the school and workplace data in this study corroborate, writing skills can't be divorced from subject matter; a student can gain full measure from a general writing course only with serious, sustained engagement with a specific subject matter (Jolliffe, 1995; Kaufer & Dunmire, 1995; Russell, 1993). Asking students to write on capital punishment one week and gay rights the next is at best asking for superficial engagement in the thinking/writing process.

In addition to having writing in school contexts be for authentic communicative purposes, the second challenge this study highlights is to make learning for transfer an educational goal of all writing classes (Anderson, Reder, & Simon, 1996). This challenge entails the other elements I've enumerated in concluding this study. The first is to extend the frames of analysis for student and professional writing beyond discourse modes, stylistics, or even genres alone to include all five areas of writing knowledge delineated in this study. While the use of heuristics for students to orchestrate writing tasks is familiar in composition studies, there is a lack of agreement among scholars on the conceptual scope for those heuristics. Some theorists (Faigley, 1992; Witte, 1992) argue for the broadest possible frame: texts as semiotic representations within culture. More typical are narrower frames that focus on traditional rhetorical concerns of audience and text function (Anson, 1988; Brandt, 1986; Ede & Lunsford, 1984; Hairston, 1986; Kinneavy, 1971). This study argues for mid-level conceptual tools such as genre and discourse community as appropriate heuristics for writers facing boundary crossings between different genres and different discourse communities.

A second element in facilitating transfer of learning is to allow students to see how abstract concepts—discourse community, genre, and rhetorical context, for example—can be applied across a variety of writing situations and to let students test out the usefulness of those concepts in different task environments inside and outside academic settings. A teacher might do as Elbow (1991) suggests and ask students to redo a piece of writing for a different rhetorical situation, or follow the suggestion of Lovitt and Young (1997) to teach the report as well as the essay in general writing skills courses. These practices will help writers see different contexts in which their schemata for writing knowledge can serve as "mental grippers" for understanding new situations.

The third element is to cultivate metacognitive thinking, or mindfulness, to increase opportunities for high-road transfer from one writing situation to the next. Portfolio assessment techniques encourage mindfulness, as do writing or research logs; end pages to assignments, which require the author to evaluate the work's strengths and weaknesses; and group debriefings on writing projects (McIsaac & Aschauer, 1990).

In my own teaching of freshman composition, currently around the theme "Constructing the Self in Time and Place," I have begun experimenting with the ideas this study proposes. I now teach analysis of genres and discourse communities. I work to create a mini-version of an academic community through engagement with serious, even difficult, subject matter on the issue of identity drawn from psychology, history, sociology, semiotics, and genetics. We publish our writing for one another (in a bound collection printed by the university bookstore), draw on each other's work for new writing projects, evaluate the criteria by which different disciplines arrive at "knowledge," and critique our own writing projects in workshop sessions. We compare popular genres with academic genres to figure out how each accomplishes a different social purpose within varying discourse communities. We examine students' writing for other classes to see how the analytical frames I expose them to can apply. I look for telltale signs of new writing behaviors, and I judge my success or failure with students on whether they've accomplished writing that was meaningful beyond the confines of the semester's course. Such extension constitutes the most critical factor in getting students to continue their growth as writers. Next semester my goal is to find a way to integrate their writing projects into some sphere of social action beyond our immediate writing community and to write with my students. And I keep working with the competing goals of creating local, grounded, socially situated practice and the long-term goal of transfer of learning to other contexts for writing.

For those who deal with training situations (more short-term learning) or with informal contexts for improving writing skills, the bad news is that this study makes the job harder—or at least longer. Teaching formal characteristics of genres alone or "principles of business writing" will not give writers the full tool kit they need for handling multiple writing situations. On the other hand, teaching workers to "read" the discourse communities in which they participate, teaching them the interrelationship of the five knowledge domains in writing and their heuristic potential, and teaching metacognitive thinking about writing *will* move writers further along the spectrum from novice to expert writing performance. But businesses need not just well-equipped trainers but managers as well who take the time to mentor their employees in writing skills in the manner laid out in this chapter.

In sum, data in this study attest both to the complexity of skills and knowledge involved in expert writing activity and to the considerable length of time necessary for acquiring writing expertise. No doubt the college papers that Birgitte, Ursula, and Pam showed me would not be considered by their professors to be the writing of "experts." Two of the writers, Ursula and Birgitte, were still figuring out syntactical and structural issues in academic writing during college. Birgitte and Pam were struggling in graduate school to handle the subject matter and the genre conventions of their disciplines. Likewise, the road to expert writing performance at JRC was a long one for all four women, spanning many months.

Finally, this study raises questions concerning where we are in our theorizing about writing and in our research methodologies for understanding writing performances. I have tried here to untangle several overlapping concepts to show their relations and their distinctiveness. The notion of discourse community has been conceived here from an anthropological perspective rather than solely in relation to texts and text production. Genres have been viewed from the standpoint of formal features and social, communicative functions within discourse communities. Rhetorical knowledge, I have argued, is a subset of genre knowledge and is best conceived in that relationship. And above all, I have argued for using multiple lenses for analyzing writing situations, for any single lens (textual analysis, rhetorical analysis, etc.) is too small to capture the whole. "Contexts for writing" has been a much written-about topic in recent years, but operationalizing theoretical discussions has been challenging (Beaufort, 1997).

Writing is an area of study intersecting with a number of other disciplines, demanding that we avoid either–or arguments—either a cognitive or a social view, either a generalist approach or a situation-specific approach. What writers do is infinitely larger and messier, requiring on the one hand that we tolerate ambiguity and on the other that we keep testing theories empirically and using terminology with as much precision as possible. Both cognitive and social dimensions are important, both knowledge structures and situated awareness are necessary, and both tacit and explicit understanding of writing activities are required. We also need to extend our notion of "learning to write" to include skill in adapting to increasingly complex, site-specific writing tasks.

My bias is toward trying to understand the bigger picture—even in hazy form if necessary—before looking at particulars. Otherwise, if we frame the study too tightly, we may miss what is outside the frame but *in* the real picture. Through the multiple lenses of culture, discourse community, genre, situated cognition, transfer theory, and theories of expert knowledge, I have tried to understand some of what was going on at one institutional site for composing and in the writing development of four individuals. Consider this work a call to use multiple lenses in writing research, focused near and far, with the shutters held open for long-term exposures.

CHAPTER 8

Getting Here from There

Ethnography is work. It is more than the collection of data or even the description and explanation of data. It is making the implicit explicit, articulating the ineffable. It means seeing the invisible and then making it visible to others.

—Andrea Fishman, *Amish Literacy*

In the opening of Chapter 7, I referred to "the story constructed thus far." That was not an attempt to shoot myself in the foot as researcher but rather a self-conscious acknowledgment of the narrative features of ethnography and my role as writer in crafting the story. In producing an ethnography about writing, one cannot avoid reflecting on the construction of text and the characteristics of the genre of ethnography. I raised in Chapter 1 the epistemological dilemma of truth telling brought on by postmodernism, which ethnographers in the 1990s must wrestle with. Where is the "Other" in the text? Am I as researcher subjugating the truth as informants see it to the truth as I see it and denying them a voice? In fact, what is meant by "truth"? Anti-positivists deny any such absolute, admitting only shades of meaning that are socially constructed.[1] This position leads to an unending series of questions concerning epistemological and methodological assumptions and ultimately places meaning in the minds of readers rather than in the text.

But postmodernism should not let the ethnographer off the hook: The only responsible position is to make as explicit as possible the process—including the research methodologies—by which the text was constructed, thereby providing another means for the reader to judge the work's merits. In this chapter I add to methodological discussions of confessional tales of ethnographers (Fishman, 1988; Latour & Woolgar, 1979;

Van Maanen, 1988; Whyte, 1943). I first address the essential character of literacy practices, which makes ethnography a methodology of choice; second, I address issues of reliability and validity, which must be considered in evaluating any form of research; third, I look at the problems and possibilities of ethnography as a genre in relation to the construction of meaning; and finally, I consider ethical issues this study raised.

WHY ETHNOGRAPHY?

Bereiter and Scardamalia (1987) point to a "conspicuous" rise of holistic approaches to composition research in the 1980s, variously labeled as phenomenological, ethnographic, hermeneutic, and qualitative. This rise in part reflects the increased recognition in the past 3 decades that literacy is culturally embedded and that written texts or acts of composing cannot be understood apart from the social systems of both producer and product.

Given the problem I wanted to investigate—that of crossing boundaries from one social context of writing to another—an ethnography of two contrasting locations for writing seemed the logical research design. I began the study by collecting ethnographic data for 6 months in a university writing program. I then searched for a workplace site where I could collect contrastive data. My choice of a nonprofit setting was based on the sense that writing would be central to the organization's activities and taken seriously. I planned to study the organization and its writers from an anthropological standpoint to understand as fully as possible the social aspects of one site of composing as compared with another.

RELIABILITY AND VALIDITY

As a preface to the discussion of establishing the reliability and validity of an ethnographic study, I want to note that in the early stages of research design an ethnographer must rely in part on hunches. Going into a site, the ethnographer has some idea of the material she may gather but will not know what material she really has at hand until she is deep into the process. After I talked with Leong, the executive director of JRC, and with the four women who would become my informants, it seemed that the site would be productive for getting at the issues I was concerned with. I had several reasons for that judgment call. For one, access to workplace settings is tricky, as most are high-pressure situations; asking that employees take time out from work to participate in a research project of the magnitude I intended required that upper management be sympathetic to an endeavor whose payoffs to the agency would be at best long-term and indirect. Due to Leong's own research background, I had that pledge of cooperation. Second, the four women did a considerable volume of writing. Each estimated that, on average, about 50% of her work week was spent on writing tasks, providing plenty of writing activity to examine.

Another judgment call at the beginning of the study at JRC was that the four informants would serve the needs of the study adequately. They were not representative of JRC employees as a whole, either in terms of writing ability or in terms of position in the organizational hierarchy. Because I was looking for employees who did a lot of writing, I was directed to the best writers in the organization, who also happened to be in the middle tier of a three-tier organizational structure. Not surprisingly, by virtue of their writing skill they had been placed in managerial positions, which demanded considerable writing.

Furthermore, after an initial interview with each woman, I saw that they represented a range of experience—from Selma and Birgitte, who had been writing in this institutional context for more than 4 years, to Ursula and Pam, who had been hired just a few months before my arrival. I hypothesized that the newcomers would be at the beginning of a steep learning curve and that the old-timers would represent the further end of the learning curve. That contrast—as well as the fact that total time lapsed since college graduation ranged from 2 to 8 years—could be instructive. Three of the four writers also had a strong interest in writing outside their jobs; I reasoned that they would be interested in the nature of the study and perhaps could benefit personally, which would aid me in getting their cooperation.

As it turned out, each of the four informants was invaluable to the study. In addition to being cooperative and articulate, each brought a different and equally helpful perspective. Selma, who had been at JRC over 5 years, was the institutional memory. She could tell me how writing practices in the organization had changed over that time and offer a historical perspective on the sociocultural aspects of the institution in its present form. Birgitte, a serious fiction writer outside JRC, could reflect most ably on her own writing processes. Trained as an ethnographer herself, Pam was helpful in reflecting on JRC's cultural aspects. And Ursula, who was both self-reflective and open with her feelings, afforded the opportunity for a close examination of the institution's impact on her writing activities and her learning processes within this setting.

In addition, three of the four writers had access to samples of their high school and college papers, so I was able to do within-subject comparisons between composing in academic and workplace settings, and to view their developmental progress as writers over a decade or more. The richness of the data set gathered at JRC led to a decision to focus this report solely on that data, leaving the data collected at the university site for a future report. I turn now to details of data collection, analysis, and interpretation of the JRC data, which I place within the larger context of issues of reliability and validity of the study.

Achieving reliability in ethnography is virtually impossible, as the research is inextricably connected to a particular time and place. By the end of the year of fieldwork, two of the informants, Birgitte and Selma, had left JRC for other jobs. Due to a variety of circumstances, personal and work-related, Ursula, Pam, and Mei also would leave the organization before this book's completion. Institutional changes at JRC have occurred as well. As Sanjek (1990) points out:

> In ethnography, "reliability" verges on affectation. We cannot expect and do not hope that another investigator will repeat the fieldwork and confirm the results before they are published. . . . As Honingmann (1976) correctly puts it: "Speaking realistically, there is practically a zero probability of ever testing the reliability of a comprehensive ethnographic report, so one ought to stop talking about replication as a technique of verification." (p. 394)

Unless a team of researchers collect the data, which was not the case in this study, little means exist for establishing reliability.

On the other hand, validity—whether the data say what I am reporting—is a core issue in evaluating ethnography. Sanjek (1990) states:

> The historic development of the ethnographic method, although underexposed, is not "non-accumulative." Nor is the method "intuitive, journalistic, unfocused, impressionistic" or merely "brilliant guesswork." (p. 395)

In fact, ethnographic methods display a well-established systematicity, which, if followed faithfully and reported fully, can be a means of assessing the report's validity. Sanjek points to three "canons" for assessing ethnographic validity: theoretical candor, the ethnographer's path, and field-note evidence.

Theoretical Candor

Theoretical candor entails stating not only the theories that informed the study at the outset, but how and when those theories were used in analyzing and interpreting the data and were themselves transformed by the data. Because of the situatedness of ethnography, a particular theoretical perspective at the outset of the study may evolve into "terrain-specific theories" (Sanjek, 1990). This study is a case in point.

Notes to myself are a partial record of the mental trailblazing required to work within and against existing theories in order to see what is going on in the data. Fishman (1988) has described well the struggle with finding the right categories for the data—juggling the need to simplify for the sake of getting to the heart of the issues and the need to represent complexity through expansive, inclusive reportage. And Whyte (1943) describes accurately the overall mental labyrinth the ethnographer encounters:

> We do not generally think problems through in a straight line. Often we have the experience of being immersed in a mass of confusing data. We study the data carefully, bringing all our powers of logical analysis to bear upon them. We come up with an idea or two. But still the data do not fall in any coherent pattern. Then we go on living with the data—and with the people—until perhaps some chance occurrence casts a totally different light upon the data, and we begin to see a pattern that we have not seen before. (pp. 279–280)

For purposes of illustrating such a mental path, I summarize here my thinking process in finding ways to explain the data set, as represented in notes and sketches to myself in the early stages of analysis.[2]

At the outset, I intended to use three primary frames for understanding the data: discourse community theory, genre theory, and learning theory. These broad concerns guided some 90 loosely structured interviews. However, problems arose when I began data analysis. Either the theories themselves were insufficiently worked out in the theoretical literature or in empirical studies to be easily applied to the data, or several theories needed to be applied at once. I will illustrate with the case of the first theoretical lens I applied, that of discourse community.

The defining elements of discourse community reported in Chapter 3 did not present themselves to me initially. When I began the tedious process of listening to the tapes, adding to field notes from the recorded data, and selecting portions of the tapes to be transcribed, I starting looking for patterns in the data and derived a rough three-pronged coding scheme: community, text, and writer. Under each of those categories I listed themes I was seeing in the data. For example, under "community" I had these subcategories: process, values, pressure, quantity, relations, rhetoric, writing function, and technology. I turned that coding scheme into a database that would allow me to access and manipulate over 1,000 pages of transcribed data. I then took the chunk of data that I thought related to discourse community practices and started a second pass through it, searching for the social factors that were influencing both what was written and how, and determining the interrelationships of those factors. I came up with four categories: (1) underlying principles, (2) process/relationships, (3) product/textual features, and (4) socialization process. At that point I realized I was dealing not with one discourse community in my data, but with five overlapping communities. My conceptual map became a Venn diagram (see Figure 3.1).

Theorizing and clarifying patterns and relationships proceeded in recursive fashion, as I thought, doodled, wrote, showed the text to others who challenged my assumptions, and wrote some more. Conceptualizing discourse communities through the data in turn helped to refine relationships with other theoretical concepts such as genre knowledge and rhetorical knowledge. For example, as I refined the notion of discourse community and was able to distinguish among the discourse communities under investigation, I saw that a single genre, such as the grant proposal, took on different characteristics depending on which discourse community it was being used in. Analyzing data and theorizing were ongoing, spiraling processes.

Goetz and LeCompte (1984) enumerate the components of theorizing well: perceiving, comparing, contrasting, aggregating, ordering, establishing linkages, and speculating. Equally true of theorizing in ethnography is Sanjek's (1990) statement:

> "Where theory?" In the field and out of the field. "When theory?" Significant theories while planning fieldwork, and theories of significance as it takes shape and direction. "Why theory?" To give ethnography meaning and purpose and to avoid opportunistic study of "everything." (p. 398)

It is also important for the reader of an ethnography to note what Fishman (1988) says: "[F]inal writing . . . starts with closure and works backwards, but doing ethnography does not. . . . [E]thnography is inductive, open-ended, and interactive/adaptive" (p. 206).

I went on with other chunks of data analysis from other theoretical standpoints (Chapters 4, 5, and 6). Existing theories, schematics for modifying theories, different data groups, and the evolving text itself cumulatively led to the realization that I was describing not just a discourse community or genre acquisition, but the characteristics of expert writing performance. The literature in cognitive psychology on novice versus expert behaviors was the overarching conceptual framework within which the data could be best understood. I recast my theoretical framework in

Chapter 1 and wrote a much different conclusion in Chapter 7 than I had anticipated as I was "chunking" and analyzing the data chapter by chapter.

The Ethnographer's Path

The ethnographer's path is the second means of assessing validity of an ethnographic study, according to Sanjek. In ethnography, the researcher is the research instrument, so human factors must be assessed: How did I as researcher influence the outcome of the study? Specifically, what in my background may have influenced the study? What were the interpersonal dynamics that developed over the course of the study, and how did those influence the outcomes? And what effect did particular methods of data collection have on the study?

I explained in Chapter 1 the personal factors that led to this study. In Chapter 7 I reported evidence of the effect of my questioning on the informants' self-reflective thinking about writing. In addition, given my personality and my firsthand experience as a writer in business environments, I was not surprised when both Ursula and Pam commented to me, about 4 months into the fieldwork, that I had become their workplace therapist. The times spent talking to me each week helped them defuse the stress accumulated on the job.

Some factors contributing to this openness in the interviews, however, were the result of intentional behaviors on my part. I wanted to create as equal a relationship with each of the women as I could, not setting myself up as an expert in any way. To that end, I did not talk about my background as a professional writer except to a very limited degree. On the other hand, I shared anecdotes from my personal life to let them see my human side; I tried to defer to their needs and wishes; I pursued every opportunity to be helpful to them. Such opportunities included bringing them cartoons clipped from the newspaper or *New Yorker* articles I thought one or another would be interested in, reading and commenting on their writing projects outside JRC, swapping information on favorite authors, or, on one occasion, researching funding agencies that might lead to new sources of grant support for Birgitte's program. Several times, in frustration, one of the women would turn to me and say, "Would you just write this for me?" But they knew the answer had to be "no." My roles were primarily friend and observer, and no one asked me to step beyond those boundaries.

Interviews were conducted in loose, conversational style. Whenever time allowed, I would take each of the women to a coffee shop or cafe for a cup of coffee. That transition time allowed some personal interaction before I turned on the tape recorder. I always began the interviews with two broad, open-ended questions: (1) what have you been working on this past week? and (2) tell me about the writing you did this past week. I talked as little as possible, letting a few open-ended remarks serve as a starting point for the individual's self-reflection. I said enough to keep the conversation going, to prompt more talk, but gave my informants the space to let their thoughts unfold in a free-association style. The less I framed the questions, the more likely I would come to understand not only what my informants said, but what they meant (Briggs, 1986; Fleischer, 1995).

I often would let the talk meander onto topics unrelated to my study for as much as 5- or 10-minute stretches and sometimes got wonderful information in the midst of seemingly "off-topic" stretches of talk. Here's a typical example: I had asked Ursula whether she had done any PR writing in previous jobs—perhaps when she was working at the repertory theater. She told me at length about the job—people, her duties, her friends. She explained that those who worked in the upstairs office of the theater didn't hang out with those who worked downstairs in the box office. I just let the tape recorder run. All of a sudden she said:

> It's the same here at JRC. Upstairs, this is where people get along really well, and there's more a sense of like professional relations up here, and downstairs there's a lot of stress . . . and interpersonal problems that don't exist up here. (1/26/93, p. 9)

With no forewarning or prompting from me, Ursula had dropped into my tape recorder a comment about the social relations and organizational structure at JRC that I had been unaware of. This loose, conversational interview style also had the advantage of sidestepping, or at least minimizing, issues a more controlled interview raises: power relations, rules for turn taking, rules for appropriate topics, and constraints of the interview as a linguistic form (Briggs, 1986).

The downside of establishing rapport is losing objectivity and/or influencing the data. I reported in Chapter 7 a few signs of my affecting the writers' thinking about writing, but these influences seemed minimal. Even when I carefully introduced the notion of genre about 5 months into the study, none began referring to "genres" in our conversations. And I could see no changes in their writing processes or written products that appeared to stem from my influence. In fact, all seemed to treat me as somewhat of an anomaly: Selma commented after reading the first draft of the research report, "Who would have ever thought you could find so much to write about in what we were doing?" (personal communication, 3/5/95). In spite of my presence at JRC, the writing appeared to remain

Table 8.1. Data Collected for the Study

	Number of Interviews	Hours of Taped Interviews	Pages of Transcript	Pages of Written Text
Birgitte	11	6.0	119	781
Pam	27	18.0	268	1,403
Selma	16	12.0	131	710
Ursula	25	13.5	215	726
Experts	11	16.0	255	90
Total	90	65.5	988	3,710

just part of the job to the four women—a normal occurrence, not particularly of interest, but a requirement to accomplish projects.

Nor did I get a sense that the four women's self-reports were, as Van Maanen (1979) reports, "presentational." As far as I was able to determine, each of the four women had no particular stake in representing herself in one way or another to me, although only Birgitte, Selma, Ursula, and Pam know the answer to that for certain.

The other means of attempting to mitigate my influence on the data was to triangulate the data—a standard ethnographic procedure—accomplished by manipulating three variables: intersecting theories, different data sources, and different time frames. As the same data were parsed differently in each chapter, using different theoretical frameworks, different and convergent views of the data emerged. In addition to open-ended interviews, I did discourse-based interviews (see Odell, Goswami, Herrington, & Quick, 1983). Each week, I would collect any writing the women had done since my previous visit and ask them to comment on the texts. In a subsequent interview, having read the texts over carefully, I would ask the writer to look over the text again and answer specific questions on its features: rhetorical strategies, word choice, structural choices, content, edits, and so on. I also would ask process questions—how the text was drafted, edited, and so on. As others also have found (DiPardo, 1994; Greene & Higgins, 1994), stimulated recall can elicit information that otherwise would not have been obtained.

Table 8.1 summarizes the actual artifacts collected and gives some indication of the scope of data collection. Other data sources also were used to verify self-reports and textual evidence: direct observation of writers at work or of key events in the organization, reports from Leong and Mei about their views of each woman's writing and learning processes, reports from individuals outside JRC who were recipients of JRC texts or support people for JRC writers, and reports of other individuals external to JRC who were writing similar documents in their own jobs. And finally, the four women read the first draft of the report and commented to me on whether it (1) was accurate from their perspectives and (2) made sense. The answer on both counts was "yes."

Because this was a long study, time became the third means to triangulate data. And at the end of the fieldwork, I asked each writer to look back over the samples I had collected and to give me her current assessment of the texts. Regardless of whether I got the same answer to questions repeated from an interview months earlier, I had yet another view of the writing situation. For example, when I asked Pam to recall her first impressions of federal grant proposals 2 years after she'd started learning how to write them, she said, "I don't think the writing daunted me at all about these things" (8/23/94, p. 6). But a year and a half earlier, she had told me:

> I'm one of these people who needs to see the overview, so that I can understand what I'm doing at each part. . . . *I didn't know what I was doing when I was writing those first [proposals]. . . . After that class I had a sense of, "Oh, I'm writing this [section] 'cause it's going to lead to this."* (2/3/93, p. 1, emphasis added)

If I had not had the advantage of looking at perceptions of writing across time, the data could have been skewed. In Chapter 4, I reported a similar change in perspective with the lapse in time, when Birgitte re-examined grant proposals written 2 years earlier and, in hindsight, was able to critique their flaws.

Field-Note Evidence

The final means for checking an ethnography's validity, according to Sanjek (1990), is field-note evidence. His bias is toward ethnographies containing as many actual field notes as possible, but he acknowledges that "the canon of field note evidence requires only that the relationship between field notes and ethnography be explicit" (p. 403) and that narrative and rhetorical decisions be accounted for in writing the report.

In describing methods of data collection and analysis, I have indicated the relationship of raw data to final text. My field and interview notes, taken in notebooks, would be unreadable to anyone else. Audio tapes and the resulting transcripts would be accessible if anyone wanted them, and for that purpose I indicated citation markers (date and page number) for excerpts of transcripts included in this text.

CONSTRUCTING THE TEXT

More important than the accessibility of field notes within the final report is the second issue Sanjek (1990) raises—the narrative and rhetorical decisions made in writing the ethnography. Claims abound that ethnography constructs reality. (For a series of essays on this matter, see Clifford and Marcus's 1986 edited collection.) Herndl (1991) states, "Ethnographies persuade readers not by the power of factual description but by employing the narrative structures, textual tropes, and argumentative topoi developed by the ethnographic genre" (p. 321). Doheny-Farina (1993) proposes a solution to this dilemma: View all research activities as rhetorical and make our research reports responsible and ethical by revealing that rhetoric. So, at the end of this report about writing in professional contexts, I attempt to explicate the rhetorical aspects of this particular ethnography.

Herndl (1991) refers to "the desires that maintain our rhetoric" (p. 322). My purposes in this study were pragmatic and altruistic—to maintain an academic appointment on the one hand, and to tackle an important problem in education on the other. Within the specific field of composition studies, I see myself as a bridge builder, connecting cognitive and social constructionist theories and research. To what extent these purposes may have biased this report, I cannot judge.

The second rhetorical consideration of any report of research, ethnography included, is the decision about audience(s) for the text and the juggling of potentially conflicting interests between writer and audience(s). I can echo Doheny-Farina's (1993) list of audiences for his report on an instance of nonacademic writing. First, actual participants in the study: How could I be truthful to my other audiences without being hurtful to this most intimate of audiences? That tension was ever present in my mind as I wrote. Anonymity was not a sufficient cover for the human need for validation. Second, disciplinary colleagues: Would those of a more positivist persuasion dispute my methods? What could I do to bolster claims of fairness in the collection and reporting of data? How would I build on others' work, showing collegiality and originality as well? Third, gatekeepers, academic presses that might publish the manuscript: How would I make this a marketable text, juggling currency of the topic and the cost per page to publish with the need to say what needed to be said and in full enough measure to be accurate? Fourth, nonacademic readers—professional writers, communications managers, and trainers: Could I keep technical jargon to a minimum, and would the conclusion include enough practical advice to make it worth their while? And what storytelling techniques or gracefulness of style could make someone ac-

customed to the one-page executive summary willing to read even a 20-
or 30-page introduction or conclusion? Fifth, bosses—department chairs,
deans, provosts—inside and outside my field of expertise: Would they
find the work of sufficient scholarly merit? And last but not least, my
internal critic: By what internal measures of thoroughness and clarity
would I decide when the text was a personal best? And could I reconcile
the artist in me with the scholar, so that the text contained a certain ele-
gance in spite of the scholarly need for minute precision? Juggling all of
these audiences and needs complicated the rhetorical decision making.

The third area of rhetorical decision making concerns how to estab-
lish the report's credibility. The philosophical arguments in academe between positivists and constructivists provide no easy answers. Nor does
the genre itself suggest a formulaic way of arranging the data, for, as Van
Maanen (1988)points out, the genre of ethnography has sprouted several
variations as the field of anthropology has evolved and been influenced
by postmodernism. In the realist tale, the ethnographer attempts to estab-
lish credibility by placing as much distance between herself and the report as possible, and at the opposite extreme the confessional tale gains
its credibility through the personalized voice of the ethnographer, who
states up front her point of view and even reports mistakes made in the
study. Ultimately, I chose a middle path between those two extremes. I
used logical appeals, combining thick description and explicit references
to theoretical frameworks for understanding the data. But pathos had its
role, too, with human stories here, tales of frustration and success, stories
within stories—the story of the research, the story of JRC, and the stories
of four women. And I used ethos as well, allowing the reader an occasional glimpse of my participation in the research: the "I was there" accounts, such as the description of my arrival at the research site on a
typical morning in Chapter 2 and the account of the fund-raising dinner
in Chapter 3, the snippets of actual dialogue throughout the chapters of
data analysis, the disclosures of relevant personal history in Chapter 1,
and the reporting of my methodological and writerly concerns in this
chapter. Nothing was written down by accident; every word was by design, with multiple purposes and multiple needs of multiple audiences
in mind. Only the relative who proclaimed he could have summed up in
two pages the chapter I gave him to read did I give up on as a potential
reader.

In the end, ethnography as a genre is part narrative, part report, part
argument. The particular mix of these three potential purposes accounts
for the variations in ethnographic accounts that Van Maanen (1979) speaks
of. Cultural critics would claim the confessional tale is all subjective story.
Social scientists would claim at least partial objectivity in realist tales. To

me, the genre is both subjective and objective and allows the writer a great deal of flexibility in deciding what form of account, or subgenre of ethnography, will best serve the intended goals and audience(s).

ETHICAL ISSUES

One final matter needs addressing before I rest my case: the ethical issues in relation to those who were the object of study. Given the depth of probing and intimacy that ultimately results between researcher and researched in the process of accomplishing an ethnography, issues of privacy and reciprocity come up.

Up front, I pledged both to the institution, JRC, and to the participants that their identities would be masked as much as possible. But the issue of privacy is intertwined with matters of truth telling, too. If a statement was made or a fact revealed that could be publicly damaging to individual or institution, should it be suppressed in the report? Would that then falsify the report? As all ethnographers know, this fine line must be walked carefully. For example, at one point an individual who participated in the study reported that another member of the community said, "This report could be turned in in crayon and it wouldn't matter." While the journalist in me loved both the color and candor of the statement, as a responsible researcher I left the statement out of the report; I could convey the meaning of the statement in a way that would not be an embarrassment to anyone involved. Some researchers have found themselves in the frustrating situation of realizing that if any portion of the truth were reported, individuals' lives could be damaged. The data remain unpublished. I am fortunate to be able to report findings that, as far as I can see, are politically and personally either neutral or positive for the individuals represented here.

The matter of reciprocity also weighs heavily on the ethnographer. Unlike experimental studies, in which the subjects' time commitment is prescribed and reasonable or compensated monetarily, ethnography requires such extraordinary amounts of time and cooperation on the subjects' part that no monetary value could be computed. A gift of graphics software to JRC at the end of the fieldwork was symbolic and token—the best tangible thanks I could give to the institution. To the individuals involved, particularly Selma, Birgitte, Ursula, and Pam, the only gift that in any way could approximate what was given to me was the offer of friendship. Ultimately, I have to hope that those who participated in this study will take some satisfaction, as Margaret Mead did, in "adding to the sum of accurate information in the world" (quoted in Schaef, 1990).

Notes

CHAPTER 1

1. All names have been changed to protect the privacy of the individuals and institutions involved in this study.

2. Connors (1981) has shown the illogic of the modes of discourse as writing models. Real writers do not set out to write description, narration, or exposition. Rather, they set out to discuss a given topic, in a given genre, for a specific purpose and audience. Further, the discourse modes may occur in various combinations in any one text. On the issue of stability of genres and whether such stable forms can be taught, see the series of articles on the topic in *Research in the Teaching of English*, 27(3), October 1993. For a report on an experimental study testing the effectiveness of giving students model texts, see Smagorinsky (1992). See also Haswell (1991, pp. 91–101) for a discussion of problems with the use of model texts for writers to emulate. The consensus on the use of models seems to be that using real texts (not the phony genres created for the purposes of teaching composition), with additional instructional support in analyzing the model and in procedural issues of composing, may help writers learning to write in new genres.

3. Experimental studies (Beach & Anson, 1988; Flower & Hayes, 1981) of novice versus expert performance on writing tasks have focused on issues of writers planning tasks and goal setting, particularly from the standpoint of defining audience and purpose. Naturalistic studies of novice versus expert writing performance have been more diverse. Herrington (1988) has studied argument structures of good and weak papers in a literary analysis course. Others also have analyzed the linguistic and rhetorical features of exemplary texts in various disciplines (Bazerman, 1981; Fahnestock, 1986; Fahnestock & Secor, 1991). Several studies (Barabas, 1990; Flower, 1989; Odell & Goswami, 1982) have pinpointed the greater expertise with rhetorical issues among expert writers. Each of these perspectives is valuable, but none constitutes the whole of what writing expertise looks like.

4. For those familiar with learning theories I add this note: Although the fundamental framework for this study is social constructionist, I also embrace

elements of cognitivist or acquisition models of learning. As Sfard (1998) points out, neither theoretical camp can describe completely the nature of learning, but each represents important elements.

CHAPTER 4

1. Here is a key to the symbols I have used for transcription of dialogue: - indicates a pause of 2 seconds or more within an utterance; [indicates overlapping utterances (used to mark the point at which an utterance in progress is joined by another interrupting utterance); = indicates contiguous utterances (used when there is no break between adjacent utterances, the second latched to, but not overlapping, the first); / indicates back channeling (when one speaker talks over the other, usually to indicate agreement with the speaker as he/she is talking).

CHAPTER 5

1. According to Crystal and Day (1969), the journalistic register also is characterized by initial adverbials, heavy use of coordinate clauses (to convey a sense of immediacy, inviting the reader as participant), and few subordinators and little embedding. However, in my analysis of two press releases written by an expert publicist, I found a number of embedded clauses that serve to condense information while at the same time making clear to the reader what information is of greatest importance. These instances may be anomalies or may suggest that the press release and news story differ stylistically.

2. Although the research study at JRC officially ended after 1 year, I maintained contact with Pam during the following year in order to obtain information on the outcome of the grant proposal she was working on at the end of the first year. That proposal represented the culmination of her learning about grant proposal writing during the first year.

3. Although he is thinking exclusively in terms of literary genres, Fowler (1982) gives comprehensive coverage to the variety and range of textual features of a given genre. His cataloguing of features includes some 15 items (see pp. 60–74).

CHAPTER 6

1. Himley (1986) and Bissex (1980) offer case studies of a single child's development over a 2- or 4-year period in the earliest stages of writing literacy—learning the mechanics of printing, spelling, vocabulary, and simple sentence structure.

Studies of performance in elementary through secondary school have characterized group performances on linguistic and rhetorical indices (Applebee, 1978, 1984; Freedman, 1987; Hunt, 1965; Langer, 1985; Loban, 1976). A few studies of high school writers have examined developmental issues in terms of syntactic, rhetorical, and cognitive maturity (Durst, 1984; Eiler, 1989; Warantz & Keech, 1982), and likewise of college writers (Geisler, 1994; Haswell, 1991; Hays, 1983).

2. Freedman and Pringle (1980) define a student's capacity to abstract as "the degree to which the primary data dealt with in the essay had been classified, ordered, and integrated by the writer within some superordinate, hierarchic, conceptual pattern" (p. 317). They suggest four levels of abstraction: report, commentary, first-level classification, and second-level classification. Moffett (1983) also suggests levels of abstraction based on the variables of time (present to future) and nearness or distance of the writer to his/her audience (known person to unknown groups of people). These scales for measuring abstraction have not had widespread empirical validation, however.

3. In a review of 2 decades of research on bilingual children, Diaz (1983) states: "When compared to monolinguals, balanced bilingual children show definite advantages on measures of metalinguistic abilities, concept formation, field independence, and divergent thinking skills" (p. 48). Pam's and Birgitte's bilingual abilities may have been a factor in their capacities to develop as strong writers, although a direct correlation cannot be inferred.

4. The 1992 study by Kirsch and Jungeblut of the Department of Labor showed a statistically significant relationship between access to reading materials in the home and desired educational goals, as well as "some empirical evidence supporting a 'causal' chain among the manipulable variables, beginning with access to reading materials, which affects reading practices, which affects literacy proficiency, which, in turn, has a positive impact on labor market outcomes" (p. 162).

CHAPTER 7

The opening quote appeared in the *San Francisco Chronicle* on September 9, 1993.

CHAPTER 8

The chapter title, "Getting Here from There," popped into my head one day while I was revising Chapter 1. Later, in referring to Fishman (1988), I discovered the source of my title. So I use it here with all due respect to Andrea for having thought of it first.

1. Cintron (1993) presents arguments on the issue of ethnography's "objectivity." On the one hand, some (Tyler, 1986) hold that ethnography cannot explain a culture scientifically but can only evoke a culture in the way that poetic writing

is evocative. However, Cintron points out that certain ethnographies, in his opinion, are successful at both depicting a body of facts and portraying the writer's rhetoric.

2. See Appendix D in Beaufort, 1995, for the notes and sketches that represent the mental path of theorizing the conceptual framework for the data.

References

Anderson, J. R., Reder, L. M., & Simon, H. A. (1996). Situated learning and education. *Educational Researcher, 25*(4), 5–11.

Anderson, P. V. (1985). What survey research tells us about writing at work. In L. Odell & D. Goswami (Eds.), *Writing in nonacademic settings* (pp. 3–83). New York: Guilford Press.

Anderson, W., Best, C., Black, A., Hurst, J., Miller, B., & Miller, S. (1990). Cross-curricular underlife: A collaborative report on ways with academic words. *College Composition and Communication, 41*(1), 11–36.

Anson, C. M. (1988). Toward a multidimensional model of writing in the academic disciplines. In D. A. Jolliffe (Ed.), *Advances in writing research: Writing in academic disciplines* (Vol. 2, pp. 1–34). Norwood, NJ: Ablex.

Anson, C. M., & Forsberg, L. L. (1990). Moving beyond the academic community: Transitional stages in professional writing. *Written Communication, 7*(2), 200–231.

Applebee, A. N. (1978). *A child's concept of story: Ages two to seventeen.* Chicago: University of Chicago Press.

Applebee, A. N. (1984). *Contexts for learning to write: Studies of secondary school instruction.* Norwood, NJ: Ablex.

Applebee, A. N. (1986). Problems in process approaches: Toward a reconceptualization of process instruction. In A. R. Petrosky & D. Bartholomae (Eds.), *The teaching of writing* (85th Yearbook of the National Society for the Study of Education, pp. 95–113). Chicago: University of Chicago Press.

Applebee, A. N., Langer, J. L., Mullis, I. V. S., Lathan, A. S., & Gentile, C. A. (1994). *NAEP 1992 writing report card* (23-W01). Washington, DC: U.S. Department of Education, Office of Educational Research and Improvement.

Bain, A. (1886). *English composition and rhetoric: A manual.* New York: American Book Company.

Bakhtin, M. M. (1986). The problem of speech genres. In C. Emerson & M. Holquist (Eds.), *Speech genres and other late essays* (pp. 60–402). Austin: University of Texas Press.

Barabas, C. (1990). *Technical writing in a corporate culture: A study of the nature of information.* Norwood, NJ: Ablex.

Bartholomae, D. (1985). Inventing the university. In M. Rose (Ed.), *When a writer can't write* (pp. 134–165). New York: Guilford Press.

Bartholomae, D., & Petrosky, A. (1986). *Facts, artifacts and counterfacts.* Portsmouth, NH: Boynton/Cook.

Barton, P., & LaPointe, A. (1995). *Learning by degrees: Indicators of performance in higher education.* Princeton, NJ: Educational Testing Service.

Basso, K. H. (1974). The ethnography of writing. In R. Bauman & J. Sherzer (Eds.), *Explorations in the ethnography of speaking* (pp. 425–432). Cambridge: Cambridge University Press.

Bazerman, C. (1981). What written knowledge does: Three examples of academic discourse. *Philosophy of the Social Sciences, 2,* 361–387.

Bazerman, C. (1988). *Shaping written knowledge: The genre and activity of the experimental article in science.* Madison: University of Wisconsin Press.

Bazerman, C. (1994). *Constructing experience.* Carbondale, IL: Southern Illinois University Press.

Beach, R., & Anson, C. M. (1988). The pragmatics of memo writing: Developmental differences in the use of rhetorical strategies. *Written Communication, 5*(2), 157–183.

Beaufort, A. (1995). *Writing the organization's way: The life of writers in the workplace.* Ethnography, Stanford University, Stanford.

Beaufort, A. (1997). Operationalizing the concept of discourse community: A case study of one institutional site of composing. *Research in the Teaching of English, 31*(4), 486–529.

Beaufort, A. (1998). Transferring writing knowledge to the workplace: Are we on track? In M. S. Garay & S. A. Bernhardt (Eds.), *Expanding literacies: English teaching and the new workplace* (pp. 179–199). Albany: State University of New York Press.

Bereiter, C., & Scardamalia, M. (1987). *The psychology of written composition.* Hillsdale, NJ: Erlbaum.

Berkenkotter, C., & Huckin, T. N. (1993). Rethinking genre from a sociocognitive perspective. *Written Communication, 10*(4), 475–509.

Berkenkotter, C., & Huckin, T. N. (1995). *Genre knowledge in disciplinary communication: Cognition/culture/power.* Hillsdale, NJ: Erlbaum.

Berkenkotter, C., Huckin, T., & Ackerman, J. (1988). Conventions, conversations and the writer: Case study of a student in a rhetoric Ph.D. program. *Research in the Teaching of English, 22,* 9–44.

Berlin, J. A. (1987). *Rhetoric and reality: Writing instruction in American colleges, 1900–1985.* Carbondale: Southern Illinois University Press.

Bernhardt, S. A., & Farmer, B. W. (1998). Work in transition: Trends and implications. In M. S. Garay & S. A. Bernhardt (Eds.), *Expanding literacies: English teaching and the new workplace* (pp. 55–80). Albany: State University of New York Press.

Bissex, G. L. (1980). *Gyns at wrk: A child learns to read and write.* Cambridge, MA: Harvard University Press.

Bizzell, P. (1982). College composition: Initiation into the academic discourse community. *Curriculum Inquiry, 12,* 191–207.

Bizzell, P. (1992). *Academic discourse and critical consciousness.* Pittsburgh: University of Pittsburgh Press.

Brandt, D. (1986). Toward an understanding of context in composition. *Written Communication, 3*(2), 139–159.

Briggs, C. L. (1986). *Learning how to ask: A sociolinguistic appraisal of the role of the interview in social science research.* New York: Cambridge University Press.

Broadhead, G. J., & Freed, R. C. (1986). *The variables of composition: Process and product in a business setting.* Carbondale: Southern Illinois University Press.

Brodkey, L. (1987). *Academic writing as social practice.* Philadelphia: Temple University Press

Brooks, L. W., & Dansereau, D. F. (1987). Transfer of information: An instructional perspective. In S. M. Cormier & J. D. Hagman (Eds.), *Transfer of learning: Contemporary research and applications* (pp. 121–150). San Diego: Academic Press.

Brown, R. L., & Herndl, C. G. (1986). An ethnographic study of corporate writing: Job status as reflected in written text. In B. Couture (Ed.), *Functional approaches to writing: Research perspectives* (pp. 11–28). London: Frances Pinter.

Bruffee, K. (1984). Collaborative learning and the "Conversation of Mankind". *College English, 46*(7), 635–652.

Carter, M. (1990). The idea of expertise: An exploration of cognitive and social dimensions of writing. *College Composition and Communication, 41*(3), 265–286.

Chin, E. (1991). *Learning to write the news.* Unpublished doctoral dissertation, Stanford University, Stanford.

Chin, E. (1994). Redefining "context" in research on writing. *Written Communication, 11*(4), 445–482.

Cintron, R. (1993). Wearing a pith helmet at a sly angle: Or, can writing researchers do ethnography in a postmodern era? *Written Communication, 10*(3), 371–412.

Clifford, J., & Marcus, G. E. (Eds.). (1986). *Writing culture: The poetics and politics of ethnography.* Berkeley: University of California Press.

Connors, R. J. (1981). The rise and fall of the modes of discourse. *College Composition and Communication, 32*(4), 444–455.

Cooper, M. M. (1986). The ecology of writing. *College English, 48,* 364–375.

Cooper, M. M. (1989). Why are we talking about discourse communities: Or, foundationalism rears its ugly head once more. In M. M. Cooper & M. Holzman (Eds.), *Writing as social action* (pp. 202–220). Portsmouth, NH: Boynton/Cook.

Crystal, D., & Davy, D. (1969). *Investigating English style.* London: Longman.

Daiute, C. (1989). Play as thought: Thinking strategies of young writers. *Harvard Educational Review, 59*(1), 1–23.

deGroot, A. D. (1965). *Thought and choice in chess.* The Hague: Mouton.

Derrida, J. (1980). The law of genre. *Critical Inquiry, 7*(1), 202–236.

Devitt, A. J. (1993). Generalizing about genre: New conceptions of an old concept. *College Composition and Communication, 44*(4), 573–586.

Diaz, R. (1983). Thought and two languages: The impact of bilingualism on cognitive development. In E. W. Gordon (Ed.), *Review of research in education* (Vol. 10, pp. 23–54). Washington, DC: American Educational Research Association.

DiPardo, A. (1994). Stimulated recall in research on writing: An antidote to "I don't know, it was fine". In P. Smagorinsky (Ed.), *Speaking about writing: Reflections on research methodology* (pp. 163–181). Thousand Oaks, CA: Sage.

Doheny-Farina, S. (1989). A case study of one adult writing in academic and non-academic discourse communities. In C. B. Matalene (Ed.), *Worlds of writing: Teaching and learning in discourse communities of work* (pp. 17–42). New York: Random House.

Doheny-Farina, S. (1993). Research in rhetoric: Confronting the methodological and ethical problems of research on writing in nonacademic settings. In R. Spilka (Ed.), *Writing in the workplace: New research perspectives* (pp. 253–267). Carbondale: Southern Illinois University Press.

Dreyfus, H. L., & Dreyfus, S. E. (1986). *Mind over machine: The power of human intuition and expertise in the era of the computer.* New York: Free Press.

Durst, R. (1984). The development of analytic writing. In A. N. Applebee (Ed.), *Contexts for learning to write: Studies of secondary school instruction* (pp. 79–102). Norwood, NJ: Ablex.

Dyson, A. (1988). Unintentional helping in the primary grades: Writing in the children's world. In B. A. Rafoth & D. L. Rubin (Eds.), *The social construction of written communication* (pp. 218–248). Norwood, NJ: Ablex.

Dyson, A. H. (1993*). Social worlds of children learning to write in an urban primary school.* New York: Teachers College Press.

Ede, L., & Lunsford, A. (1984). Audience addressed/audience invoked: The role of audience in composition theory and pedagogy. *College Composition and Communication, 35*(2) 155–171.

Ede, L., & Lunsford, A. (1990). *Singular texts/plural authors: Perspectives on collaborative writing.* Carbondale: Southern Illinois University Press.

Eiler, M. A. (1989). Process and genre. In C. B. Matalene (Ed.), *Worlds of writing: Teaching and learning in discourse communities of work* (pp. 43–63). New York: Random House.

Elbow, P. (1981). *Writing with power: Techniques for mastering the writing process.* New York: Oxford University Press.

Elbow, P. (1991). Reflections on academic discourse: How it relates to freshmen and colleagues. *College English, 53*(2), 135–155.

Fahnestock, J. (1986). Accommodating science: The rhetorical life of scientific facts. *Written Communication, 3*(3), 275–296.

Fahnestock, J., & Secor, M. (1991). The rhetoric of literary criticism. In C. Bazerman & J. Paradis (Eds.), *Textual dynamics of the professions: Historical and contemporary studies of writing in professional communities* (pp. 76–96). Madison: University of Wisconsin Press.

Faigley, L. (1980). Names in search of a concept: Maturity, fluency, complexity, and growth in written syntax. *College Composition and Communication, 31*(3), 291–300.

Faigley, L. (1992). *Fragments of rationality: Postmodernity and the subject of composition.* Pittsburgh: University of Pittsburgh Press.

Faigley, L., & Hansen, K. (1985). Learning to write in the social sciences. *College Composition and Communication, 34,* 140–149.

Faigley, L., & Miller, T. P. (1982). What we learn from writing on the job. *College English, 44*(6), 555–569.

Fish, S. (1980). *Is there a text in this class? The authority of interpretive communities.* Cambridge, MA: Harvard University Press.

Fishman, A. R. (1988). *Amish literacy: What and how it means.* Portsmouth, NH: Heinemann.

Fishman, A. R. (1990). Becoming literate: A lesson from the Amish. In A. Lunsford, H. Moglen, & J. Slevin (Eds.), *The right to literacy* (pp. 29–38). New York: Modern Language Association.

Fleischer, C. (1995). *Composing teacher-research: A prosaic history.* Albany: State University of New York Press.

Florio, S., & Clark, C. M. (1982). The functions of writing in an elementary classroom. *Research in the Teaching of English, 16*(2), 115–130.

Flower, L. (1989). Rhetorical problem solving: Cognition and professional writing. In M. Kogen (Ed.), *Writing in the business professions* (pp. 3–36). Urbana, IL: National Council of Teachers of English and Association for Business Communication.

Flower, L. (1994). *The construction of negotiated meaning: A social cognitive theory of writing.* Carbondale: Southern Illinois University Press.

Flower, L., & Hayes, J. R. (1981). A cognitive process theory of writing. *College Composition and Communication, 32*(4), 365–387.

Flower, L., Schriver, K. A., Carey, L., Haas, C., & Hayes, J. R. (1989). *Planning in writing: The cognition of a constructive process* (Technical Report No. 34). Berkeley, CA: Center for the Study of Writing.

Foertsch, J. (1995). Where cognitive psychology applies: How theories about memory and transfer can influence composition pedagogy. *Written Communication, 12*(3), 360–383.

Foucault, M. (1977). What is an author? In D. Bouchard (Ed.), *Language, countermemory, practice: Selected essays and interview by Michel Foucault* (pp. 101–120). Ithaca, NY: Cornell University Press.

Fowler, A. (1982). *Kinds of literature: An introduction to the theory of genres and modes.* Cambridge, MA: Harvard University Press.

Freed, R. C., & Broadhead, G. J. (1987). Discourse communities, sacred texts, and institutional norms. *College Composition and Communication, 38*(2), 154–165.

Freed, R. C., & Roberts, D. D. (1989). The nature, classification, and generic structure of proposals. *Journal of Technical Writing and Communication, 19*(1), 317–351.

Freedman, A. (1987). Development in story writing. *Applied Psycholinguistics, 8*, 153–170.

Freedman, A. (1993). Show and tell? The role of explicit teaching in the learning of new genres. *Research in the Teaching of English, 27*(3), 222–251.

Freedman, A. (1994, April). *Legitimate peripheral participation and the acquisition of genre.* Paper presented at the American Educational Research Association, New Orleans.

Freedman, A., Adam, C., & Smart, G. (1994). Wearing suits to class: Simulating genres and simulations as genre. *Written Communication, 11*(2), 193–226.

Freedman, A., & Medway, P. (1994a). Introduction: New views of genre and their implications for education. In A. Freedman & P. Medway (Eds.), *Learning and teaching genre* (pp. 1–22). Portsmouth, NH: Boynton/Cook.

Freedman, A., & Medway, P. (Eds.). (1994b). *Learning and teaching genre*. Portsmouth, NH: Boynton/Cook.

Freedman, A., & Pringle, I. (1980). Writing in the college years: Some indices of growth. *College Composition and Communication, 31*(3), 311–324.

Freedman, S. W. (1984). The registers of student and professional expository writing: Influence on teachers' responses. In R. Beach & L. S. Bridwell (Eds.), *New directions in composition research* (pp. 334–347). New York: Guilford Press.

Geertz, C. (1973). *The interpretation of cultures*. New York: Basic Books.

Geisler, C. (1994). *Academic literacy and the nature of expertise: Reading, writing and knowing in academic philosophy*. Hillsdale, NJ: Erlbaum.

Gick, M. L., & Holyak, K. J. (1987). The cognitive basis of knowledge transfer. In S. M. Cormier & J D. Hagman (Eds.), *Transfer of learning: Contemporary research and applications* (pp. 9–46). San Diego: Academic Press.

Goetz, J. P., & LeCompte, M. D. (1984). *Ethnography and qualitative design in educational research*. San Diego: Academic Press.

Greene, S., & Higgins, L. (1994). "Once upon a time": The use of retrospective accounts in building theory in composition. In P. Smagorinsky (Ed.), *Speaking about writing: Reflections on research methodology* (pp. 115–140). Thousand Oaks, CA: Sage.

Greenwood, S. (1994). Purposes, not text types: Learning genres through experience of work. In A. Freedman & P. Medway (Eds.), *Learning and teaching genre* (pp. 237–242). Portsmouth, NH: Boynton/Cook.

Gundlach, R. (1998). Personal communication.

Gunnarsson, B. L. (1997). The writing process from a sociolinguistic viewpoint. *Written Communication, 14*(2), 139–188.

Hairston, M. (1986). Different products, different processes: A theory about writing. *College Composition and Communication, 37*, 442–452.

Halliday, M. A. K. (1973). Explorations in the functions of language. London: Edward Arnold.

Harris, J. (1989). The idea of community in the study of writing. *College Composition and Communication, 40*(1), 11–22.

Haswell, R. H. (1991). *Gaining ground in college writing: Tales of development and interpretation*. Dallas: Southern Methodist University Press.

Hays, J. N. (1983). The development of discursive maturity in college writers. In J. N. Hays, P. A. Roth, J. R. Ramsey, & R. D. Foulke (Eds.), *The writer's mind: Writing as a mode of thinking*. Urbana, IL: National Council of Teachers of English.

Heath, S. B. (1981). Toward an ethnohistory of writing in American education. In M. F. Whiteman (Ed.), *Writing: The nature, development and teaching of written communication: Vol. 1. Variation in writing: Functional and linguistic-cultural differences* (pp. 25–45). Hillsdale, NJ: Erlbaum.

Heath, S. B. (1982). Protean shapes in literacy events: Ever shifting oral and literate traditions. In D. Tannen (Ed.), *Spoken and written language: Exploring orality and literacy* (pp. 91–117). Norwood, NJ: Ablex.

Heath, S. B. (1983). *Ways with words.* Cambridge: Cambridge University Press.

Heath, S. B. (1993). Rethinking the sense of the past: The essay as legacy of the epigram. In L. Odell (Ed.), *Theory and practice in the teaching of writing: Rethinking the discipline* (pp. 105–131). Carbondale: Southern Illinois University Press.

Heath, S. B., & Branscombe, A. (1985). "Intelligent writing" in an audience community: Teacher, students, and researcher. In S. W. Freedman (Ed.), *The acquisition of written language* (pp. 3–31). Norwood, NJ: Ablex.

Herndl, C. G. (1991). Writing ethnography: Representation, rhetoric, and institutional practices. *College English, 53*(3), 320–332.

Herrington, A. (1988). Teaching, writing and learning: A naturalistic study of writing in an undergraduate literature course. In D. Jolliffe (Ed.), *Advances in writing research: Vol. 2. Writing in academic disciplines* (pp. 133–166). Norwood, NJ: Ablex.

Hill, C. A., & Resnick, L. (1995). Creating opportunities for apprenticeship in writing. In J. Petraglia (Ed.), *Reconceiving writing, rethinking writing instruction* (pp. 145–158). Mahwah, NJ: Erlbaum.

Himley, M. (1986). Genre as generative: One perspective on one child's early writing growth. In M. Nystrand (Ed.), *The structure of written communication: Studies in reciprocity between writers and readers* (pp. 137–157). Orlando, FL: Academic Press.

Honingmann, J. J. (1976). The personal approach in cultural anthropological research. *Current Anthropology, 17*, 243–261.

Hunt, K. W. (1965). A synopsis of clause-to-sentence length factors. *English Journal, 54*, 300–309.

Hunt, R. (1994). Speech genres, writing genres, school genres and computer genres. In A. Freedman & P. Medway (Eds.), *Learning and teaching genre* (pp. 243–262). Portsmouth, NH: Boynton/Cook.

Hutson, B. A. (1987). Literacy at school and literacy at work. In D. Bloome (Ed.), *Literacy and schooling* (pp. 225–257). Norwood, NJ: Ablex.

Hymes, D. (1974). *Foundations in sociolinguistics: An ethnographic approach.* Philadelphia: University of Pennsylvania Press.

Jameson, F. (1981). *The political unconscious: Narrative as a socially symbolic act.* Ithaca, NY: Cornell University Press.

Johns, L. C. (1989). The file cabinet has a sex life: Insights of a professional writing consultant. In C. B. Matalene (Ed.), *Worlds of writing: Teaching and learning in discourse communities of work* (pp. 153–187). New York: Random House.

Jolliffe, D. A. (1995). Discourse, interdiscursivity, and composition instruction. In J. Petraglia (Ed.), *Reconceiving writing, rethinking writing instruction* (pp. 197–216). Mahwah, NJ: Erlbaum.

Kaufer, D. S., & Dunmire, P. L. (1995). Integrating cultural reflection and production in college writing curricula. In J. Petraglia (Ed.), *Reconceiving writing, rethinking writing instruction* (pp. 217–238). Mahwah, NJ: Erlbaum.

Kaufer, D., & Young, R. (1993). Writing in the content areas: Some theoretical complexities. In L. Odell (Ed.), *Theory and practice in the teaching of writing: Rethinking the discipline* (pp. 71–104). Carbondale: Southern Illinois University Press.

Kent, T. (1991). On the very idea of a discourse community. *College Composition and Communication, 42*(4), 425–445.

Kinneavy, J. L. (1971). *A theory of discourse: The aims of discourse.* New York: Norton.

Kirsch, I. S., & Jungeblut, A. (1992). *Profiling the literacy proficiencies of JTPA and ES/ UI populations.* Washington, DC: U.S. Department of Labor.

Kirtley, M. (1994). Genres for out-of-school involvement. In A. Freedman & P. Medway (Eds.), *Learning and teaching genre* (pp. 227–236). Portsmouth, NH: Boynton/Cook.

Kitzhaber, A. R. (1963). *Themes, theories, and therapy: The teaching of writing in college.* New York: McGraw-Hill.

Knoblauch, C. H. (1989). The teaching and practice of "professional writing". In M. Kogen (Ed.), *Writing in the business professions* (pp. 246–264). Urbana, IL: National Council of Teachers of English and Association for Business Communication.

Langer, J. A. (1985). Children's sense of genre: A study of performance on parallel reading and writing tasks. *Written Communication, 2*(2), 157–187.

Latour, B., & Woolgar, S. (1979). *Laboratory life: The construction of scientific facts.* Princeton, NJ: Princeton University Press.

Lave, J. (1993). The practice of learning. In S. Chaiklin & J. Lave (Eds.), *Understanding practice: Perspectives on activity and context* (pp. 3–32). New York: Cambridge University Press.

Lave, J., Murtaugh, M., & de la Rocha, O. (1984). The dialectic of arithmetic in grocery shopping. In B. Rogoff & J. Lave (Eds.), *Everyday cognition: Its development in social context* (pp. 67–94). Cambridge, MA: Harvard University Press.

Lave, J., & Wenger, E. (1991). *Situated learning: Legitimate peripheral participation.* Cambridge: Cambridge University Press.

Loban, W. (1976). *Language development: Kindergarten through grade twelve* (Research Report 18). Urbana, IL: National Council of Teachers of English.

Lofty, J. S. (1992). *Time to write: The influence of time and culture on learning to write.* Albany: State University of New York Press.

Lovitt, C. R., & Young, A. (1997). Rethinking genre in the first-year composition course: Helping student writers get things done. *Profession,* 113–125.

May, C. B., & Menelaides, S. L. (1993). Good writing counts. *Journal of Accounting, 17*(7), 77–79.

McCarthy, L. P. (1987). A stranger in strange lands: A college student writing across the curriculum. *Research in the Teaching of English, 21*(3), 233–265.

McIsaac, C., & Aschauer, M. A. (1990). Proposal writing at Atherton Jordan, Inc. *Management Communication Quarterly, 3*(4), 527–560.

Mikulecky, L., Albers, P., & Peers, M. (1994). *Literacy transfer: A review of the literature* (NCAL Technical Report TR94-05). University of Pennsylvania, National Center on Adult Literacy.

Miller, C. R. (1984). Genre as social action. *Quarterly Journal of Speech, 70,* 151–167.

Miller, S. (1991). *Textual carnivals: The politics of composition.* Carbondale: Southern Illinois University Press.

Moffett, J. (1983). *Teaching the universe of discourse.* Boston: Houghton Mifflin.

Murray, D. M. (1980). Writing as process: How writing finds its own meaning. In T. R. Donovan & B. W. McClelland (Eds.), *Eight approaches to teaching composition* (pp. 3–20). Urbana, IL: National Council of Teachers of English.

Myers, G. (1985). The social construction of two biologists' proposals. *Written Communication, 2*(3), 219–245.

Newell, A., & Simon, H. A. (1972). *Human problem solving.* Englewood Cliffs, NJ: Prentice-Hall.

Nystrand, M. (1990). Sharing words: The effects of readers on developing writers. *Written Communication, 7*(1), 13–24.

Nystrand, M., Greene, S., & Weimelt, J. (1993). Where did composition studies come from? An intellectual history. *Written Communication, 10*(3), 267–333.

Odell, L., & Goswami, D. (1982). Writing in a non-academic setting. *Research in the Teaching of English, 16*(3), 201–223.

Odell, L., & Goswami, D. (Eds.). (1985). *Writing in nonacademic settings.* New York: Guilford Press.

Odell, L., Goswami, D., Herrington, A., & Quick, D. (1983). Studying writing in non-academic settings. In P. B. Anderson, R. J. Brockman, & C. R. Miller (Eds.), *New essays in technical and scientific communication: Research, theory, practice* (Vol. 2, pp. 17–40). Farmingdale, NY: Baywood.

Odell, L., Goswami, D., & Quick, D. (1983). Writing outside the English composition class. In R. W. Bailey & R. M. Forsheim (Eds.), *Literacy for life* (pp. 175–194). New York: Modern Language Association.

Perelman, L. (1986). The context of classroom writing. *College English, 48,* 471–479.

Perkins, D. N., & Salomon, G. (1989a). Are cognitive skills context-bound? *Educational Researcher, 18*(1), 16–25.

Perkins, D. N., & Salomon, G. (1989b). Teaching for transfer. *Educational Leadership, 46*(1), 22–32.

Perry, W., Jr. (1968). *Forms of intellectual and ethical development in college years: A scheme.* New York: Holt, Rinehart and Winston.

Petraglia, J. (Ed.). (1995). *Reconceiving writing, rethinking writing instruction.* Mahwah, NJ: Erlbaum.

Piaget, J (1970). *Science of education and the psychology of the child* (D. Coltman, Trans.). New York: Orion Press.

Piazza, C. L. (1987). Identifying context variables in research on writing: A review and suggested directions. *Written Communication, 4*(2), 107–137.

Polanyi, M. (1966). *The tacit dimension.* Garden City, NY: Doubleday.

Porter, J. E. (1992). *Audience and rhetoric: An archaelogical composition of the discourse community.* Englewood Cliffs, NJ: Prentice–Hall.

Prior, P. (1995). Tracing authoritative and internally persuasive discourses: A case study of response, revision, and disciplinary enculturation. *Research in the Teaching of English, 29*(3), 288–325.

Rafoth, B. A. (1988). Discourse community: Where writers, readers, and texts come together. In B. A. Rafoth & D. L. Rubin (Eds.), *The social construction of written communication* (pp. 131–146). Norwood, NJ: Ablex.

Rafoth, B. A. (1990). The concept of discourse community: Descriptive and explanatory adequacy. In G. Kirsch & D. H. Roen (Eds.), *A sense of audience in written communication* (Vol. 5, pp. 140–152). Newbury Park, CA: Sage.

Resnick, L. B. (1987). Learning in school and out. *Educational Researcher, 16*(9), 13–20.

Rivers, W. E. (1989). From the garrett to the fishbowl: Thoughts on the transition from literary to technical writing. In C. B. Matalene (Ed.), *Worlds of writing: Teaching and learning in discourse communities of work* (pp. 64–79). New York: Random House.

Rogoff, B. (1990). *Apprenticeship in thinking: Cognitive development in social context.* Oxford: Oxford University Press.

Rogoff, B. (1994). Developing understanding of the idea of communities of learners. *Mind, Culture, and Activity, 1*(4), 209–229.

Russell, D. R. (1993). Vygotsky, Dewey, and externalism: Beyond the student/discipline dichotomy. *Journal of Advanced Composition, 13,* 173–197.

Salomon, G., & Globerson, T. (1987). Skill may not be enough: The role of mindfulness in learning and transfer. *International Journal of Educational Research, 11,* 623–637.

Sanjek, R. (1990). On ethnographic validity. In R. Sanjek (Ed.), *Fieldnotes: The makings of anthropology* (pp. 385–418). Ithaca, NY: Cornell University Press.

Schaef, A. W. (1990). *Meditations for women who do too much.* San Francisco: HarperCollins.

Schön, D. A. (1983). *The reflective practitioner: How professionals think in action.* New York: Basic Books.

Schryer, C. F. (1993). Records as genre. *Written Communication, 10*(2), 200–234.

Scribner, S., & Cole, M. (1981). Unpackaging literacy. In M. F. Whiteman (Ed.), *Variation in writing: Functional and linguistic-cultural differences* (Vol. 1, pp. 71–88). Hillsdale, NJ: Erlbaum.

Sfard, A. (1998). On two metaphors for learning and the dangers of choosing just one. *Educational Researcher, 27*(2), 4–13.

Shea, G. F. (1992). A case for clear writing. *Training and Development, 46*(1), 63–66.

Singley, M. K., & Anderson, J. R. (1989). *The transfer of cognitive skill.* Cambridge, MA: Harvard University Press.

Smagorinsky, P. (1992). How reading model essays affects writers. In J. W. Irwin & M. A. Doyle (Eds.), *Reading/writing connections: Learning from research* (p. 160). Newark, DE: International Reading Association.

Smagorinsky, P., & Smith, M. W. (1992). The nature of knowledge in composition and literary understanding: The question of specificity. *Review of Educational Research, 62*(3), 279–305.

Sommers, N. (1980). Revision strategies of student writers and experienced adult writers. *College Composition and Communication, 31*(4), 378–388.

Sternberg, R. J., & Forsythe, B. (1994, April). *The role of tacit knowledge in the professions.* American Educational Research Association Conference.

Sternberg, R. J., & Frensch, P. A. (1993). Mechanism of transfer. In D. K. Detter-man & R. J. Sternberg (Eds.), *Transfer on trial: Intelligence, cognition, and instruction* (pp. 25–38). Norwood, NJ: Ablex.

Stratman, J. F., & Duffy, T. M. (1990). Conceptualizing research on written management communication: Looking through a glass onion. *Management Communication Quarterly, 3*(4), 429–451.

Swales, J. M. (1990). *Genre analysis: English in academic and research settings.* Cambridge: Cambridge University Press.

Swales, J. M. (1992). *Re-thinking genre: Another look at discourse community effects.* Unpublished paper, Carleton University Conference on Genre.

Teich, N. (1987). Transfer of writing skills: Implications of the theory of lateral and vertical transfer. *Written Communication, 4*(2), 193–208.

Tyler, S. (1986). Post-modern ethnography: From document of the occult to occult document. In J. Clifford & G. E. Marcus (Eds.), *Writing culture: The poetics and politics of ethnography* (pp. 122–140). Berkeley: University of California Press.

U.S. Department of Labor. (1992). *Skills and tasks for jobs: A SCANS report for America 2000.* Washington, DC: Author.

Van Maanen, J. (1979). The fact of fiction in organizational ethnography. *Administrative Science Quarterly, 24,* 539–550.

Van Maanen, J. (1988). *Tales of the field: On writing ethnography.* Chicago: University of Chicago Press.

Voss, J. F. (1989). On the composition of experts and novices. In E. P. Maimon, B. F. Nodine, & F. W. O'Connor (Eds.), *Thinking, reasoning, and writing* (pp. 69–84). New York: Longman.

Vygotsky, L. S. (1978). *Mind in society: The development of higher psychological processes* (E. Hanfmann & G. Vakar, Trans.). Cambridge: Massachusetts Institute of Technology Press.

Walvoord, B. E., & McCarthy, L. P. (1990). *Thinking and writing in college: A naturalistic study of students in four disciplines.* Urbana, IL: National Council of Teachers of English.

Warantz, E., & Keech, C. L. (1982). Beyond holistic scoring: Rhetorical flaws that signal advance in developing writers. In J. R. Gray & L. Ruth (Eds.), *Properties of writing tasks: A study of alternative procedures for holistic writing assessment* (pp. 509–542). Berkeley: University of California, Graduate School of Education, Bay Area Writing Project.

Watters, A., & Ford, M. (1995). *A guide for change: Resources for implementing community service writing.* New York: McGraw-Hill.

Wertsch, J. V. (1991). *Voices of the mind: A sociocultural approach to mediated action.* Cambridge, MA: Harvard University Press.

White, E. B. (1938). *One man's meat.* New York: Harper & Row.

Whyte, W. F. (1943). *Street corner society: The social structure of an Italian slum.* Chicago: University of Chicago Press.

Witte, S. P. (1992). Context, text, intertext: Toward a constructivist semiotic of writing. *Written Communication, 9*(2), 237–308.

Witte, S. P., & Davis, A. S. (1983). The stability of T-unit length in the written discourse of college freshmen: A second study. *Research in the Teaching of English,* *16*(1), 71–84.

Woolever, K. R. (1989). Coming to terms with different standards of excellence for written communication. In C. B. Matalene (Ed.), *Worlds of writing: Teaching and learning in discourse communities of work* (pp. 3–16). New York: Random House.

Yates, J. (1989). *Control through communication: The rise of system in American management.* Baltimore: Johns Hopkins University Press.

Yates, J., & Orlikowski, W. J. (1992). Genres of organizational communication: A structurational approach to studying communication and media. *Academy of Management Review, 17*(2), 299–326.

Index

About the Author

Anne Beaufort received her Ph.D. in Education in 1995 from Stanford University's Language, Literacy and Culture program. She is currently assistant professor and director of the College Writing Program in the Department of Literature at American University in Washington, D.C. In addition to teaching writing and training graduate students to teach writing at American, she has revised the university's writing curriculum, instituted the Writer as Witness program in Fall 1998, and has begun a cross-disciplinary pilot project studying transfer of learning issues in writing courses linked with general education courses. Her current research continues her interest in the developmental processes of writers at the postsecondary level and transfer of learning issues for writers entering new discourse communities.

Prior to pursuing her doctoral studies, Beaufort taught in a wide range of programs, from middle school to the university level. The early influence in her teaching career of the Bay Area Writing Project led to her focus on writing instruction and training teachers of writing. She had a 10-year career in corporate communications, working as an in-house writer and editor of management publications, and as a communications trainer for hospital administrators, Silicon Valley salespeople, financial analysts, and public relations specialists before pursuing the doctorate. She lives in Washington, D.C., with her husband, Guy Wulfing.